P9-BJM-392

JACQUES
DERRIDA

RELIGION AND POSTMODERNISM

a series edited by Mark C. Taylor

Geoffrey Bennington
and Jacques Derrida

JACQUES DERRIDA

Translated by
Geoffrey Bennington

The University of Chicago Press
Chicago and London

Geoffrey Bennington, professor of French literature at the University of Sussex, is the author of, among other books, *Lyotard: Writing the Event* and cotranslator of Derrida's *Of Spirit: Heidegger and the Question* and *The Truth in Painting*. **Jacques Derrida** is professor at the Ecole des Hautes Etudes en Sciences Sociales, Paris, and the author of numerous books. Among them, *Of Spirit, The Truth in Painting, The Post Card,* and *Writing and Difference* are published by the University of Chicago Press.

The University of Chicago Press, Chicago 60637
The University of Chicago Press, Ltd., London

Printed in the United States of America
02 01 00 99 98 97 96 95 94 93   5 4 3 2 1

ISBN (cloth): 0–226–04261–8

Originally published in French, under the same title.

Library of Congress Cataloging-in-Publication Data
Bennington, Geoffrey.
[Jacques Derrida. English]
Jacques Derrida / Geoffrey Bennington and Jacques Derrida; translated by Geoffrey Bennington.
p. cm.
Translation of: Jacques Derrida.
Includes bibliographical references.
1. Derrida, Jacques. I. Derrida, Jacques. II. Title.
B2430.D484B4613 1993
194—dc20   92-11186
CIP

♾The paper used in this publication meets the minimum requirements of the American National Standard for Information Sciences—Permanence of Paper for Printed Library Materials, ANSI Z39.48–1984.

Dès qu'il est saisi par l'écriture,
le concept est cuit.
Jacques Derrida

Geoffrey Bennington

DERRIDABASE

Jacques Derrida

CIRCUMFESSION

Fifty-nine periods and periphrases
written in a sort of internal margin, between
Geoffrey Bennington's book and work in preparation
(January 1989–April 1990)

CONTENTS

This book presupposes a contract. And the contract, itself established or stabilized on the basis of a friendly bet (challenge, outbidding, or raising the stakes), has determined a number of rules of composition. G. B. undertook to describe, according to the pedagogical and logical norms to which he holds, if not the totality of J. D.'s thought, then at least the general system of that thought. Knowing that there was to be text by J. D. in the book, he saw fit to do without any quotation and to limit himself to an argued exposition which would try to be as clear as possible. The guiding idea of the exposition comes from computers: G. B. would have liked to systematize J. D.'s thought to the point of turning it into an interactive program which, in spite of its difficulty, would in principle be accessible to any user. As what is at stake in J. D.'s work is to show how any such system must remain essentially open, this undertaking was doomed to failure from the start, and the interest it may have consists in the test, and the proof, of that failure. In order to demonstrate the ineluctable necessity of the failure, our contract stipulated that J. D., having read G. B.'s text, would write something escaping the proposed systematization, surprising it. It goes without saying that G. B. was not allowed, in order to take account of this new text, to revise his work: which—he tells himself after the event, surprised—was only done to provoke and welcome this surprise.

WITH TIME

We ought, then, to show how Derrida is a "contemporary."

We would say, for example, that since the sixties he has published some twenty books which have had a definite impact, more abroad than in France, that there have been countless colloquia and publications devoted to his work worldwide (this is no doubt one of the reasons why, as an Englishman, I find myself in this curious situation of having to introduce him to a French audience), that he continues to write at a speed that is a little intimidating for his readers, and that we are still far from having taken the measure of a thought whose richness and complexity is equal to that of the great names of the philosophical tradition.

In doing this, we would be setting ourselves two distinct but complementary tasks: on the one hand, that of justifying, as it were, Derrida's contemporaneity by describing this impact in order to show its topi-

1 The crude word, fight with him in this way over what's crude, as though first of all I liked to raise the stakes, and the expression "raise the stakes" belongs only to my mother, as though I were attached to him so as to look for a fight over what talking crude means, as though I were trying relentlessly, to the point of bloodshed, to remind him, for he knows it, *cur confitemur Deo scienti,** of what is demanded of us by what's crude, doing so thus in my tongue, the other one, the one that has always been running after me, turning in circles around me, a circumference licking me with a flame and that I try in turn to circumvent, having never loved anything but the impossible,

cality without reducing it to a phenomenon of fashion; and on the other, that of placing this thought in a tradition or a filiation in order to say how Derrida is new, to define an originality with respect to predecessors from whom Derrida would stand out in some way. We should thus have a description with two complementary dimensions: a synchronic one, for the place of Derrida in the galaxy of contemporaries, at least the French ones (what place does Derrida occupy with respect to Deleuze, Foucault, Lacan, Levinas, Lyotard, to mention only the most obvious?); and a diachronic one, for the history that alone carries the contemporary in what he contributes to "our modernity" (how does Derrida go beyond Hegel, Heidegger, Husserl, Freud, Marx, Nietzsche?). If we took Derrida more as a philosopher, we would carry out these two tasks by attempting to reconstruct the system of his thought: to get our bearings from time to time, we would recall the proper names of accredited thinkers (pretending to believe that the studious reader is acquainted with their positions, having already read volumes such as this one

the crudeness I don't believe in, and the crude word lets flow into him through the channel of the ear, another vein, faith, profession of faith or confession, belief, credulity, as though I were attached to him just to look for a quarrel by opposing a naive, credulous piece of writing which by some immediate transfusion calls on the reader's belief as much as my own, from this dream in me, since always, of another language, an entirely crude language, of a half-fluid name too, there, like blood, and I hear them snigger, poor old man, doesn't look likely, not going to happen tomorrow, you'll never know, superabundance of a flood after which a dike becomes beautiful like the ruin it

Photograph with automobile (I)

Rue Saint Augustin, Algiers

"...compulsion to overtake each second, like one car overtaking another, doubling it rather, overprinting it with the negative of a photograph already taken with a 'delay' mechanism, the memory of what survived me to be present at my disappearance, interprets or runs the film again..." (*Circumfession,* 7). The racing of a car is filmed or photographed, always on the verge of having an accident, from one end of J. D.'s work to the other (for example: *The Post Card,* pp. 17, 26, 43, 60, 115, 162, 174, 200; "Ulysses Gramophone," *in fine; Mémoires d'Aveugle,* p. 11).

for all the others) and point out briefly how Derrida's thought is distinguished from them. In this way, we would gradually delimit what is proper to Derrida and none other, his originality, his idiom or signature, what with a bit of luck we would manage to state concisely and clearly in conclusion, so that the reader could thereafter tell him- or herself that Derrida is the one who, after Nietzsche and/or Heidegger, but contrary to Foucault and/or Lacan, demonstrates (or at least claims) that…, to be completed by a statement in apodictic form, probably "There is nothing outside the text."

Which is more or less what we are going to do. But it cannot in principle suffice in Derrida's case, even supposing that it does in other cases. First, because almost the whole of what Derrida has written consists in "readings" (in a sense to be specified) of philosophical and literary texts from the tradition, rather than in a system of theses proper to him. One can imagine Derrida as very modest, entirely occupied by reading and re-reading his predecessors with minute attention, de-

will always have walled up inside it, cruelty above all, blood again, *cruor, confiteor,* what blood will have been for me, I wonder if Geoff knows it, how could he know that that morning, a November 29, 1988, a sentence came, from further away than I could ever say, but only one sentence, scarcely a sentence, the plural word of a desire toward which all the others since always seemed, confluence itself, to hurry, an order suspended on three words, *find the vein,* what a nurse might murmur, syringe in hand, needle upward, before *taking blood,* when for example in my childhood, and I remember that laboratory in the rue d'Alger, the fear and vagueness of a glorious appeasement both

termined to spend the time it takes over the slightest detail, the slightest comma, guardian of the letter of the old texts, putting nothing forward that he has not already found written by an other, scarcely our contemporary—and this is true. But one can also imagine him, on the contrary, as immodesty itself, forcing these same old texts to say something quite different from what they had always seemed to say, constantly putting out theses or hypotheses on the totality of what he calls "Western Metaphysics," sure of having diagnosed the hidden and unthought truth of all the others, our most contemporary contemporary, the only one to have emerged from age-old philosophical blindness—and this is not false (DIA, 81). Derrida is the object of simultaneous adulation and denunciation on both sides of this imagination, on both sides of the Atlantic. Our task is not to take sides according to these possibilities, but to show up their insufficiency; not to say "He is one or the other, you have to choose," nor "He's a bit of both, you must love and hate him for both reasons at the same time" (although these sentences are legitimate

took hold of me, took me blind in their arms at the precise moment at which by the point of the syringe there was established an invisible passage, always invisible, for the continuous flowing of blood, absolute, absolved in thc sense that nothing seemed to come between the source and the mouth, the quite complicated apparatus of the syringe being introduced in that place only to allow the passage and to disappear as instrument, but continuous in that other sense that, without the now brutal intervention of the other who, deciding to interrupt the flow once the syringe, still upright, was withdrawn from the body,

too), but something like "Only Derrida can give us the means to understand this situation."

"Contemporary," *contemporaneus, cum tempus,* with (the) time(s). Derrida thinks with (the) time(s), not at all in that he represents the spirit of the times ("post-modern," "post-philosophical," so they say), but in that the time he thinks dislocates all contemporaneity. Unhappy he who claims to be his own contemporary. Derrida does not: I would imagine him, rather, with Plato and a few others, at Heliopolis, in Egypt.

REMARK

Programmed excuses: it is, of course, impossible to write a book of this sort about Derrida. I do not mean the—real—difficulties of reading or comprehension that his texts appear to put up against a first approach, difficulties which this book, by its destination, is supposed to reduce. This sort of book lives on just those difficulties, and this one is no exception to that rule. In

quickly folded my arm upward and pressed the swab inside the elbow, the blood could still have flooded, not indefinitely but continuously to the point of exhausting me, thus aspirating toward it what I called: the glorious appeasement.

*"Why we confess to God, when he knows (everything about us)." This title is given to chapter 1 of book 9 of Saint Augustine's *Confessions* in the 1649 French translation by Robert Arnauld d'Andilly. It was in this very free translation that I first read the *Confessions*. In spite of my attachment for this bilingual

general we accept without qualms the pedagogical role assigned to us here: we are trying to understand, and explain as clearly as possible, "Derrida's thought," up to the point where the terms "understand," "explain," and "thought" (or even "Derrida") no longer suffice.

So not those difficulties, which in the end are quite banal. But a difficulty which is as it were structural, which has nothing to do with the competence of such and such a reader of Derrida (me, as it happens). This difficulty hangs on the fact that *all* the questions to which this type of book must habitually presuppose replies, around for example the practice of quotation (LI, 40ff.; SI, 126–8), the relationship between commentary and interpretation (AT, 10; GR, 159: SP, 31, 53), the identification and delimitation of a corpus or a work (GR, 99, 161–2), the respect (GL 216a; NM, 37–8; WD, 121) owed to the singularity (PS, 560; WD, 22, 169ff.) or the event (PC, 304; TW, 146) of a work in its idiom (GL, 1496; SI, 24), its signature (GL, 3ff.; M, 230–1; SI passim), its date (SCH passim) and its context (LI, 60ff.; M, 316ff.), without simply making them into examples or cases (GR, 29; LG, 206ff.; PC,

edition (Garnier, 1925) in which, so long ago, I discovered the prayers and tears of Augustine, I henceforth use the translation in the edition of the Bibliothèque Augustinienne, by E. Tréhorel and G. Bouissou (Desclée de Brouwer, 1962). [Translator's note: English translations are taken, with some minor alterations, from the version by Vernon J. Bourke (Washington: Catholic University of America Press, 1953).]

425–6; SI, 88–90; TP, 79–109; WD, 170ff.)—*all* these questions (to say nothing of the question itself [OS passim; WD, 79–81]) are *already* put to us by the texts we have to read, not as preliminary or marginal to the true work of thought, but as this work itself in its most pressing and formidable aspects. Our little problems of reading-protocol cannot therefore remain enclosed in the space of a preface: they are *already* [*déjà*] the whole problem. This *déjà,* in which we might be tempted to recognize the signature we are trying to respect, is of course also interrogated by Derrida, as what precedes every interrogation and makes it possible (AL, 420; DES, 29–30; GL, 79b, 84b, 165–6b; PS, 97). The remark we wanted to make before beginning turns out to be already in some sense a quotation and an anticipation of our most intractable problems. This structure is related to what Derrida has called the remark, precisely (D, 251ff.). Beyond what we may find intimidating or even paralyzing about this (LG, 218–99), beyond even the jealousy and admiring resentment it cannot fail to inspire (GL, 134b; TW 147–8), this structure of the remark assigns us the task of understanding why without

2 From the invisible inside, where I could neither see nor want the very thing that I have always been scared to have revealed on the scanner, by *analysis*—radiology, echography, endocrinology, hematology—a crural vein expelled my blood outside that I thought beautiful once stored in that bottle under a label that I doubted could avoid confusion or misappropriation of the vintage, leaving me nothing more to do, the inside of my life exhibiting itself outside, *expressing* itself before my eyes, absolved without a gesture, dare I say of writing if I compare the pen to a syringe, and I always dream of a pen that would be a syringe, a suction point rather than that very hard weapon with

Post Card or *tableau vivant:* with Geoffrey Bennington at Ris Orangis, during the preparation of these pictures—and of this book, "a hidden pretext for writing in my own signature behind his back" (*Derridabase,* p. 316).

all this, without this already-there which obliges us to adopt a certain passivity toward the given, the gift, the *there is* of the text of the other which says to us "Come" and which we now have to read, no reading could open and we would have no chance of beginning to understand. The fact that this beginning is already a quotation or a general rehearsal (of what Derrida has written and of what we shall be attempting to develop in this book) already implies, at the limit, everything we can hope to explain in the following pages. And that the whole book is thus condemned to being in some sense a quotation has made us decide to adopt the rule of never directly quoting Derrida's texts (whereas he always quotes so abundantly the texts he reads) and of satisfying ourselves with references, as precise as we can make them, to the published texts: for if this book aims to be a faithful repetition of a work without equal (without example, without precedent [TP, 185–6]), we must not give in to the dangers of literal repetition, knowing, as we do since Borges, that it (re)produces something quite different from the original (WD, 296; see too, for jealousy, EO, 101). Like it or not, we are

which one must inscribe, incise, choose, calculate, take ink before filtering the inscribable, playing the keyboard on the screen, whereas here, once the right vein has been found, no more toil, no responsibility, no risk of bad taste nor of violence, the blood delivers itself all alone, the inside gives itself up and you can do as you like with it, it's me but I'm no longer there, for nothing, for nobody, diagnose the worst, you'd be right it'll always be true, then the glorious appeasement at least, at least what I call glorious appeasement, depends on the volume of blood, incredible amount for the child I remain this evening, should expose outward, and thus to its death, what will have

here in the diabolical domains of the simulacrum where paradox is the law: in order to say the same thing as Derrida, we are obliged to go in for reconstruction (where we would like to speak deconstruction), we are constrained to analytic dryness (where we would like to communicate the breadth and genius of a writing), and we expose ourselves to the necessary risk of making mistakes (where we would like to be sure and exact). This *double bind* (DES, 34; LOB, 118 ff.; SI, 56, 64; UG, 154ff.) just is the law of repetition: what repeats must be the same (there is sameness only if it repeats, and the only repetition is of the same), but can in no case be the identical (D, 123, 127; SI, 88; WD, 294–300). It's the same thing with Derrida's work, which, we can say without prejudice to him, repeats itself. This work, which is remarkable for its diversity *and* its consistency, its powers of dispersion *and* of gathering, its *formation* (PS, 9), cannot be divided into styles or periods: even the quite widespread idea that there are first of all very philosophical texts and then, after *Glas* (1974), a more "literary" and less "serious" tendency, is doubtful as to its empirical accuracy and irrelevant to

been most alive in me, the vein I wonder if Geoffrey Bennington can have found, and it's as though Geoff, very close, pronounce it Djef, because I love him and from the depths of my admiration without memory, as though I were insinuating to him the principle of a reply to this improbable question of what blood has been for me since ever, since, seeking a sentence, I have been seeking myself in a sentence, yes, I, and since a circumbygone period at the end of which I would say I and which would, finally, have the form, my language, another, of what I have turned around, from one periphrasis to the next, knowing that it took place but never, according to the strange turn of the

our understanding. From one end to the other of what we cannot prejudge to be an *oeuvre,* this repetition, with varied rhythms, to be sure, but without breaks or repudiations (EO, 141) forbids us, or saves us, from the linear presentation of some "intellectual itinerary," and pushes us to give our references in alphabetical order of title, rather than in chronological order of publication. (This is also why the following text is the linear version—one version among many possible versions—of a book without prescribed order of reading, written in Hypertext, to appear subsequently in electronic form.) Without allowing ourselves the facile cliché whereby a great thinker slaves away for a whole life to think *his* thought, *his* thing, to follow *his* path, nor accepting the idea that there is *one* unthought per great thinker (OS, 9, 13), we can say that things repeat in Derrida's work, in a series of events each time singular, and that it is in this same repetition, this repetition of the same, that there is something new: or, better, for to talk of something new is perhaps already to presuppose too much, that there is invention of the other (PIO, 62). In this opening of the other (toward the other,

event of nothing, what can be got around or not which comes back to me without ever having taken place, I call it circumcision, see the blood but also what comes, cauterization, coagulation or not, strictly contain the outpouring of circumcision, one circumcision, mine, the only one, rather than circumnavigation or circumference, although the unforgettable circumcision has carried me to the place I had to go to, and circumfession if I want to say and do something of an avowal without truth turning around itself, an avowal without "hymn" (hymnology) and without "virtue" (aretalogy), without managing to close itself on its possibility, unsealing abandoning the circle open, wander-

called by the other), without which the same would not be, there is the chance of something happening. It turns out that what makes our work a priori impossible is precisely what simultaneously makes it possible. Give the chance of this encounter a chance.

THE BEGINNING

We must begin somewhere, but there is no absolutely justified beginning (GR, 162; M, 6–7). One cannot, for essential reasons that we shall have to explain, return to a point of departure from which all the rest could be constructed following an order of reasons (POS, 4) nor following an individual or historical evolution (POS, 48–9). At most one can give a *strategic* justification for the procedure.

A (metaphysical) thought, which begins by searching for origins or foundations and proceeds to a reconstruction in order, infallibly finds that things have not happened as they ought: for there to be the need to begin everything again on a secure basis (when it is al-

ing on the periphery, taking the pulse of an encircling phrase, the pulsion of the paragraph which never circumpletes itself, as long as the blood, what I call thus and thus call, continues its venue in its vein.

3 If I let myself be loved by the lucky vein of this word, this is not for the *alea* or the mine it's enough to exploit by hacking out writing on the machine, nor for the blood, but for everything that all along this word vein lets or makes come the chance of events on which no program, no logical or textual

ready—always—so late [see OS, 99; TW, 145]), one must assume that somewhere things have gone wrong, and accept the task of explaining why and how this was even possible. To simplify outrageously, let us say that this evil, this turning, this departure, can be thought of either as come from the outside, as accident or catastrophe, or as already at work on the inside, as monstrosity (see GR, 41). The first hypothesis explains nothing, but simply invokes an absolute contingency (cf. GR, 256–7): in the second, we no longer have a very secure foundation, because this foundation is already inhabited by the principle of its decline. Consequence: "idealisms" (but "materialisms" do not escape this). The more naive believe in a paradise lost, the more cunning restore order by claiming to think, in order, the absence or loss of order. For Derrida, as for Heidegger, in both cases (with their innumerable variations and nuances) one is constructing things on an unquestioned value: *presence*. The metaphysics of presence thinks in two (logical and often historical) moments: presence first, of the world to a gaze, of a consciousness to its own inspection, of a meaning to a

machine will ever close, since always in truth has operated only by not overcoming the flow of raw happenings, not even the theologic program elaborated by Geoff who remains very close to God, for he knows everything about the "logic" of what I might have written in the past but also of what I might think or write in the future, on any subject at all, so that he can rightly do without quoting any singular sentences that may have come to me and which that "logic" or "alogic" would suffice to account for, transcendental deduction of me, so that I should have nothing left to say that might surprise him still and bring something about for him, who you would be tempted to compare to Augustine's God when he asks whether there is any sense in

Saint Augustine with his mother Monica. "When the day on which she was to depart this life was near at hand (Thou knewest the day; we did not)...she and I were standing alone...talking to each other alone, very sweetly" (*Confessions,* IX, x, 23). Ary Scheffer, *Saint Augustine and Saint Monica* (Paris: Musée du Louvre).

mind, of life to itself, of a breast to a mouth; absence next—the world veiled, consciousness astray, non-sense, death, debauchery, language, weaning. By thinking the second moment as derived with respect to the first, one returns, if only in thought, the complex to the simple, the secondary to the primary, the contingent to the necessary. This is the very order of reason and meaning, of the *logos,* and one does not escape it as easily as seem to think those who quickly invoke the unconscious or matter (POS, 64–7, 93–6; WD, 293–5), madness (WD 31–63 passim) or even the other (WD, 79–153 passim). A thought no longer ordered according to these schemas and their continuous complication would no longer be, strictly speaking, philosophy, and would give rise to formulations that would be unacceptable and ridiculous for philosophy, about an absolute past that has never been present (GR, 66; WD, 300), an originary repetition (AL, 389–90; WD 202, 299), a finite infinite (SP, 102), a supplement which "produces" what it supplements (GR, 144–5; SP, 89), and to scandalous affirmations, that perception does not exist (SP, 45a), that the proper name cannot

confessing anything to him when He knows everything in advance, which did not stop my compatriot from going beyond this *Cur confitemur Deo scienti,* not toward a verity, a severity of avowal which never amounts merely to speaking the truth, to making anything known or to presenting oneself naked in one's truth, as though Augustine still wanted, by force of love, to bring it about that in *arriving* at God, something should happen to God, and *someone* happen to him who would transform the science of God into a learned ignorance, he says he has to do so in *writing,* precisely, after the death of his mother, over whom he does not deplore the fact of not having wept, not that I dare link what he says about confession with the deaths of our re-

be proper (EO, 106–8; GR, 109–114), that the *cogito* is mad errancy (WD, 58), that there is nothing outside the text (D, 35–6; GR, 158–63; NA, 26), that in the beginning was the telephone (AL, 270), or that I am perhaps dead (SP, 95). These scandalous statements, which one would be quite wrong to attribute to a will to shock, or even to a desire to get out of philosophy (which would still be a philosophical desire), go with the assertion that there is no absolutely justifiable starting point, if not derivable from that assertion (for there is here no order of continuous derivation). By explaining some of these claims, we will understand why we have to begin somewhere without really knowing where. Which we have now done. But in beginning at the "beginning" we have, precisely, not begun at the beginning; everything had *already* begun.

—You claim that there is no given starting point, so you start in the most traditional way imaginable with the problem of beginning, and you proceed with a game that is puerile and predictable, reflexive, narcissistic, you attempt to enclose us from the start in writ-

spective mothers, I am not writing about Saint Georgette, the name of my mother, whom her brother sometimes used to call Geo, nor about Saint Esther, her sacred name, the one not to be used, the letters of a name I have used so much so that it might remain, for my mother was not a saint, not a Catholic one in any case, but what these two women had in common is the fact that Santa Monica, the name of the place in California near to which I am writing, also ended her days, as my mother will too, on the other side of the Mediterranean, far from her land, in her case in the cemetery in Nice which was profaned in 1984, and the son reports her wishes, i.e., that *nos concurrimus, sed cito reddita est sensui et aspexit astantes me et fratrem meum et ait nobis quasi quaerenti similis: "ubi eram?" deinde nos intuens maerore attonitos:*

ing and the text, a whole complacent baroque discourse based on well-known and quite banal paradoxes of self-reference. Lucky you don't quote us that text by Ponge that Derrida wants to make his own: "With the word *with,* then, begins this text/ Whose first line tells the truth" (PIO, 30ff.; PS, 648; SI, 102). We've already gone random, everything is already played for and lost, farewell clarity and meaning, we'll never understand anything, and what's more there's nothing to understand, that's your only secret (HAS, 19–20).

—Let's start again. Saying that there is no secure starting point does not mean that one starts at random. You always start somewhere, but that somewhere is never just anywhere. Denouncing or even demanding a "just anywhere" is already ruled by a philosophical demand: one can only identify the "just anywhere" (and therefore the random) on the—at least promised—basis of a true foundation, which alone can make you believe in the freedom or irresponsibility of a "just anywhere." The somewhere where you always start is overdetermined by historical, political, philosophical, and phan-

*"pontis hic" inquit "matrem uestram." ego silebam et fletum frenabam,** sentences I quote in Latin, I have taught a lot about these subjects, and if I must not continue doing so here, I owe it to autobiography to say that I have spent my life teaching so as to return in the end to what mixes prayer and tears with blood, *salus non erat in sanguine.*

* "We hastily gathered about her, but she returned to consciousness quickly and looked at me and my brother as we stood by. Rather like a person in search of something, she said to us: 'Where am I?' Then, seeing that we were overcome with grief, she said: 'Bury your mother here.' I remained silent and restrained my tears" (IX, xi, 27).

Before J. D's birth, his mother and elder brother on the balcony of the rue Saint-Augustin, Algiers.

tasmatic structures that in principle can never be fully controlled or made explicit (GL, 5a). The starting point is in a way radically contingent, and that it be thus contingent is a necessity. This necessity (of the contingent) is that of the *déjà,* which means that the starting point is always given, that we are responding to the "Come" that is received and suffered as necessity itself. It is imposed, but never stops mingling with contingency, and to that extent wanders (EO, 116; WD, 11, 292): that's its chance. As for being narcissistically enclosed in writing and the texts that remark it, we shall see the opening that that can imply (D, 202–86; PAR, 15; PIO, 19ff. [read it again]), because what is on the program doesn't happen, but disappears in its predictability, has no force as an event.

—That's monstrous.

—Indeed... (G2, 161ff.; GR, 5; SCH, 342; WD, 293).

—Is that all you have to say?

4 Consign them here, but why I wonder, confide to the bottom of this book what were my mother's last more or less intelligible sentences, still alive at the moment I am writing this, but already incapable of memory, in any case of the memory of my name, a name become for her at the very least unpronounceable, and I am writing here at the moment when my mother no longer recognizes me, and at which, still capable of speaking or articulating, a little, she no longer calls me and for her and therefore for the rest of her life I no longer have a name, that's what's happening, and when she nonetheless seems to reply to me, she is presumably replying to someone who happens to be me without her knowing it, if knowing means anything here, therefore

—In a sense that's all there *is* to say: there remains all that there is to write (D, 65).

—So everything is programmed and nothing will happen...

—We can't avoid that risk: we can't predict the event, which if we could would not be one (PAR, 15). We have to see after the event if something will have happened. I hope at least that you'll testify that this preface really was written before the book it precedes?

—Yes, yes: but in that case it isn't a preface (D, 1–59).

THE SIGN

Derrida, for his part, did not begin at the beginning, if we believe in classical beginnings. Set off on a study of "The Ideality of the Literary Object" (PUN, 36), which is an entirely marginal object for philosophy in the main lines of its tradition, he tarries over problems

without my knowing henceforth any more clearly myself who will have asked her such and such a question like the other day in Nice when I asked her if she was in pain ("yes") then where, it was February 5, 1989, she had, in a rhetoric that could never have been hers, the audacity of this stroke about which she will, alas, never know anything, no doubt knew nothing, and which piercing the night replies to my question: "I have a pain in my mother," as though she were speaking *for* me, both in my direction and in my place, although in the apparently amnesiac confusion in which she is ending her days the memory of *her* mother is very present to her, and although she looks more and

to do with the sign and meaning and finds that philosophy never gets out of these problems. Starting with the sign is starting with secondariness itself, already the detour. According to the logic of logic (of the *logos*), the sign is a sign of something, it stands in for the thing in its absence, representing it in view of its return: the sign stands between two presents, and can only be understood in relation to the priority of the presence of these two presents (M, 9–10). But not only does Derrida begin with the sign in the order of his published work, *he asserts, from the beginning, that the sign is at the beginning*. Which will imply very rapidly that there is no beginning, thing, or sign. Here's how:

1. The sign must stand in for the thing in its absence, represent it at a distance, detached enough from it to be its delegate, but still attached enough to it to be its sign, to refer, in principle, to it alone. The time of the sign is reduced to the time of this referral and, in the presence of its thing, the sign disappears.

2. That is the broadest schema, in which the word "thing" is itself a sign which refers to two possible things—usually called "referent" and "sense" (or sig-

more like her, I mean like my grandmother, a woman just as attentive to her appearance, her clothing, her makeup and her manners, then the evening of the same day, when she was alone with me in that house and I was in a different room, she had several times successively exposed herself naked, having nervily torn off the clothes that were hampering her in her bed, then as soon as I asked her why she replied to me, in just as *improbable* a way for anyone who had known her: "Because I'm attractive," and because she no longer articulates very clearly, her refusal to keep false teeth in not helping matters, I wondered if I had heard aright, had she said "Because I'm attractive," had she really,

nified). Without a distinction such as this, the whole of language would be reduced to a list of proper names of things, and would not in fact be a language (we shall be returning to the proper name). Between the word and the thing, the level of sense, signified, ideas, or concept (the distinctions between these terms are unimportant here) means that we can call a cat a cat rather than Marmaduke. The sign refers to the concept which refers to the world, allowing us a grasp of the world which is other than chaotic and evanescent.

3. For simplicity's sake, let us provisionally accept Saussure's terminology. The function of the sign is to represent the thing during its absence. But for this description to be plausible, what is absent must be the referent, not the signified, as otherwise the sign would not function. Signifier and signified are indissociable, detached from the referent to represent it at a distance, without ever being completely detached from it. The unity of signifier and signified makes the sign.

4. This attachment/detachment is not unproblematic, which implies that we would be wise to beware of the word "representation." At least we must recog-

however true it might be, spoken such an improbable sentence, but instead of pursuing this story, I stop for a moment over this word "improbable" and over a pang of remorse, in any case over the admission I owe the reader, in truth that I owe my mother herself for the reader will have understood that I am writing *for* my mother, perhaps even for a dead woman and so many ancient or recent analogies will come to the reader's mind even if no, they don't hold, those analogies, none of them, for if I were here writing for my mother, it would be for a living mother who does not recognize her son, and I am periphrasing here for whomever no longer recognizes me, unless it be so that one

nize that there is no *natural* link of resemblance between signifier and referent (Saussure quickly discards the possibility of a natural motivation of signs, and especially of onomatopoeias: too quickly [GL, 90.bff.; GR, 47]) and a fortiori between signifier and signified (what could a signified look like? and therefore, what could look like a signified?): so we assert that the sign is *arbitrary* or *unmotivated.* We shall say that signs are instituted or conventional, so long as we understand that "convention" cannot imply a foundational moment in which everyone gathered round to agree about signs. Language, says Saussure, is always *received,* like the law.

5. Let us say, for simplicity, that this tripartite division (which so far has nothing specifically Saussurian about it, but which Saussure receives, like the law, from the tradition) gives us the appearance of a reign of ideality (signified, concept, the intelligible) which touches on both sides a realm of materiality. Upstream, in first position, things, the world, reality; downstream, in third position, the signifier, the phonic or graphic body that linguistics has always thought of, despite its denials, as that of a *word* (GL, 91; GR, 31; M,

should no longer recognize me, another way of saying, another version, so that people think they finally recognize me, but what credulity, for here's the basis of the improbable, improbable is here below the name.

5 I posthume as I breathe, which is not very probable, the improbable in my life, that's the rule I'd like to follow and which in the end arbitrates the duel between what I am writing and what G. will have written up there, beside or above me, *on* me, but also *for* me, in my favor, toward me and in my place, for you will have noted that his hymn of burning ice will basi-

96; PAR, 47; RM, 15; SP, 16, 74), when it is not that of a *name* (M, 230ff.). Following a specular structure, we can valorize either the domain of ideality (to the point, for example, of thinking things as creations on the prior model of the idea or *eidos* [GR, 11–12]) or the "hard" materiality of things and, via a perilous extension, of the signifier. We can distribute as we wish the values of truth and illusion in these two realms without escaping the basic schema: the sign has always been thought of on the basis of this distinction between the sensible and the intelligible, and cannot be thought of otherwise (GR, 13; WD, 281).

6. However insufficient such a schema turns out to be, it allows us to understand why philosophy has been able to determine itself as philosophy of language (though we shall see that Derrida's thought is not essentially a philosophy of language), and why language can reveal what Derrida calls the closure (which is not the end [AT, 26, 30; GR. 4, 14; POS, 13; SP, 102; WD, 250]—we shall come back to this) of metaphysics. For we see that in this classical description, the sign has the privilege—and therefore runs all the risks—of joining

cally have said, foreseen, *predicted* if I translate myself into his language everything, he has apparently, will he have, produced it without quotation, without the least element of literality torn, like an event having taken place only once, from what might be called in the university my corpus, this is my corpus, the set of sentences I have signed of which he has literally not quoted one, not one in its literality, that was the choice, he explains himself about it, a strange choice when one is writing a book *on* someone who writes books, well he has not retained intact a single fragment of my corpus and if he has cut or lifted out some pieces, it's just so as not to keep them, to let them drop like skins useless to the understanding of my texts, to erase them in short,

the two realms. Whether it work in the service of ideality or materiality, of concepts or things, of *theoria* or *praxis,* the sign has to compromise with the other realm: idealism must take the risk of speaking or writing (as in Marx and Engels's famous *boutade*) and thus entrust spirit, however minimally, to a material support, however evanescent (M, 82ff.), and materialism must have recourse to idealities in order to signify.

7. A doctrine of "the materiality of the signifier," which has sometimes, wrongly, been attributed to Derrida, seems at first to consecrate the triumph of materialism. This, basically, was the position of the *Tel Quel* group. If we take again the description of the sign proposed by Saussure, we may wonder how a given sign retains its identity, remaining the sign that it is through its repetitions. We cannot, without begging the question, invoke the referent as an answer: for how are we to be sure of the identity of the referent to which we are referring if we are not sure of the identity of the sign used to refer to it? We know, moreover, what aporias are attendant on any theory of ostension (Wittgenstein), and more generally we can say that if the refer-

after having selected, decided to forget, to incinerate cold, carrying off with him, like my mother doesn't speak my name, the uniqueness, literally, of my sentences if not of each of my words for he keeps words, precisely, French words, he cuts out and circumscribes the words and even concepts but words or concepts do not make sentences and therefore events, and therefore proper names, supposing that sentences are proper names, let's say that they lay claim to be proper names, which words are never supposed to do, and he has decided, by this rigorous circumcision, to do without my body, the body of my writings to produce, basically, the "logic" or the "grammar," the law of production of every past, present, and why not future statement

Rembrandt, *Circumcision* (First version, 1654: Paris: Petit Palais). Circumcision and drawing: the passage of the *trait.* "The Epistle to the Galateans associates ... the theme of *conversion* (always an experience of the inner gaze turned toward the light at the moment of revelation, i.e. the moment of truth) to the theme of *circumcision.* The latter becomes pointless after the revelation or the 'unveiling' of Christ ('For in Christ Jesus not circumcision is good, nor the foreskin either, but faith, which is at work through charity' [5, 6])," *Mémoires d'aveugle,* p. 117.

ent gave *direct* access to sense, there would be neither sign nor language at all (Frege, Merleau-Ponty). And it is difficult to appeal to the signified as such without getting into a caricatural Platonism, or a physiological determinism which would deny language any originality and would again fall victim to Wittgensteinian arguments ("private language"). It will be remembered that, according to Saussure, signified and signifier are indissociable, *recto* and *verso* of a single sheet of paper: so it appears to follow that only the signifier can allow the sign to have an identity. The signifier is by all accounts the material face of the sign: that's how to avoid a vulgar materialism without avoiding materialism altogether.

8. This argument is false, or at least radically unsatisfactory. Of course we must say that the sign gets its identity from the signifier, but without accepting the consequence, which is incorrect. We shall indeed refuse to think of the signified as an entity or unity that could in principle be separated from its signifier. We shall not reduce the signifier to the simple status of an "acoustic image," as Saussure had it, and we shall go so far as to

that I might have signed, now future is the problem since if G., as I believe he was right to do and has done impeccably, has made this theologic program capable of the absolute knowledge of a nonfinite series of events properly, not only the enunciation of this law can ultimately do without me, without what I wrote in the past, or even what I seem to be writing here, but do without, foreseeing or predicting what I could well write in the future, so that here I am deprived of a future, no more event to come from me, at least insofar as I speak or write, unless I write here, every man for himself, no longer under his law, improbable things which destabilize, disconcert, surprise in their turn G.'s program, things that in short he, G., any more than my

say that the signified is just a signifier put in a certain position by other signifiers (GR, 7, 73), and that the difference between signifier and signified is *nothing* (GR, 23). It is not out of the question to talk of a "body of the signifier" when the context makes misunderstanding improbable (WD, 210). But we cannot in all rigor speak of a materialism of the signifier: first because the signifier is not material; second because there is no signifier.

The fact that the second of these two propositions erases the first does not imply that the first is useless: the second proposition would be meaningless if we did not demonstrate the first. This necessity of passing through an unsatisfactory formulation in order to advance further is not however a simply pedagogical or heuristic necessity, but an essential one: for we are here not advancing toward a triumphant truth or a finally adequate expression of a difficult thought—here, for example, the second proposition is not "better" than the first, and in fact, as such, as a *thesis,* it is perfectly untenable. We shall attempt later to thematize this situation. It implies at the least, and among other things,

mother or the grammar of his theologic program, will not have been able to recognize, name, foresee, produce, predict, *unpredictable things* to survive him, and if something should yet happen, nothing is less certain, it must be *unpredictable,* the salvation of a backfire.

6 Salvation being at this price, which has no other future alas than the name without literature, people will say that I'm giving G. a jealous scene, G. whom I love and admire, as will rapidly have been understood, whom I prefer, oh yes, and I could never have accepted, jealous as I am, to write a book, a

that Derrida's thought is not organized in the terms of a traditional conception of truth.

9. The doctrine of the materiality of the signifier, and, by the same token, the thought of the sign in general, runs aground on the thought of difference, also advanced by Saussure. For in fact we should never succeed in identifying the same sign through its nonidentical repetitions (important variations of accent, tone, graphism, etc.) if we had to count on its materiality alone. We must be able to recognize that it is the same sign in spite of all these variations, and this implies that what insures the sameness through the repetitions must indeed be an ideal-ity: the signifier is thus never purely or essentially sensible, even at the level of its phonological or graphological description. Derrida is perfectly clear on this point (GR, 10, 29, 91), which already blurs the distinction that is essential to the thought of the sign.

10. This ideality does not provide the sign with an identity quite as straightforwardly as this: ideality in repetition compromises with difference between repetitions, but also with differences in the system, Saus-

book about me, with anybody else, fighting with him over the right to deprive me of my events, i.e. to embrace the generative grammar of me and behave as though it was capable, by exhibiting it, of appropriating the law which presides over everything that can happen to me through writing, what I can write, what I have written or ever could write, for it is true that if I succeed in surprising him and surprising his reader, this success, success itself, will be valid not only for the future but also for the past for by showing that every writing to come cannot be engendered, anticipated, preconstructed from this matrix, I would signify to him in return that something in the past might have been withdrawn, if not in its content at least in the sap of the idiom, from the effusion of the signature, what I was calling a

sure's "system of differences without positive terms." The identity of the sign, even its ideal identity, is insured only by its difference with respect to other idealities. This difference *between* apparently sensible units cannot, by definition, be itself sensible (one cannot see [touch, hear, etc.] a difference as such). Given this, the matter or stuff from which it seemed that the signifiers were cut out, as it were, disappears from the essential definition of the sign, even on its signifier side. This is what ruins the tendency of linguistics to privilege one "substance of expression" (voice) over another (writing), and begins the deconstruction of phonocentrism, a prelude to the deconstruction of logocentrism (GR, 52–3).

11. There remains the privilege of the signifier which we have recognized in principle. In the system of differences that language is, every signifier functions by referring to other signifiers, without one ever arriving at a signified. Look up the signified of an unknown signifier in the dictionary and you find more signifiers, never any signifieds. As we have already said, a signi-

moment ago by the name of name and that I would be trying, against him, that would be my rule here, my law for the duration of these few pages, to reinscribe, reinvent, obliging the other, and first of all G., to recognize it, to pronounce it, no more than that, to call me finally beyond the owner's tour he has just done, forgetting me on the pretext of understanding me, and it is as if I were trying to oblige him to recognize me and come out of this amnesia of me which resembles my mother while I say to myself when I read this matrix there's the survivress signing in my place and if it is right, and it is, faultless, not only will I no longer sign but I will never have signed, is this not basically what I have always meant to say, and given that, for something to happen and for me finally to sign something for

fied is only a signifier placed in a certain position by other signifiers: there is no signified or meaning, but only "effects" of them (POS, 66–7). But this privilege given to the signifier destroys it immediately: for the signifier "signifier" only signifies in its differential relation with (the signifier) "signified," which is immediately placed in a position of priority. "Signifier" and "signified" imply each other, just as they imply "sign" and "referent." It is impossible for us to stipulate (with a gesture that is sometimes made by analytical philosophy) that "signifier" will henceforth no longer imply "signified" as its corollary, on pain of falling, like Humpty Dumpty, into the illusion of conventionalism, and of forgetting that we receive language and its sedimentations rather than creating it. This relation to language, which has always already begun before us, implies the whole of deconstruction, and we shall return to it more than once.

12. So we need to find a new language. But this runs the risk of being a scarcely less naive fantasy than the one that wants to continue to use the old terms,

myself, it would have to be against G., as though he wanted to love in my stead, and to stop him I was finally admitting some perjury that his programming machine couldn't providentially account for, a thing all the more improbable in that his matrix, i.e. mine, that which faultlessly he formalizes and which in the past seized hold of me, but when will this giving birth have begun, like a "logic" stronger than I, at work and verifiably so right down to so-called aleatory phenomena, the least systemic, the most undecidable of the sentences I've made or unmade, this matrix nevertheless opens, leaving room for the unanticipatable singularity of the event, it remains by essence, by force, nonsaturable, nonsuturable, invulnerable, therefore only extensible and transformable, always unfinished, for even if I wanted to

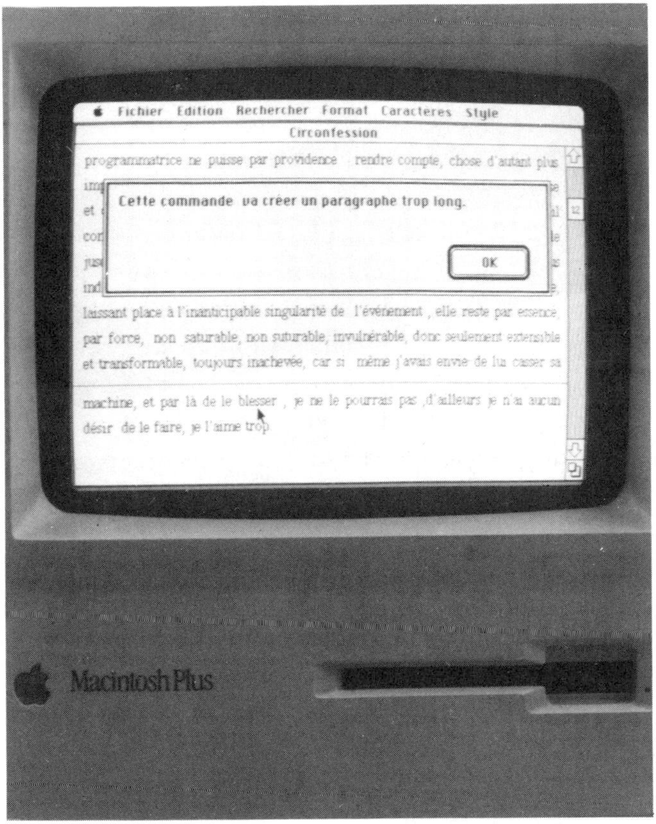

"Between the aleatory and the calculable ... chance and necessity": the provisional law of *Circumfession,* a machine—with which breath had to be calculated, each period punctuated, the contour of the periphrasis arrested, in a word, circumcision performed so that the event might challenge or surprise the *other* machination. Not a single sign more after the warning: command counter command."

changing their use all at once by simple decree. Let us imagine that we replace "signifier" with a new symbol, say "#." We would have changed nothing at all insofar as this symbol would take the same place in the network of differences as that occupied by "signifier," while giving our description a purely mystificatory look of scientificity or algorithmicity. And if this symbol managed to take the place of "signifier" and made us lose all memory of the reasoning we have just sketched out, then we could bet that the new symbol would function, amnesically, just as metaphysically as the old. The point is to shake up the system, not just to replace a few terms. Of course we must invent new terms, but we cannot create them ex nihilo by divine performative: rather take up the terms which are already a problem for metaphysical thought (writing, trace), and accentuate their power of diversion—while knowing a priori that we shall never find anything but nicknames, fronts (LI, 37), pseudonyms (LOB, 114).

13. So here we are faced with a dilemma: having shown that, by virtue of its apparently "material" priv-

break his machine, and in doing so hurt him, I couldn't do so, and anyway I have no desire to do so, I love him too much.

7 If it is invulnerable, this matrix, and some would say that that's its defect, what on earth can happen to it, from what wound is it waiting for me, me who, among other remorse with respect to my mother, feel really guilty for publishing her end, in exhibiting her last breaths and, still worse, for purposes that some might judge to be literary, at risk of adding a dubious exercise to the "writer and his mother" series, subseries "the

ilege in the structure of the sign, not only is the signifier not material but there is no signifier, we find that this last proposition cannot function as the triumphant conclusion of a chain of deductions which is nonetheless rigorous. In spite of appearances, these deductions have not destroyed the sign in favor of something quite different. We cannot simply decide to do without the concept of the sign, nor simply replace it with that of signifier, for—this major problem awaits us—if we did so we should deprive ourselves of the means of understanding translation (POS, 20). Our deductions have indeed demonstrated a sort of incoherence in the very construction of the concept "sign," but this incoherence affects just as much the concept "concept," which complicates irremediably all the traditional notions of critique, progress (but we shall see this progressively), and even of truth and history. The deconstruction of the sign thus affects *all* these other cornerstones of the conceptual edifice of metaphysics, up to and including the values of construction and edifice. This deconstruction is not something that someone does *to* metaphys-

mother's death," and what is there to be done, would I not feel as guilty, and would I not in truth *be* as guilty if I wrote here about myself without retaining the least trace of her, letting her die in the depth of another time, if I remember that December 24, 1988, when already she was hardly saying anything articulate anymore, nor apparently fitting the situation, nothing that thus seemed to answer to the normal rule of human exchange, she pronounced clearly, in the midst of confused groanings "I want to kill myself," and precisely what G. up there, very close or too late, cannot let you understand or guess, and that no doubt my writings can manifest but as though illegibly, follow-

ics, nor something that metaphysics does to *itself.* If things have "gone wrong," as we said at the beginning, this is neither because a catastrophe external to its system has come to spread trouble and ruin in it, nor because metaphysics has more or less slowly rotted according to a law of internal decline: on the contrary, *metaphysics only subsisted from its very beginnings through this deconstruction* (cf. DR, 273–4). It lives in it before dying of it, or, rather, it lives in it only by dying of it. Metaphysics lives only in what we have imprudently called an incoherence: we do not have the means to correct this incoherence, for it carries with it everything that gives us our measure of coherence. In following the sign through metaphysics, we have been obliged to borrow all our language and criteria of coherence—and we are attached to them—from the metaphysics of the sign: we are working in a milieu where possibility and impossibility imply one another, in a complexity that we are only beginning to glimpse.

14. So it is impossible to avoid complicity with metaphysics. This situation is one of necessity, and a lot

ing some rule of reading still to be formulated, is that "I want to kill myself" is a sentence of mine, me all over, but known to me alone, the mise en scène of a suicide and the fictive but oh how motivated, convinced, serious decision to put an end to my days, a decision constantly relaunched, a rehearsal which occupies the entire time of my internal theater, the show I put on for myself without a break, before a crowd of ghosts, a rite and an effusion which have a limit all the less for the fact that their invisibility is guaranteed, the very secret in which I keep this ritualized effusion, beginning with prayer and tears, and I wonder if those reading me from up there see my tears, today, those of the

of time has been lost discussing it as though it expressed an ethical or even political choice on Derrida's part. All ethical and political choices are made a priori in the milieu of this complicity, and every evaluation must take place within it too (which means that this complicity is not really a complicity) (GR, 14, 24; OS, 109–10; WD, 282). The metaphysical concept of "sign" is indispensable to everything that we have said so far, and serves as a good revealing agent or guiding thread for a demonstration that shakes up this concept and every other concept at the same time. There is no reason to deprive ourselves of the resources of this metaphysical concept (we could not; they are the only resources, resource itself, at the source [GR, 269–316; M, 273–306]). This demonstration is nonetheless not a simple exposition of the metaphysical concept of the sign, even though all it does is expose that concept. The metaphysical concept of the sign poses the distinction signifier/signified on the foundation given by the sensible/intelligible distinction, but works toward the reduction of that distinction in favor of the intelligible:

child about whom people used to say "he cries for nothing," and indeed, if they guess that my life was but a long history of prayers, and the incessant return of the "I want to kill myself" speaks less the desire to put an end to my life than a sort of compulsion to overtake each second, like one car overtaking another, doubling it rather, overprinting it with the negative of a photograph already taken with a "delay" mechanism, the memory of what survived me to be present at my disappearance, interprets or runs the film again, and already I catch them out seeing me lying on my back, in the depth of my earth, I mean, they understand everything, like the geologic program, except that I have lived

it thus reduces or effaces the sign by posing it as secondary from the start. Any attempt to reduce the distinction in the other direction works within the same logic, and, wanting to make the intelligible sensible, only manages to make the sensible intelligible according to a structure we shall explain later under the name of *transcendental contraband*. Deconstruction also reduces the sign in a sense (according to the demonstration we have summarized) precisely by *maintaining* it *against* this metaphysical reduction (SP, 51; WD, 281): this *maintenance* is achieved by insisting, in an obviously untenable way, on the priority of the sign with respect to the referent (which implies that there is no thing in itself outside the networks of referrals in which signs function [GR, 48–50]), and, in the sign, on the priority of the signifier with respect to the signified (which implies that there is no signified and therefore no signifier)—in general, on *the originarity of the secondary:* it is obvious that this formulation is a non-sense in the very simple sense of going against the very sense of sense. A secondary origin can be neither originary nor secondary, and there is therefore no origin. As we announced

in prayer, tears and the imminence at every moment of their survival, terminable survival from which "I see myself live" translates "I see myself die," I see myself dead cut from you in your memories that I love and I weep like my own children at the edge of my grave, I weep not only for my children but for all my children, why only you, my children?

above, we find that there is no thing, no sign, and no beginning.

This "example" of deconstruction, which we shall supplement in a moment by analyzing what is no doubt the most celebrated deconstruction by Derrida, bearing on speech and writing, and of which the analysis of the sign is only a part, can already help us to understand why Derrida's work has often been received as a virtuoso and sophistical manipulation of paradoxes and puns, which takes an evil pleasure in mocking a whole metaphysical tradition, leading to a nihilism which paralyzes thought and action or, at best, to an "artistic" practice of philosophy and a literary aestheticism. Of course, there is no need to deny the virtuosity, or the pleasure (POS, 6–7), nor, perhaps more marked in these early, so "serious" texts, a demand for play and dance (M, 27; WD, 290, 292–3), even though this demand is always complicated beyond the choice that at first sight is offered us. But these paradoxes are not imported into metaphysics by Derrida; on the contrary, they constitute metaphysics and in some sense speak its

8 As if I loved only your memory and confession of me but who would I be, me, if I did not begin and end by loving you in my private language deprived of you, that very one, the untranslatable one, in which the joke leaves us floored, winners and losers like the day on which a premeditation of love had dictated to me for immortality, no, for posterity, no, for the truth that you are, *et lex tua ueritas, et ueritas tu,** "don't forget that I will have loved you" ["*n'oublie pas que je t'aurai aimé*"] thinking myself at that point cunning enough to avoid the conditional by specifying so loud, "A I [pronounced *haï,* 'hated'], of course," Jackie, the vowels, my voice of your name or the name of my only sister, and perceiving only after the event this very advance or this delay through which a hatred effaces itself

truth: what is shocking is that this "truth" of metaphysical truth can no longer be thought of as truth (SP, 54n.4)—which does not prevent one from thinking.

WRITING

The deconstruction of the sign was able to assert itself by insisting on what metaphysics thinks of as a certain materiality or exteriority of the signifier. More generally, deconstruction gets going by attempting to present as primary what metaphysics says is secondary. If metaphysics constructs the sign in general as secondary, it thinks of writing as *even more* secondary, as the sign of the sign or, more exactly, as the (graphic) signifier of the (phonic) signifier (GR, 7, 43). According to its traditional determination (especially in the *telos* assigned to writing by Western thought, i.e., not only "phonetic" but "alphabetic" writing [GR, 3ff., 299ff.; SCR, 24]), writing has no direct signified or referent (whence wariness and fascination for those writing systems called pictographic or ideographic), but refers to

in contraband to exchange itself with the love of you, with the gift of me, *ego uereo cogitans dona tua, deus invisibilis,***, from the same poker play in which I was born, as they told me I was born, while my mother, *qualis illa erat,**** up to the last moment, that is my very birth, in summer, in what in El-Biar they called a villa, refused to interrupt at dawn a poker game, the passion of her life, they say, her passion of life, and here among her last words, in the insensate flow I'm speaking of, while amnesiac she no longer recognizes me or remembers my name, I hear her murmur, March 7, 1989, "I'm losing," then reply "I don't know" to the question "what does that mean?", and what I'm failing to translate here, under what death agony came to magnify in these words, is the almost quotidian tone of a verdict

the phonic signifier of which it is supposed to be no more than the transcription. If, then, one wishes to insist on what metaphysics thought of as secondary and external, writing—secondary with respect to the secondary, outside the outside, supplement of a supplement—merits our attention.

There is nothing surprising in this position of writing, which there is no question of *criticizing* as such. We write when we cannot speak, when contingent obstacles, which can be reduced to so many forms of distance, prevent the voice from carrying. Writing is a form of telecommunication (M, 311–13): we know all its advantages, which are not without serious problems too, just as well known. There is no question of contesting experience here: everyone knows that the written word hugely extends the scope of language in space and time, and that what we commonly call history, at least thought of as progress or decline, only begins with it. Everyone also knows that for all sorts of reasons writing exposes thought to risks which sometimes, if not most often, seem to be more important than the advantages. I may well take my time writing,

that I still hear being said, "I'm losing," cards in hand, over there, on the other shore, in the middle of a poker game a summer's evening or just before the end, the one I'm running after, wondering at every moment if she will still be alive, having nonetheless stopped recognizing me, when I arrive at the end of this sentence which seems to bear the death that bears her, if she will live long enough to leave me time for all these confessions, and to multiply the scenes in which I see myself alone die, pray, weep, at the end of a circumnavigation trying to reach its bank in a story of blood, at the point where I am finally this cauterized name, the ultimate, the unique, right up against what, from an improbable circumcision, I have lost by gaining, and when I say that I want to gain my name against G., that does not mean

revise and hone my work, etc., and even find in it a certain freedom that speech denies me (WD, 101–2), but I can be sure neither of the success of the destination of my text or my letter (which are in principle readable by anyone at all, even if I write in code [M, 315]), nor of the correct understanding of my message, supposing it does arrive at its destination: for on the one hand writing does not transcribe all the phonetic qualities of my speech which can contribute to the transport of my thought (intonation, accent: phonetic writing is never phonetic through and through [M, 4–5]), and on the other, I am not there to take up obscure sentences or reply when the interlocutor perceives an ambiguity where I thought I was being clear, and asks me what I meant. And whereas speech fades instantaneously in the very time of its pronunciation, writing lasts and can always return to commemorate or damn me. And even if I am prudent or modest enough to write nothing compromising, writing is essentially falsifiable: if one is not a priori certain of reaching the right addressee, neither is the addressee a priori certain of the identity of sender or signatory.

the opposite of losing, whether one understand winning in the sense of a game, winning at poker, or in the sense of a voyage, of arriving, winning the bank, or in the sense of toil, of earning, winning one's life, the horrible expression that *I win,* that's what they will never have understood, I like neither the word nor the thing, whence the indefinite referral, so-called negative theology, the play with the names of God, the substitution of one bank for the other, the hemophiliac panic which interrupts itself on the order come from on high and opposite at once, the rhythmic injunction to which I give in without having to be asked.

*"And 'Thy law is the Truth' and 'Thou art the Truth' " (IV, ix, 14).

Much more than the spoken signifier, writing thus seems to accentuate the risk of the detour via the sensible world implied in every signifier. Of course, speech goes out from me into the world, but scarcely so, and when I speak to myself it appears not to leave me at all: but writing *remains* in a monumentality which we shall soon see linked to death.

It is therefore scarcely surprising that Derrida has been able to pick out, throughout the tradition, so many warnings against writing, virulent condemnations even, or simply implicit debasements of writing in the promotion of the excellence of speech: these texts, which go from Plato to Lacan and the theorists of speech acts, via all the great names of the tradition, and which essentially repeat the Platonic schema whereby writing is the bastard or even parricidal son of the *logos,* are lengthily quoted and commented on by Derrida with an attention and meticulousness whose modalities and necessity we shall interrogate later. Where we find texts which appear to contradict this norm—and they are frequent, even among the authors who denounce writing the most violently elsewhere—

**"But, thinking over Thy gifts, O Invisible God... [remembering what I had known of the great concern which she had exhibited in regard to the burial place which she had arranged and prepared for herself beside the body of her husband]" (IX, xi, 28).

***"Such a person was she, [under the influence of Thy teaching as an inner Teacher in the school of her breast]" (IX, ix, 21).

9 Among the sentences that G. is right not to quote, all of them in short, there is one, the only one, I recall it myself, but precisely as though I had not written it then, more than ten years ago, as though I had not yet read the address thus kept in

Derrida has no trouble in showing that such passages (in which there is recourse to the "metaphor" of writing to state, in opposition to secondary writing, the inscription of truth itself in the soul, of the moral law in the heart, of natural law in general) give a sense to this valorized writing which brings it close again to voice and breath: "pneumatological" rather than "grammatological" writing (GR, 17). The possibility of such a "metaphor" will pose us some difficult problems later, both as *scriptural* metaphor and as scriptural *metaphor.* The frequency and consistency of this configuration in this whole tradition, through all the epochs one might distinguish in it, suggest that this relationship with writing must have something to do with what linked these texts into a tradition which has wanted to be *one* tradition: and, as we shall see, the idea that the traditionality of tradition cannot be thought outside a certain relation with writing, which seems to be a hypothesis, is in fact an analytical consequence. A little later, we shall refute the historian's objection which protests against what it takes to be a flattening out of history and a refusal of differences and discontinuities in this

reserve for the counterexample or the denial I want constantly to oppose to G., in other words to the eternal survivress, to the theologic program or maternal figure of absolute knowledge for which the surprise of no avowal is possible, and this sentence says that "one always asks for pardon when one writes,"* so as to leave suspended the question of knowing if one is finally asking pardon in writing for some earlier crime, blasphemy, or perjury or if one is asking for pardon for the crime, blasphemy, or perjury in which consists presently the act of writing, the simulacrum of avowal needed by the perverse overbidding of the crime to exhaust evil, the evil I have committed in truth, the worst, without being sure of having even sponged it from my life, and it's the worst, but my compatriot had a premonition of

massive description of a whole Western "tradition." Let us say immediately that these reproaches, which emanate mostly, but not solely, from the human sciences rather than from philosophy, in a polemical haste that we shall have to interrogate in itself, tend more or less crudely to aim at the wrong target and to mix up levels (and especially times, rhythms) of analysis with no control (WD, 129n.46)—and as such confusion sometimes thinks it can draw authority from Derrida himself, we shall need time and prudence (in fact an infinite vigilance, as we shall see) to account for these misunderstandings.

So let us accept for the moment Derrida's assertions about the debasement of writing in the Western tradition. The most obvious and least interesting conclusion (which people have been tempted to take as Derrida's own conclusion) is that philosophy is thus caught in what is called a "performative contradiction," because philosophers nonetheless *write* these indictments of writing. This is not nothing, of course, but nothing prevents philosophy from recognizing, perhaps to go on to deplore it, that its own discourse is

it, if a writing worthy of the name avows so as to ask pardon for the worst, literally, *et nunc, domine, confiteor tibi in litteris,*★★ and turns away from God through the very piece of writing addressed to his brothers on the death of their mother, even were it supposedly to call them back to charity in the presence of God, *legat qui uolet et interpretetur, ut uolet, et si peccatum inuenerit, fleuisse me matrem exigua parte horae, matrem oculis meis interim mortuam, quae me multos annos fleuerat, ut oculis tuis uniuerem, non inrideat, sed potius, si est grandi caritate, pro peccatis meis fleat ipse ad te, patrem omnium fratrum Christi tui,*★★★ no matter, writing is only interesting in proportion and in the experience of evil, even if the point is indeed to "make" truth in a style, a book and before witnesses, *uolo eam [ueritatem] facere in corde meo coram te in*

written, while nonetheless prescribing living speech as the ideal *telos* of language. It would be necessary to show that philosophy is *essentially* written if we wished to make this a serious argument. Which is what Derrida will do, and the argument will entail consequences which go well beyond the slightly mocking irony toward the tradition that has sometimes been attributed to him.

> Among these consequences, we shall find the origin of space and time, a refutation of humanism, a deconstructive articulation of the empirical and the transcendental, and other things too. I use the word "consequences" out of provisional convenience, and it would be just as accurate to say that the order is the reverse, and that what will be expounded first (or even what has already been expounded) is in fact the consequence of what is here presented as its consequence. The solidarity implied here is not that of a linear deduction, nor of a circle or a table: we must reserve the possibility of finding other ways of describing what is going on here, but the reader will have understood that there is something irreducibly arbitrary in our procedure as much as

---

*confessione, in stilo autem meo coram multis testibus,***** *and make* the truth in this case that I'm not sure comes under any religion, for reason of literature, nor under any literature, for reason of religion, making *truth* has no doubt nothing to do with what you call truth, for in order to confess, it is not enough to *bring to knowledge,* to make *known what is,* for example to *inform* you that I have done to death, betrayed, blasphemed, perjured, it is not enough that *I present myself* to God or you, the presentation of what is or what I am, either by revelation or by adequate judgment, "truth" then, having never given rise to avowal, to true avowal, the *essential* truth of avowal having therefore nothing to do with truth, but consisting, if, that is, one is concerned that it consist and that there be any, in asked-for pardon, in a request

in Derrida's, that to a certain variable but inevitable extent we are progressing without navigational aids, following our noses (GR, 162), and that a work such as this is uncomfortable with the order of the book, and aspires to the condition of a computer program with multiple entries, for example.

The famous and much misunderstood generalization of the term "writing" or "archi-writing," in tight collaboration with the terms "trace," "différance," and "text," proceeds according to a striking clarity and simplicity, given the enormous difficulties it implies. First of all, the features which distinguish the traditional concept of writing are isolated, then it is shown that these elements apply to the traditional concept of speech as much as to writing; finally there is a justification of the maintenance of the term "writing" for this general structure. Briefly: "writing" implies repetition, absence, risk of loss, death; but no speech would be possible without these values; moreover, if "writing" has always meant a signifier referring to other signifiers, and if, as we have seen, *every* signifier refers only to other signifiers, then "writing" will name properly

rather, asked of religion as of literature, *before* the one and the other which have a right only to this time, for pardoning, pardon, for nothing.

* *The Post Card—from Socrates to Freud and Beyond,* I think.

** "And now, O Lord, I am confessing to Thee in writing" (IX, xii, 33).

*** "Let him who wishes read and interpret it as he wishes. If he finds it a sin that I wept for my mother during a little part of an hour, the mother who was dead for the time being to my eyes, who had wept over me for many years that I might live before Thy eyes—let him not be scornful; rather, if he is a person of

the functioning of language in general. We shall see why only the hypothesis of the proper name is false here, and that to say so implies that we shall in some sense transgress the limits of language, which will explain why, as we have already announced, Derrida's thought is not essentially a philosophy of language.

Writing communicates my thought to far distances, during my absence, even after my death. At the moment of reading my letter, the addressee knows that I might have died during the time, however minimal it may be, between the moment at which the letter was finished and the moment of its reception. The "delay" affecting writing gave rise, in the seventeenth and eighteenth centuries, to a whole literary debate as to the posibility of writing without falsity or impropriety the sentence "I am dead" in a letter written just before a suicide or execution: and the same question could be asked of a will. (And we shall see that the question of literature hangs on this point too.) All sorts of accidents can prevent my letter surviving me de facto: but de jure a letter which was not readable after my death

great charity, let him weep himself for my sins, before Thee, the Father of all the brethren of Thy Christ" (IX, xii, 33).

**** "I desire to do this [the truth] in my heart, before Thee in confession; and in my writing, before many witnesses" (X, i, 1).

10 Chance or arbitrariness of the starting point, irresponsibility even, you will say, inability I still have to answer for my name, even to give it back to my mother, remains (the fact) that I am here now, let us suppose, for I shall never be able to demonstrate the fact, the counterexample in series of what I might have written or what G. might know about it, and the fear that has gripped me since always, for to that at least I am

would not be a letter. It is not necessary for me to be dead for you to be able to read me, but it is necessary for you to be able to read me even if I am dead. Derrida calls this sort of possibility (here, the possibility that I be dead) an *essential* or *necessary* possibility (LI, 47ff.; M, 316). My mortality (my finitude) is thus inscribed in everything I inscribe (GR, 69; SP, 54ff.). What is here called "death" is the generic name we shall give to my absence in general with respect to what I write—whether this absence be real or an absence of attention or intention or sincerity or conviction... When you read me, not only do you not know whether or not I am dead, but whether what I write is really what I meant, fully *compos mentis,* at the moment of writing, etc. That there be this fundamental and irreducible uncertainty is part of the essential structure of writing.

So much for me. The argument is not essentially different for you. I write in your absence, because you are far away, and I must know at the moment I write that you could be dead before my text reaches you. I write "you" to re-mark the fact (already marked in the mark) that my text presupposes an addressee. But the

faithful, discords with itself, threatens itself from two apparently contradictory imminences, that of the writer who is afraid of dying before the end of a long sentence, period, without signing the counterexample, and that of the son who, dreading seeing her die before the end of the avowal, for this confession promised unto death, trembles then too at the thought of departing before his mother, this figure of absolute survival he's talked so much about, but also the one who literally could not weep for him, it would be an excess of suffering for one who has already lost two sons, one before me, Paul Moïse, who died in 1929 when less than one year old, one year before my birth, which must have made me for her, for them, a precious but so

fact that it functions does not depend on the empirical existence of this or that addressee in particular, not even you. Even if it is uniquely and exclusively addressed to you, my letter must remain readable in principle after your death as much as after mine. It loses at the same stroke its uniqueness and exclusivity. To write is to know a priori that I am mortal, but that the addressee is mortal too: to read is to know a priori that the author is mortal, but that I, the reader, am mortal too. Which suggests that the two "activities" of writing and reading interact otherwise than in the obvious symmetry that constitutes their usual concept, but also that we must beware of celebrating too quickly the "death of the author" and believing that this death can be paid for by the "birth of the reader." We should have to say, rather, that the death of the reader (and therefore of interpretation in its usual form) is an analytic consequence of the death of the author: no doubt every author writes in relation to his own mortality—but for the survival of his name: we shall come back to this—and that of his immediate readers, but all the while fantasizing a totalized addressee, called posterity (or the

vulnerable intruder, one mortal too many, Elie loved in the place of another, then the other after me, Norbert Pinhas, dead aged two when I was ten, in 1940, without the least image of his circumcision that I nonetheless remember, and I saw then the first mourning as the mourning of my mother who could not, then, literally weep for me, me the sole replacement, weep for me as my sons will have to, whereas my sole desire remains that of giving to be read the interruption that will in any case decide the very figure, this writing that resembles the poor chance of a provisional resurrection, like the one that took place in December 1988 when a phone call from my brother-in-law sent me run-

judgment of history)—it would be necessary to show that this fantasy, which is made possible by the structure that we have begun to pick out, is simultaneously rendered unrealizable by it.

For these arguments have a paradoxical consequence: the distinction that starts them off is threatened by their rigorous development; this is a movement that we have already seen at work in the analysis of the sign and which we shall see repeat itself as the movement of deconstruction (itself). Here, the customary divisions between author and reader, sending and reception, dispatch and arrival are not watertight. As author, I am *already* addressee at the moment I write. One can of course maintain, with Blanchot, that no author can really read himself, but the fact remains that in order to write I must read myself, if only in a minimal sense, in the moment that I write. The act of writing is from the first divided by this complicity between writing and reading, which immediately prevents one from considering this act so easily as an act, and blurs at the same time the activity/passivity (or production/consumption) distinction that underlies the usual understanding

ning for the first plane to Nice, tie, dark suit, white *kippa* in my pocket, trying in vain not only to cry but, I don't know, to stop myself crying, *et fletum frenabam,** to get myself out of all the programs and quotations, when the unforeseeable did not fail to happen, surprising me absolutely but like what goes without saying, inflexible destiny, i.e, that having been incapable of recognizing me that evening and, according to the doctors only due to survive a few hours, in the early morning at the moment when, having slept alone in her house, I arrived first in the white room at the clinic, she saw me, heard me and, so to speak, came round, as though immortal, SA also had this experience, went

of writing. As in the deconstruction of the sign, the deconstruction we see here (and which, although never made explicit by Derrida, is suggested at various points [WD, 11–2, 226–7]) will give rise to propositions that are unacceptable in the language of metaphysics (i.e., that of common sense). For we move easily from this originary complication of the opposition writing/reading to the idea of the absolute priority of a certain writing one reads (and in the end the already-thereness of language), which *souffle* what I write, in the double sense of dictating my text to me and simultaneously dispossessing me of my writing in its act before it begins (WD, 169–95)—what is usually called inspiration. There would thus be a fundamental passivity (GR, 66) preceding the activity/passivity opposition. Further on we will attempt, a little naively, to get the measure of this passivity before passivity.

This situation would require extremely delicate analyses if one wished to respect the very different modalities that this mutual implication of writing and reading can take (*A la recherche du temps perdu* is perhaps simply the very example of such a delicacy and re-

through it, was its *Savoir Absolu,* SA tells us, *cito reddita est sensui,*** and I write between two resurrections, the one that is given then the one that is promised, compromised to this almost natural monument which becomes in my eyes a sort of calcinated root, the naked spectacle of a photographed wound—the bedsore cauterized by the light of writing, to fire, to blood but to ash too.

*"[She said: 'Bury your mother here.' I remained silent] and restrained my tears" (IX, xi, 27).

spect): as we are trying to show a priori, the deconstruction of metaphysical oppositions does not lead to an undifferentiated and homogeneous confusion or chaos, as people have sometimes made out, but to a situation in which absolutely singular configurations have a chance to be events. The fact remains that the unity of the act of writing and/or reading is divided; the gap thus introduced between the agencies of "sender" and "addressee" (but also within each of these agencies) implies, at the least, that writing can never fully "express" a thought or realize an intention (D, 225, 248; LI, 55ff., 128; M, 159, 223, 322; POS, 33–4): not, as we shall see, that we can henceforth cross the words "intention" and "expression" from our lexicon—but they are already carried off or away in writing.

The necessary possibility of the death of the writer, in this extended sense, thus makes every sender an addressee, and vice versa. This "death" opens writing to the general alterity of its destination, but simultaneously forbids any sure or total arrival at such a destination: the presumed unity of a text, marked in prin-

** "[We hastily gathered about her], but she returned to consciousness quickly [and looked at me and my brother as we stood by. Rather like a person in search of something, she said to us: 'Where am I?' Then, seeing that we were overcome with grief, she said: 'Bury your mother here']" (IX, xi, 27).

11 No point going round in circles, for as long as the other does not know, and know in advance, as long as he will not have won back this advance at the moment of the pardon, that unique moment, the great pardon that has not yet happened

ciple by its author's signature, thus has to wait on the other's countersignature (we shall come back to this). But every determinate addressee, and thus every act of reading, is affected by the same "death," it therefore follows that every countersignature has to wait on others, indefinitely, that reading has no end, but is always to-come as work of the other (and never of the Other—a text never comes to rest in a unity or meaning finally revealed or discovered. This work must also be a work of mourning. In truth, only this situation allows a text to have a "life" or, as we shall say later, an "afterlife." For the moment, let us hang on to the fact that the written text presupposes this mortality of empirical writers and readers; it is therefore indifferent to their real death: to this extent the text is inhuman (soon we shall say that it is a machine) and in its very principle exceeds the resources of any humanist analysis.

Nothing limits these consequences to the written text. They depend on a power of repetition in alterity—an *iterability* (LI passim)—which is in principle infinite. This marks the finitude of every author and every reader. (Further on we shall have to complicate

in my life, indeed I am waiting for it as absolute unicity, basically the only event from now on, no point going round in circles, so long as the other has not won back that advance I shall not be able to avow anything and if avowal cannot consist in declaring, making known, informing, telling the truth, which one can always do, indeed, without confessing anything, without *making* truth, the other must not learn anything that he was not already in a position to know for avowal as such to begin, and this is why I am addressing myself here to God, the only one I take as a witness, without yet knowing what these sublime words mean, and this grammar, and *to,* and *witness,* and *God,* and *take,* take God, and not only do I pray, as I have never stopped doing all my life, and pray to him, but I take him here

The façade of the Lycée de Ben Aknoun, a former monastery, near El-Biar. J. D. starts there in the first year, is expelled the following year (October 1942) with the application of the anti-Jewish laws. The school is transformed into a military hospital on the arrival of the Allies. J. D. joins the school again after the war and finishes his secondary studies there.

this relation of finite and infinite, still too implicit here.) From this point of view, writing has only a heuristic privilege. For every sign, be it spoken or written, must be repeatable—a "sign" which was essentially singular and which could be used only once would not be a sign (LI, 48ff.; SP, 50). It is a matter of complete indifference to know whether we are talking here of written or spoken signs: long before the invention of the tape recorder and other repetition machines, speech was already essentially repeatable. And therefore as indifferent to the death of the speaker as to that of the hearer. Once again, the fact that the vast majority of statements has not in fact been recorded or repeated in the usual sense in no way stops the possibility of repetition from constituting their primary possibility, and this from the very "first" time.

This power of repetition, and the mortality it recalls, can appear to deny any possibility that a statement be singular: we are tempted to say that the argument about repetition is situated on the level of language (of *langue* in Saussure's sense), but that the

and take him as my witness, I give myself what he gives me, i.e. the *i.e.* to take the time to take God as a witness to ask him not only, for example, like SA, why I take pleasure in weeping at the death of the friend, *cur fletus dulcis sit miseris?,** and why I talk to him in Christian Latin French when they expelled from the Lycée de Ben Aknoun in 1942 a little black and very Arab Jew who understood nothing about it, to whom no one ever gave the slightest reason, neither his parents nor his friends, but why do I address her like him, my God, to avow, while he is the very thing who, I know nothing else about him when I prepare for avowal, must already know, and indeed he knows that very thing, as you well know, *cur confitemur Deo scienti,* you the knower, in your science required by desire and the first impulse

level of speech (*parole*) just is that of singularities, where what is said is said once, here and now, in such and such a place, at such and such a date. And this is not false: but that these "once only" events of speech are made possible by iterability is the whole problem, and it is a problem complex enough to cast into doubt the very distinction between *langue* and *parole*.

For one could indeed object that it is only on the level of *langue* that the demonstrations about iterability and death take place. No one is likely to be surprised that the distinction between speech and writing is not pertinent at that level: it is clear, and Saussure's inconsistencies in this respect matter little (we will happily express our gratitude to Derrida for having brought out these inconsistencies), that *langue* as a system (be it determined, as by Saussure, as a repertoire of elements or, in more Chomskian fashion, as a set of rules) goes beyond any given user of that system, and that it functions in the same way for events of speech as for events of writing. But, one might conclude, to claim to draw from this an argument for blurring the speech/writing

of avowal, the witness I am seeking, for, yes, for, without yet knowing what this sublime vocable, *for,* means in so many languages, for already having found him, and you, no, according to you, for having sought *to* find him around a trope or an ellipsis that we pretend to organize, and for years I have been going round in circles, trying to take as a witness not to see myself being seen but to re-member myself around a single event, I have been accumulating in the attic, my "sublime," documents, inconography, notes, learned ones and naive ones, dream narratives or philosophical dissertations, applied transcription of encyclopedic, sociological, historical, psychoanalytical treatises that I'll never do anything with, about circumcisions in the world, the Jewish and the Arab and the others, and excision,

distinction *at the level of parole,* let alone treat all acts of *parole* as writing or text, is to encourage the worst forms of confusion.

Let us recall Derrida's procedure. The point is to show, against the dominant currents of the philosophical tradition, that the features habitually attributed to writing (distance, death, repetition in the absence of an animating intention, ambiguity, etc.) are just as applicable to speech. Not in order to give writing all the virtues usually attributed to speech, nor even to praise other virtues of writing or in general to recommend its excellence (GR, 56–7). But to show that the generally admitted relations between speech and writing (and the traditional primacy of speech) rest on a dubious argumentation, to the extent that these relations must draw their possibility from an earlier root: we call this root "writing" or "archi-writing" because the current concept of writing names obliquely some of its components, while enclosing them far from living speech. A certain conception of language encourages this analysis, but we can push its consequences to the point where even the difference between *parole* and *langue,*

with a view to my circumcision alone, the circumcision of me, the unique one, that I know perfectly well took place, one time, they told me and I see it but I always suspect myself of having cultivated, because I am circumcised, *ergo* cultivated, a fantastical affabulation.

* "Why tears are sweet to those in misfortune?" (IV, v, 10).

between event and institution, becomes enigmatic. We will accept the apparently transcendental situation of *langue* with respect to *parole,* but this effect of transcendentality, and therefore what distinguishes *langue* from *parole,* is produced by the logic of repetition and death we have just picked out (M, 315–16; SP, 54–5), and cannot therefore dominate that logic. The "linguisticist" objection fails, then, while telling us something about the relationship between deconstruction and the "human sciences" in general: it is possible to show that the latter must always presuppose the validity of certain philosophical distinctions if they are to do their work, that they always give rise to (later we shall say that they *vomit*) at least one transcendental term that they are constitutively incapable of questioning, at the very moment at which they attempt to absorb or reduce philosophy to the status of being no more than a more or less illusory product of anthropological, sociological, or linguistic operations. We must allow for what in Derrida can sometimes look like a quite classical defense of philosophy (cf. LI, 125) against the pretensions of the human sciences. This is the case, notably, of texts on

12 I have not yet closed her eyes but she will not see me again, whereas I see her eyes wide open, for my mother can no longer see, I had forgotten to say so, she can hardly see now, one can't really tell, her gaze no longer focuses, scarcely following the direction of the voices, less and less every day, and in telling you last night's dream, those two blind men fighting one another, one of the two old men turning aside to take me on, to take to task and take by surprise the poor passer-by that I am, now here he is harassing me, blackmailing me, pulling me down with him, grabs me again with such agility that I suspect him of being able to see at least through one half-open eye, he's still got me, playing with one hold after another and ends up using the arm against which I have no defense, a threat against

Lévi-Strauss (GR, 101–140; WD, 278–94) and on Benveniste (M, 177–205), but it is also the rule of the complex relations of Derrida's work with psychoanalysis. But we must add that this apparent defense is itself complex: the point is not to claim that we must choose philosophy over the human sciences, but that, if we fail to respect certain philosophical demands and fail to go through transcendental questions, then we risk falling back into naiveté (GR, 60–1). It is the rhythm of such a going through that we should like to communicate here.

We have shown how it is possible to extend to speech certain predicates habitually reserved for writing. We have seen that a certain form of objection, which invokes the distinction between *langue* and *parole,* falls away as soon as what is being elaborated under the name of "writing" is shown to precede such a distinction. We might still have a strong sense of unease, and a stubborn conviction that if our common experience of writing answers quite well to these descriptions, our experience of speech obstinately refuses this movement of generalization to the whole of language.

my noncircumcised sons, telling you this dream without understanding anything more than the return of a family, a family of words to be taken, I became aware of having, in yesterday's pulsion, like in a tributary basin, in the same blood, taken in this syllable "pri" in which are mixed up all the essences of taking [*pris* is the past participle of *prendre,* to take] and praying [*prier*], if indeed I pray the other as witness not to see me being seen but to come down to the one, and then I remember having gone to bed very late after a moment of anger or irony against a sentence of Proust's, praised in a book in this collection "Les Contemporains," which says: "A work in which there are theories is like an object on which one has left the price tag," and I find nothing more vulgar than this Franco-Britannic decorum, European in

The point, however, is that this movement of generalization does not stop at language, opposite or against our experience, but infiltrates "experience" itself. For example, we will say that consciousness and, therefore, the common conception of experience are constructed on the basis of a certain representation of living speech as an experience of hearing oneself speak (GR, 20; SP, 10, 15), and that thus we will be unable to establish the truth of this situation by appealing to experience. However, we must follow the most rigorous attempt (that of Husserl, according to Derrida) to safeguard this unity of voice and consciousness in the presence of the living present, first to show that it is impossible to withdraw a kernel of presence from what we are beginning to call writing, but also to guard against the temptation of believing that it is sufficient to invoke the unconscious to escape these problems. The point will not be to refute Husserl, but to *cross* his text and leave in it the trace or wake of this crossing (GR, 62): we will have understood nothing of deconstruction if we think of these crossings of the text of the other as means to an end, to conclusions in the forms of theses. There are

truth, I associate with it Joyce, Heidegger, Wittgenstein, and a few others, the salon literature of that republic of letters, the grimace of a good taste naive enough to believe that one can efface the labor of theory, as if there wasn't any in Pr., and mediocre theory at that, to believe that one must and above all that one can efface the price to be paid, the symptom if not the avowal, I always ask what the theory is a symptom of and I admit that I write with the price on, I display, not so that the price be legible to the first-comer, for I am for an aristocracy without distinction, therefore without vulgarity, for a democracy of the compulsion to the highest price, you have to pay the price to read the price displayed, one writes only at the moment of giving the contemporary the slip, with a word, the word for word,

only crossings. Which does not imply that all crossings are equivalent.

HUSSERL

Saussure is looking for an object of sufficient definition to ground a science of language, and believes he has found it in *la langue,* the language system. Husserl, as a philosopher, must question everything, including the foundations of a science in general, which he does by looking toward the sense-giving acts of a transcendental consciousness. He cannot be content with saying, like Saussure, that language is received like the law, but must try to understand the constitution of that language and/or that law. In a word, it will be found that only idealities can give a foundation to sciences, but there is ideality only through and by repetition: this repetition brings with it an alterity that forbids the unity of the foundation it was supposed to insure.

According to Husserl, there are two sorts of signs: indications and expressions. Indications are all caught

you'll see, giving the slip to all those I've just named, i.e. to the sociological program and so many others, that's the condition for it to take (*pour que ça prenne*), untranslatable locution, losing one's head between two values, on the stage where it takes because one believes in it, one has believed in it, in blasphemy, simulacrum, imposture, supplement of perjury called avowal but also on the scene where it takes, just now, like that chaos of red lava that hardens to put itself to work, only by not coagulating.

up in a facticity which compromises their ideality and forbids all certainty: the canals on Mars are *perhaps* an indication of intelligent life, my blushing *perhaps* betrays an embarrassment, but meaning is here subject to mistake and is at best no more than probable; meaning is not *expressed* in such signs, which are not the product of meaning-*giving* acts. Indications may *say* something, but do not *mean* to say anything, have no *meaning* in that sense. In interlocution too, my words, which attempt to express my intentions or my meaning, only indicate them to the other party, represent what is properly present to myself alone, must go outside into facticity and the physical side of the sign. This indication cannot be the essence of signification, for I can also speak to myself, indicating nothing, not going outside to communicate my thought, without for all that losing meaning. Even if meaning is de facto almost always caught up in indication, indication cannot be the genus of which expression would merely be a species: to show this, we must therefore find examples of expression pure of all indication.

In its purity, expression expresses in the self-

13 At the moment when it takes, I know, respectfully but dead jealous, I am the contemporary of none of those I named yesterday, in the last blood-taking, nor of all the others, today for me meaning this day on which they begin to be unbearable, and beyond the contretemps I belong to the blind man blackmailing me, on the verge of a recitative, like this: "When a song expresses, for example, a sadness caused by a loss, we can rightfully ask immediately: what has been lost?", sucking up the blood through a lightweight cloth, the tight filter of a white dressing round the penis, on the seventh day, when they would put on orange-flower water in Algeria, with the theory, among

presence of consciousness. The internal voice with which I express myself to myself in the silent self-presence of my consciousness preserves meaning in its purity, with respect to which all the forms of indication must be considered as secondary and derivative. In my inner life I do not *communicate* with myself, even if that is how I imagine it: we must distinguish between *real* communication (which always implies indication) from the *imaginary* communication with myself in soliloquy, in which I speak with a voice that does not fall outside into the space of the world, and which is at the furthest possible remove, for example, from writing. But how are we to be sure of this distinction between the real and the imaginary? Every sign, if it is to be a sign, must presuppose the possibility of repetition (iterability). Because of this possibility, the present presentation of meaning by expression is *haunted* by its repetition. Its reproduction or representation is always possible. The sign is a sign only in this milieu of *re-* in which the distinction Husserl needs between a true communication and a "communication" with myself which would be merely imaginary or represented can-

so many others, that by mingling with the blood right on that wound that I have never seen, seen with my own eyes, this perfumed water attenuates the pain which I suppose to be nil and infinite, and I can still feel it, the phantom burning, in my belly, irradiating a diffuse zone around the sex, a threat which returns every time the other is in pain, if I identify with him, with her even, with my mother especially, and when they claimed that orange-flower water had an anesthetic virtue, they were believed, anesthetic they said for the wounded baby, of course, not for the mother kept at bay, sometimes in tears, so that she could

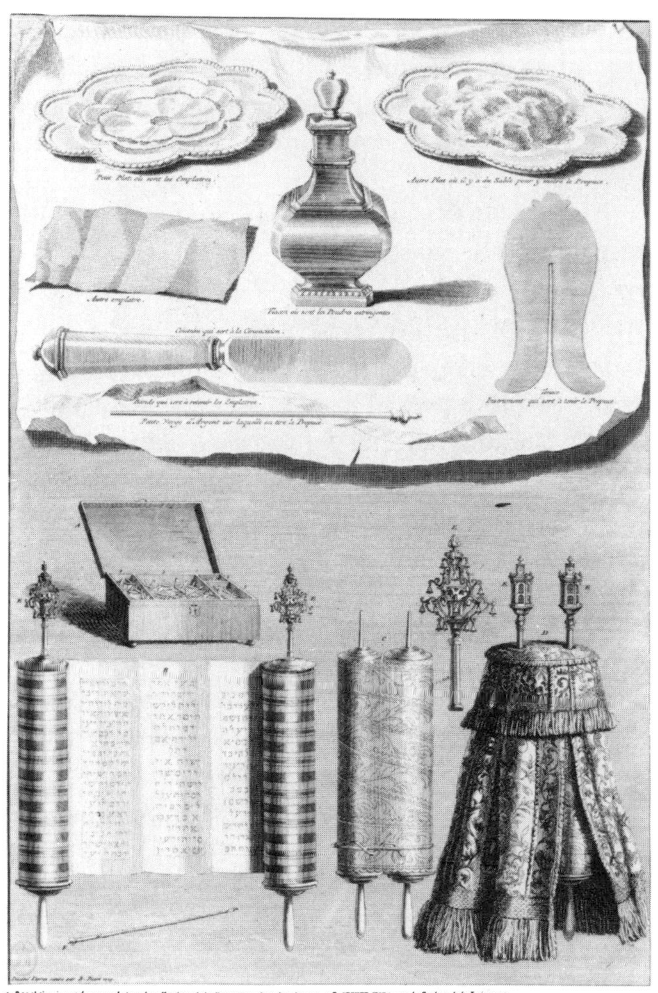

Top: Instruments of circumcision. *Cérémonies et Coutumes religieuses de tous les peuples du monde,* illustrations by B. Picard, Amsterdam, 1723.

not be made: as soon as there is a sign, the difference between first time and repetition, and therefore between presence and non-presence, has already begun to blur (SP, 45ff.). The sign is (only) its own representation.

And yet Husserl, who wants to preserve a purity of self-presence to consciousness, also needs, if he is to save the ideality of meaning, the repetition which casts this same purity into doubt. Without this ideality, meaning could no longer be subordinated to truth. The presence of meaning to a consciousness free from all facticity cannot be a function of me as empirical and finite individual: the presence of the present, the form of an experience in general, is not my personal doing, it outlives me, and that is the measure of its transcendentality. If I want to establish any purity of expression and maintain it in the horizon of truth, I must therefore recognize in it an originary capacity of repetition beyond my death. And for there to be tradition and progress in the pursuit of truth, there must be written transmission (mathematical objects are the most ideal objects; but without a written tradition there would be

not see, in the next room, and I spread out here this white cloth all bloodied in consoling a mother in order to console myself without forgetting all the theories according to which circumcision, another word for peritomy, that cutting of the surround, is instituted by the mother, for her, the cruelty basically being hers, and sometimes the very act of cutting off that sort of ring, I'm thinking of Catherine of Siena, of the stone, the knife, tomes in reserve to reconstitute the subject, even the remains would belong to the mother of whom it is said that in the past, in my ancestors' country, the descendant of Zipporah, the one who repaired the failing of a Moses incapable of circumcising

no progress in mathematics, and each generation of researchers would be condemned to find the same things over again—writing, which threatens ideality with exteriority and death, becomes more necessary as ideality becomes more ideal [OG, 87ff.]).

It is impossible to reconcile the privilege of presence with the necessity of repetition: and yet this privilege is constitutive of metaphysics. So we shall say that just as in Saussure the thought of language in terms of difference turned out to be "stronger" than the denunciation of writing, in Husserl the thought of ideality insured only in repeatability turns out to be "stronger" than the demand for presence. The blink of the present instant (the *Augenblick*) is thus haunted from the start by a past and a future. And so it cannot maintain its privilege as a philosophical foundation (all thought about time is shaken by this [M, 31–67]). But the point is not to bring out contradictions, nor to choose one strand of Husserl's thought over another; for if we cannot in all rigor accept the presupposition of the possibility of an originary presentation to a consciousness, no more can we retain ideality in the Husserlian form

his own son, before telling him, "You are a husband of blood to me," she had to eat the still bloody foreskin, I imagine first by sucking it, my first beloved cannibal, initiator at the sublime gate of fellatio, like so many *mohels* for centuries had practiced suction, or *mezizah,* right on the glans, mixing wine and blood with it, until the thing was abolished in Paris in 1843 for reasons of hygiene but let us not forget that an avowal is always a denouncing of self and there I am still weaving the cloths of an affabulation that I have to date first from *Spurs,* 1972, the thing is named in it, from *Glas* especially, '74, and the first notebook opens December 27, 1976, from *The Postcard* especially, from

as *telos* of language. For this thought of ideality rests on the Idea of a progress to infinity: the Idea of a possible replacement of everything in language that is indication by objective expressions of an infinite and immortal rational consciousness—this would be truth. But the iterability of the sign in general, without which there would be no ideality, implies, through its indifference to whether I am alive or dead, the finitude of any subject or consciousness, and the originary possibility of representation and *fiction* (truth just is such a "fiction"). Which forbids any discourse, even that of philosophy, from being essentially directed by truth, and justifies the assertion that the falsity of the statement "I am immortal," whose presupposed truth organizes metaphysical thought, is the truth of the classical concept of truth (SP, 54n.4).

DIFFÉRANCE

This is a witticism of Derrida's: in French, the difference between "différence" and "différance" is only

the second last words of *Envois,* "turn around," so that, this is my theory at least, I am beginning to weave the simulacrum of that cloth on the warp of four moments at least.

14 For example, and I'm dating this, this is the first page of the notebooks, "*Circumcision, that's all I've ever talked about, consider the discourse on the limit, margins, marks, marches, etc., the closure, the ring (alliance and gift), the sacrifice, the writing of the body, the* pharmakos *excluded or cut off, the cutting/sewing of* Glas, *the blow and the sewing back up, whence the hypothesis according-*

marked in writing, which thus takes a certain revenge on speech by obliging it to take its own written trace as its reference if, during a lecture for example (M, 3–27), it wants to say this difference. This witticism, this invention, tries to gather up the strange unity of the arguments resumed thus far, along with a certain number of arguments announced or promised for later: "différance" also refers to the inevitability of just such an anticipation of what we have put off until later. We would have liked to proceed in order, explain everything in its place, composedly, without having to invoke what will only be expounded later: this is the moment to point out again the impossibility of any such ambition, and the inevitability of *precipitation* (GL, 7a; cf. TP, 262).

Différance attempts to name (M, 3–27; POS, 8–9, 26–9, 39–41):

1. not what Saussure calls differences in the system of *langue*, but the differentiality or being-different of those differences, their "production," the "force" that maintains the system gathered in its dispersion, its *maintenance;*

2. the delay or lateness that means that meaning is

ing to which it's that, circumcision, that, without knowing it, never talking about it or talking about it in passing, as though it were an example, that I was always speaking or having spoken, unless, another hypothesis, circumcision itself were merely an example of the thing I was talking about, yes but I have been, I am and always will be, me and not another, circumcised, and there's a region that is no longer that of an example, that's the one that interests me and tells me not how I am a case but where I am no longer a case, when the word first of all, at least, CIRCUMCISED, *across so many relays, multiplied by my 'culture,' Latin, philosophy, etc., as it imprinted itself on my language circumcised in its turn, could not have not worked on me, pulling me*

always anticipated or else reestablished after the event: for example, in the structure of the sentence, tending toward its end, which will retrospectively have organized its elements—but also in the structure of a book (WD, 24), of a work (GL, 16a), of a life or a tradition, in which every present element (which is thus never really elementary or present) is stretched or spread between a "past" and a "future" which themselves will never have been present (and which are thus not really a past and a future [GR, 66–7; SP, 60–9]). This is what we have already seen for writing and reading, destination and "posterity." One might be tempted to think that this second sense of "différance" belongs on the side of *parole,* the first being on the level of *langue:* but this second sense infiltrates the first, complicates the distinction made by Saussure between synchrony and diachrony at the level of language, and complicates thereby the distinction between *langue* and *parole*—for it is only through *parole* that diachrony affects language. But if this second sense forbids us from thinking of language as identically present to itself in any synchronic "present," it has therefore already intro-

backward, in all directions, to love, yes, a word, milah, *loves another, the whole lexicon that obsesses my writings,* CIR-CON-SI, *imprints itself in the hypothesis of wax* [cire], *no, that's false and bad, why, what doesn't work, but saws* [mais scie], *yes and all the dots on the i's, I've greatly insisted on it elsewhere, Mallarmé, Ponge, but that's really what I was talking about, the point detached and retained at the same time, false, not false but simulated castration which does not lose what it plays to lose and which transforms it into a pronounceable letter, i and not I, then always take the most careful account, in anamnesis, of this fact that in my family and among the Algerian Jews, one scarcely ever said 'circumcision' but 'baptism,' not Bar Mitzvah but 'communion,'*

duced diachrony into synchrony (one can no longer in principle think of diachrony as a succession of synchronic states, which then ruins, in a movement we have already seen at work, the very distinction between the synchronic and the diachronic), and *parole* into *langue;*

3. the possibility of any conceptual distinction, for example that holding between the sensible and intelligible which we have already interrogated and which must presuppose our first meaning of *différance* to the extent that it is considered to be established, and our second meaning for that establishment.

You see how artificial our numbering of meanings is: *différance* also names the relation between what we have isolated as three meanings, as much for their localizable difference as for the movement of anticipation and *après-coup* which means that the first meaning anticipates the third, which in return says something about the relation between the first two, etc. The word or concept *différance* is thus itself spread out, *in différance,* plunged into what it attempts to name and understand. It follows that this "word" or "concept" can be

with the consequences of softening, dulling, through fearful acculturation, that I've always suffered from more or less consciously, of unavowable events, felt as such, not 'Catholic,' violent, barbarous, hard, 'Arab,' *circumcised circumcision, interiorized, secretly assumed accusation of ritual murder*" (12–20–76), the quoted time of this notebook pulls the white threat of a period cutting across the three others, at least, 1. the theologic program of SA, 2. the absolute knowledge or geologic program of G., and 3. the presently present survival or life by provision of Georgette Sultana Esther, or Mummy if you prefer, which cuts across everything, a synchrony running the risk of hiding what's essential, that is that

neither a word nor a concept, naming the condition of possibility (and therefore impossibility) of *all* words and concepts: but at the same time it is only a word/concept that is not sheltered from its own effects: this doubling spreads panic among *all* words and concepts, allowing them to be what they are only by simultaneously forbidding them from so being in the sense that has always been given to the word (and the concept) "word," and to the concept (and the word) "concept."

Once again, then, we have the production of propositions which are unaccaptable to logic. Let us note that if these paradoxes are indeed produced by the application of a "concept" to itself (*différance* is subject to *différance*), the result is not at all an interiority closed in upon itself, but a metonymic contamination (AL, 397; DRB, 263ff.), and therefore opening. We shall need to find more accurate descriptions of this structure, which we shall soon be calling, for example, "remark," "decapitation," "double chiasmatic invagination of the edges." But we can already name the *trace*. For if every element of the system only gets its identity in its difference from the other elements, every element is in this

the restrained confession will not have been my fault but hers, as though the daughter of Zipporah had not only committed the crime of my circumcision but one more still, later, the first playing the kickoff, the original sin against me, but to reproduce itself and hound me, call me into question, me, a whole life long, to make her avow, her, in me.

way marked by all those it is not: it thus bears the trace of those other elements. As we have already seen that the elements of the system are not at all atomic (at least in the classical sense), we must say that these "elements" are nothing other than *bundles* (M, 3) of such traces. These traces are not what a certain linguistics calls distinctive features, being nothing other than the traces of the *absence* of the other "element," which is moreover not absent in the sense of "present elsewhere," but is itself made up of traces. Every trace is the trace of a trace. No element is anywhere present (nor simply absent), there are only traces. These traces are not, as the word might suggest, traces of a presence or the passage of a presence. We are led inevitably to this thought by everything we have said about the sign and its immotivation: in every "element" all that is "present" is the other, "absent" element, which must, for language to be possible, present this alterity *as* alterity. This "presentation" of absence "as such" does not make of it a presence, and at the same stroke overtakes the opposition presence/absence (GR, 46–7): for we must not suppose that because Derrida questions pres-

15 I shall always have been eschatological, if one can say so, in the extreme, I am the last of the eschatologists, I have to this day above all lived, enjoyed, wept, prayed, suffered as though at the last second, in the imminence of the flashback end, and like no one else I have made the *eschaton* into a coat of arms of my genealogy, the lips' edge of my truth but there is no metalanguage will mean that a confession does not make the truth, it must affect me, touch me, gather me, re-member me, constitute me, without that meaning, as always, putting an end to, and speaking before you, confiding in you at present what in another period I called my synchrony, telling you the story of my stories, I ask *numquid . . . cum tua sit aeternitas, ignoras, quae tibi*

ence he must therefore be a thinker of absence, emptiness, nothing. We must find sentences that outplay this opposition, and so we shall say, for example, that the trace *n'arrive qu'à s'effacer* (RM, 29), arrives only by effacing itself, manages only to efface itself. "Trace" attempts to name this entwinement of the-other-in-the-same which is the condition of the same itself [*le même même*], which would perhaps be the most general statement of what we arc trying to understand here. Neither can the trace be thought of as an *entity,* if "entity" always implies a presence somewhere: whence the temptation, two or three times, to write the verb "to be" with a cross through it, "under erasure" (GR, 19, 44). There is no need to dramatize these moments: everything we have seen up until now implies already a certain "under erasure" in the obligation in which we have found ourselves to use certain words (sign, signifier, writing) to think something which in principle exceeded these same words. In truth, this is not only a "deconstructive" strategy, but a condition of thought in general. The fact that an analysis of language obliges us to treat the verb "to be" in such a way, that language

*dico,** why it takes me the time that you give me, and *cur ergo tibi tot rerum narrationes digero,*** not for the truth, of course, nor the knowledge of it, *non utique ut per me noueris ea, sed affectum meum excito in te et eorum, qui haec legunt, ut dicamus omnes,**** said what exactly if not the secret that I am jealously seeking as the last word of my very jealousy, and as long as I have not thought, i.e. altered in my body, at the bottom of the bedsore open to the sky or on the edge of the crater whose lavas have bloodied my life, jea-lou-sy, or even the temptation to interpret it on the basis of some reassuring truth such as for example a betrayal of my mother, I will have continued to turn around it without knowing the secret of my suffering, and "*I still do not know, today* [12–

thus exceeds its own resources, and especially the question "what is...?," which grounds philosophy, implies a fold or twist in which the totality of entities is delimited, and we are no longer simply "in" language.

There would be a whole list to be made of what in Derrida is said to suspend, exceed, or precede this question "what is . . .": here, provisionally: writing (D, 146; GR, 75); literature (D, 177); woman (5, 71); propriation (S, 111–17), *Aufhebung* (GL, 34a); the sign (GR, 18–9; SP, 25); the date (AL, 388ff.), the "yes" (AL, 296; OS, 94ff. and n.5); art (TP, 20ff.): it will immediately have been understood that these variations do not imply a hesitation of thought or a groping toward a true name (even if the two passages that name the sign say that it is the only thing to escape in this way), and also that these names organize more or less openly our own progression.

Without following these possibilities for the moment, let us suppose more modestly that this structure is the truth of language, written or spoken. In this case, the signifier "différance" or ("trace") would refer us to a signified to which, in the last analysis, all the other

23–76] *how you say 'circumcision' in pretty much any language other than French, scarcely, obviously, in Hebrew, and at the moment I am beginning this 'book,' we must note that everything that the experience of this 'book' must transform runs the risk of making us forget it*" or else "*if this book does not transform me through and through, if it does not give me a divine smile in the face of death, my own and that of loved ones, if it does not help me to love life even more, it will have failed, whatever signs there may be of its success, I do not want it to fail by playing at success as a failure in which only losing means salvation, a game that's too well known, I want it to succeed* decidedly *and for me to be the* first, *or even the* only one *really to know it,*" where "*the limit is circumcision, the thing, the word, the book, to be torn off, no*

signifiers of the language would refer us too. Every concept would refer to the concept of "différance" as its final guarantee: "différance" would thus be the first or last word in the language, and the first or last concept, the keystone of the system. Or else we might say that "différance" was the center that allowed the play of differences among themselves, while withdrawing itself from that play (WD, 278–80). In this case "différance" would be put forward as a new foundation, the latest truth at the end of a long list of failed attempts to name that truth (ibid.): "différance" would denounce the inadequacy of these attempts or, at best, would allow them some anticipatory value. From the height of its splendid transcendence, "différance" would control the whole affair, which it would, moreover, have produced or, as we should have to say if we were to be logical, created ex nihilo. "Différance" would thus be a name of God.

Everything we have said so far refutes this possible objection by confirming it in a different way. The deconstruction of the sign entails the absence of any such transcendental signified: *every* signifier refers to other

that's not it, but to be treated, loved in such a way that I can write, or better, live without needing to write anymore... the desire for literature is circumcision, with which I want to finish (the loss of my father's ring, two years after his death, and what followed, reconstitute everything in detail, menu, *diminished, what one eats, the text read does not suffice, has to be eaten, sucked, like the foreskin) which will remain absolutely secret in this book, I'm talking about conscious secrets, carried by what is known, as known, and not about the unconscious one, no one has yet said anything about the secret as known*" (the same day).

* "Since eternity is Thine, O Lord, dost Thou not know what I am saying to Thee?" (XI, i, 1).

signifiers, we never reach a signified referring only to itself. Only this absence of a transcendental signified allows the deconstruction of the distinction between signifier and signified, and permits us to follow the movement of the signifier to the point of its dissolution. We can say that the idea of God is, precisely, inseparable from the traditional idea of the sign (GR, 13) as the final signified putting an end to the movement and resolving *différance* into presence (GR, 71): the point is not to kill God nor to even to declare once more that He is dead (GR. 68; WD, 235), but, by showing that He is produced by and in *différance,* as the name of what would put an end to it, to inscribe Him in what He is supposed to go beyond. This reinscription of God in the world (WD, 107), in history (WD, 115–6), in finitude and mortality (SP, 54–5) is already done by *différance,* which does as much for all the names that have been put in His place, including *différance* itself. It will always be possible to accuse Derrida of setting up as master-words, in spite of himself, terms such as "différance" (or "dissemination" [cf. PC, 151]): but all these terms remark and affect with *differ-*

**"Why, then, do I tell Thee the detailed story of so many things?" (XI, i, 1).

***"Certainly, not for Thee to learn them through me, but to arouse my feeling of love toward Thee, and that of those who read these pages, so that we may all say: ['Thou art great, O Lord, and greatly to be praised']" (XI, i, 1).

ance the whole list of terms to which they belong (they speak the possibility of such a list), and equally all the terms proposed in the history of metaphysics in the position of transcendental signified. *Différance,* then, cannot be simply the last attempt in a series of attempts to speak the truth of language or being, and it therefore does not take its place at the end of a linear history of philosophy, for example. But we are not yet ready to approach this question, which, later, we shall be content to describe as the unapproachable itself. The fact remains that we cannot simply make of *différance* a new name of God, or make of Derrida's thought a theology (even a negative one) (D, 5; HAS passim; M, 6, 282; WD, 146, 271), unless we displace the philosophical (onto-theological) position of God—which (nothing excludes this a priori) can also be done by theologians (HAS, 28–9; OS, 110–3).

Différance is never pure. One cannot make it into an absolute (on pain of falling into Hegel's absolute difference and reverting to identity [POS, 43–5; WD, 153no.91, 265]): it is always in between or in-the-process-of, never itself, never present. Let us attempt

16 Now she is becoming—I'm with her this 18th of June—what she always was, the impassability of a time out of time, an immortal mortal, too human inhuman, the dumb god the beast, a sleeping water in the henceforth appeased depth of the abyss, this volcano I tell myself I'm well out of, *in istam dico uitam mortalem, an mortem uitalem, ? nescio,** she does not move much on her bed, only her fingers, she looks without seeing, can scarcely hear and as "the analyses are good," as she "is eating and sleeping well," what future remains to her, indefinitely one would say for one can no longer count, on her or in anything else and this is therefore real life, her life therefore reassures and worries the others, her nearest and dearest, at the only sign of

Elijah, the most "eschatalogical" and thus the most awaited of the prophets, had condemned the Israelites for breaking the alliance. God supposedly then appointed him to be present at each circumcision as at the renewal of the alliance. *The Ascension of the Prophet Elijah,* 18th Century, Sophia, Archeological Museum.

provisionally to think of it as a *force,* as Derrida appears to in his first texts (notably WD, 3–30 passim), the force that produces and shakes up form. But one quickly sees that if this force is thought of as a "living energy" (WD, 5), one runs the risk of making it a new presence (cf. WD. 279–80, where Derrida includes *energeia* in a list of the names of presence, and *dynamis* does not escape the system of presence either [M, 51; 303; cf. EO, 5–6]). We shall be hard put to do without this language of force (cf. PS, 95–103), but we must understand that one can only really understand force on the basis of *différance*—the idea of force only makes sense in a relationship of forces, therefore of differences of forces, of forces in *différance* (M, 17). *Différance* cannot be *one* force, but the tension of at least two forces (later we shall talk of band and contraband, striction and counterstriction, before wondering whether it is not *rhythm* that we are talking about here): a pure force would not be a force, it only becomes one faced with another force, resistance (WD, 202). *Différance* "is" this relation, and thus precedes de jure any given force.

evolution that still has the color of desire, history or event, in other words blood, called by a name I am learning to learn, from head to toe, the *escarre* [bedsore], an archipelago of red and blackish volcanoes, enflamed wounds, crusts and craters, signifiers like wells several centimeters deep, opening here, closing there, on her heels, her hips and sacrum, the very flesh exhibited in its inside, no more secret, no more skin, but she seems not to be suffering, she does not see them as I do when the nurse says "they're looking good" to mark the fact that their rawness, the not yet necrosed character of the tissue allows one to hope that they will scar over, and I try to make her speak: "What have you got to say?—Don't know.—...—What?", or "What have you

This difficulty around the use of a word such as "force" can easily give rise to the false idea according to which *différance* would be ineffable, and reduce us to regretting the lamentable insufficiency of language for saying this ineffability. But this would be to make deconstruction into a negative theology again, whereas it invites no such pathos—we shall have to explain why paleonymy, the use of "old names" (including "force" and even "différance" [SP, 103]) is not a limitation which prevents deconstruction from being fully itself, nor even a provisional stage on an inevitable or desirable route toward a postdeconstruction. These words, imperfect though they are, are perfect, now.

It is true that certain of Derrida's formulations seem to invite such a "revolutionary" reading, and notably a reference to the gleam beyond the closure (GR, 14): nothing can prevent such a mistake, which is not fundamentally different from that which gets indignant about the proposition that there is nothing outside the text, on the pretext that the world is not made up of printed words. Our reaction to such mistakes, based on

got to tell me?—What have I got to tell you?—Yes—Nothing," but she responds better on the telephone, whose apparatus comes down to making the world sink away to leave the passage of the pure voice toward the depth of memory, and thus a little while ago she pronounced my name, Jackie, in echo to the sentence from my sister passing her the receiver, "hello Jackie," something she had not been able to do for months and will perhaps do no more, beyond the fact that through her whole life she scarcely knew the other name, "*Elie: my name—not inscribed, the only one, very abstract, that ever happened to me, that I learned, from outside, later, and that I have never* felt, borne, *the name I do not know, like a number (but what a number! I was going to say* ma-

a few sentences extracted from their place in the text, always consists in reestablishing the context of these statements.

CONTEXT

Différance is not God because it is not a supreme entity: it is nothing outside differences and *différends*. It is not a force but what makes force possible while dividing it—there are only forces and differences in the plural. *Différance* is *nothing* outside these relationships. It follows that in its apparent generality it is always singular, being nothing outside *these* forces and *these* differences: this is why there is no absolute starting point—and yet we started—and why (we're not there yet) Derrida's work is always carried out in relation to texts by others, in their singularity. We have begun to cast doubt on everything that can apparently limit deconstruction to language (this is our only chance of understanding that there is nothing outside the text): a classical concept which habitually serves to think the limit between text

tricule, *thinking of the plaque of the dead Elie that Marguerite wears or of the suicide, in 1955, of my friend Elie Carrive) anonymously designating the hidden name, and in this sense, more than any other, it is the* given *name, which I received without receiving in the place where what is received must not be received, nor give any sign of recognition in exchange (the name, the gift), but as soon as I learned, very late, that it was my name, I put into it, very distractedly, on one side, in reserve, a certain nobility, a sign of election, I am he who is elected* [celui qu'on élit], *this joined to the story about the white taleth (to be told elsewhere) and some other signs of secret benediction*" (12–23–76), my very *escarre*.

and what is outside it is that of context, which is applied, often in an obscure and unthought-out manner, as much to the strictly discursive context (sometimes also called "cotext") as to the "real," extra-discursive, political, social, in general "historical" contexts. The "historian's" objection to Derrida, whose refutation we announced earlier, must invoke a necessity or obligation to put things (back) in their context in order to understand them, and the exchange between Derrida and Foucault around Descartes hangs in part on this question. Faced with such a demand, the point is not at all to claim the liberty to read out of context, which would be meaningless (one always reads in one or several contexts), but to interrogate the coherence of the concept of context deployed in this way.

One can always quote out of context. In fact one quotes by definition out of context. No natural necessity prevents any statement from being lifted from "its" context and grafted onto another (M, 317). Once more, it is writing which best illustrates this general property of language: writing is by definition destined to be read in a context different from that of the act of

*"... I mean, of dying life, or living death?... [And behold, my babyhood is long since dead, yet I live. But Thou, O Lord, art ever living and in Thee nothing dies]" (I, vi, 7–9).

inscription. Usually people work with a loose enough concept of context to suppose that there is a vague contemporaneity of writing and reading, but any rigorous concept must recognize that writing is from the start breaking with its context of "production" and with every determined context of reception. Positive studies on the reception of a given work at a given time, however enlightened and enlightening they may be compared with an older insistence on the context of production as the only pertinent one, cannot think contextuality in general, which functions in such studies, according to a mechanism whose logic we have begun to sketch out, as what we shall later call transcendental contraband.

The necessary possibility of quoting out of context depends on the arguments we have already elucidated, on mortality and intention, and, just like these arguments, it can be generalized, from writing, to language in general. A statement that could not be quoted in another context would not be a statement, for a statement exists only through the possibility of repetition in alterity—iterability—on which we have already insisted for

17 Deep in the history of penitence, from repentance to regret and contrition, from public avowal with expiation to private avowal and confession, from public reconciliation to reparation then to absolution, between blood and water, and baptism, and white and red veils, Tertullian the African, the council of Latran and Saint John Nepomucenus, martyr of the secret of confession, and Saint Augustine, of whom I read that "having returned to God, he probably never confessed, in the modern sense of the word," never having had, any more than I, beyond even truth, "the opportunity to 'confess,'" which precisely does not prevent him from working at the delivery of lit-

the sign in general. We say "quote in another context" rather than "quote out of context" to mark the fact that there are always contexts: the logic of the trace makes the idea of a sign or statement outside any context unthinkable, while making possible an exploitation of very open contexts (whence the fascination for titles, which often function in a rather unsaturated context [LI, 31n.1; MEM, 115; T, passim]). This is again why there is no absolute point of departure: any point of departure is already in a context, as we are always already in language (according to a "-ject" to be followed) before we even speak.

It will however be objected, and this is a way of returning to the suspicion we have already voiced around *langue* and *parole,* that a statement or a sentence is nonetheless a singular event which can precisely *not* be repeated, which takes place at a point in space-time whose coordinates (what is called the context) guarantee its singularity. In the logic of this objection, everything that Derrida says is put on the side of the conditions of possibility (there would be no event of *parole* if there were not a system [*langue, episteme,* etc.] making

erary confessions, i.e. at a form of theology as autobiography, I wonder, interested in the depth of the bedsore, not in writing or literature, art, philosophy, science, religion or politics but only memory and heart, not even the history of the presence of the present, I wonder what I am looking for with this machine avowal, beyond institutions, including psychoanalysis, beyond knowledge and truth, which has nothing to do with it here, beyond even the "scandalously beautiful" hypothesis of my secret name, Elie, around which the first notebooks from 1976 circled, drawing pads with thick leaves whose cover bore an *escarre,* i.e. a coat of arms with two lions, and, written on the edge of an

it possible, agreed), but it is claimed that the identity of the event is not touched by that fact, and that respecting this event, this speech act in Searle's sense or this *énoncé* in Foucault's, demands that we reestablish the context in question.

Derrida would not deny this at all. But he would certainly point out that the objection rests on the traditional distinction between the empirical and the transcendental: our earlier exposition has made us suspect that the logic of iterability precedes that distinction, which depends on a hidden relation with repetition and finitude. If the distinction invoked to refute iterability is only thinkable on the basis of iterability, then the refutation is not one, and cannot fail to confirm what it is claimed to destroy. Which is what we shall show, in the hope too of beginning to understand a little better why deconstruction is not essentially a Kantian type of philosophy, and cannot be content with the idea of conditions of possibility and everything that that idea entails.

Let us note first that the task of reestablishing a context is in principle infinite and would lead to the paradoxes illustrated in Borges's story "Funes the Me-

open square the words *skizze, croquis, sketch, schizzo, schets, kpoki,* and I added by hand, in Hebrew, the word for word, מִילָה, pronounce it *milah,* which names the word and circumcision, trying to find out already whom at bottom Elie would have loved, from whom, "last loved face" he would have chosen to receive his name like an absolution at the end of a confession without truth, for the love of you, to make the love of you, to make what I am making here for the love that you would have for Elie, *amore amoris tui facio istuc,*★ thus "*the fact that this forename was not inscribed* [*on my birth certificate, as were the Hebrew names of my family*] *(as though they wanted to hide it, still more than*

Cover of the first of the notebooks preparatory to a book on circumcision, "The Book of Elijah," projected from 1976. End of the *Envois* section of *The Post Card* (1979): "I shall wonder what, from my birth or thereabouts, *to turn around* has meant."

morious." Every element of the context is itself a text with its context which in its turn... etc. Or else every text is (only) part of a context. There are only contexts, and one cannot proceed to make the usual text/context distinction unless one has already taken the text in itself, out of "its" context, before demanding that it be placed back in that context. And if one accept what has already been said about consciousness and intention, which rules out the possibility of ever deciding rigorously what a text "means," then we must accept that every demand to put things back in context is already interested and cannot be neutral (LI, 131). Deprived of the resort in the last instance to intention (which is reconstituted after the event to justify—always already too late—the reading that has already been made), even if it be the intention of an unconscious or a collective subject, or even a spirit (of the times or of the world), one can no longer really organize or center a context (M, 327). To the extent that every trace is the trace of a trace, no text is "itself" enough to do without a context; but by the same token no context can really be closed (LOB, 81), and we will read indefinitely a sen-

the other Hebrew names, placed after the others), was as though effaced, held back, signified several things mixed together: first of all that they wanted to hide me like a prince whose parentage is provisionally concealed to keep him alive (I've just thought, trying to explain this gesture to myself [my parents never talked to me about it, I never asked them about it, it remains secondary and occupies so much space here only because of the thread I have chosen to follow] that a brother died when a few months old, less than a year before my birth, between my elder brother, René [Abraham], and me. He was called Paul Moses), keep him alive until the day that his royalty could [...] be openly exercised, without risk for the precious semen; and then that I should not openly wear any Jewish sign" (12–23–76).

tence such as "I forgot my umbrella" without ever getting to the end of it (S, 123–35).

Reading would be impossible otherwise: from the moment one manages to read a text, even at a level of elementary decipherment, one is, however minimally, part of its context. This is a version of the argument that earlier stated the inevitability of a certain complicity with metaphysics, and of that which cast into doubt any radical distinction between writing and reading. In order to read a text out of context, one must already be in its context. It is within these implications that we must distinguish different forces of reading, and only within (which is thus no longer really an inside) that there is the slightest possibility of resistance to what one reads. Up to a certain point, one must share the language of what one is reading (such an assertion obliges us to talk about translation later), always out of context, always in context, on pain of depriving oneself of the minimum of identification required for there to be reading (EO, 87). This necessary encroaching forbids any rigorous metalinguistic hold of a reading over a text: there can be no indivisible dividing line between

* "In the love of Thy Love am I doing this" (XI, i, 1).

18 *Escarre,* oh my jealousy, and so long as I have not understood you, i.e. sutured you, oh my jealousy, as *escarre* closes on the blood to make a new skin, so long as I will not know whence you come to explode, my jealousy, whence you expose the inside of the burning alive of my body at the worst, twisting it with pain like this face which for three days now (6–28–89) has been paralyzed in a hideous grimace, the grimace of my lucidity, left eye open and fixed under the effect of a virus about which I concluded a few months ago,* recalling that the

object-language and metalanguage, any more than there can be one between ordinary language and philosophical language (M, 327)—which does not imply total confusion, as might be feared, but passage and entwinings, to be negotiated.

Here, for example, we shall say that the impossibility of a sharp distinction between object-language and metalanguage implies "there is only metalanguage" as much as "there is no metalanguage": there is nothing outside the text, therefore every text is text on a text under a text, without any established hierarchy. Taking account of this situation ought to have effects on common reading practices: one could no longer expect a theory to dominate a practice, of reading or writing. If we have disqualified every reading that claims to leave the text to state its final signified, we must recognize that any theory is another text in an unstable network of texts in which every text bears the traces of all the others—so if we do not attempt a psychoanalytic reading of Rousseau, for example, this is in part because psychoanalysis is inscribed in the same network as Rousseau and us (GR, 160–1).

virus will have been the only object of my work, "the virus is ageless," and I was talking about computer viruses as well as about Aids, so long as I have not written a treatise *marking* the origin and end of my jealousy, *Of the indubitable foundation or the* cogito *of my jealousy,* or again *The Confessions of a Mother,* I will have failed my life and written nothing, farewell salvation, incurable facial paralysis, mask, hypocrisy, unfathomable perjury, dark glasses, water dripping back out of my mouth, anger of the handicapped, multiplication, on the mother's body and on mine, of *escarres,* of the thing and of the words, I love words too much because I have no language of my own, only false *escarres,*

But if we thus place in doubt the distinctions between text and context on the one hand, object-language and metalanguage on the other, we are not flattening everything into a single homogeneous text: on the contrary, we are multiplying differences within the text, whose unity and closure were given only by the context supposed to surround it. We shall say now that the context is already remarked in the text, the object-language already infiltrated with metalanguage: to this extent we ought to be able, up to a point, to find resources for reading "in" the text being read. We thus recognize that no text is homogeneous, that every text proposes its own reading and even an institution which will insure its reading (DP, 422) but must, in doing this, leave unexploited resources which can very well trouble or even contradict that reading. Our reading instrument for the chapter on writing in Saussure's *Course* will be the doctrine of that same Saussure which defines language in terms of differences. Or else we shall say that certain sentences by Rousseau attempt to fix the meaning of other sentences by Rousseau, which does not prevent these latter from being open to the

false foci (*eskhara*), those blackish and purulent crusts which form around the wounds on my mother's body, under her heels, then on the sacrum and the hips, numerous, living, crawling with homonymies, all these *escarres,* altar hearths for gods and sacrifices, brazier, campfire, vulva, escharosis of the word itself engendering an enormous family of etymological bastards, progenitures, which change name and whose homonymous *escarre,* the square on the square coat of arms, gives rise to genealogies *en abîme* that I shall not misuse but I can't stop here without noting the link with the English *scar,* or with the Old High German for cut, *scar,* the eschatology of my circumcision, for this

chance of other interpretations (GR, 307; cf. D, 95–6). Or we will find in Plato's "chora" the means to overrun the limits of Platonism (CH passim; D, 160–1) More generally, we find that the term "supplement" in Rousseau functions, beyond the interpretation that Rousseau himself provides, in such a way as to describe the very textuality which contains this term (GR, 163); that the words "blank" and "fold" in Mallarmé are not merely themes among others, but describe the very possibility of what is called a theme in general, and how such a "theme" can thematize the thematic as such (D, 227–86 passim). In general, Derrida draws his reading instruments from the texts he is reading, extracts terms that he then plunges back into the very text they serve to read. Let us say that there are terms which show a metalinguistic tendency (but no doubt no term is absolutely exempt from this) with respect to the (con)text "in" which they are to be found, and therefore with respect to other texts too (we already know that a text is not an entity closed on itself). The "meta-" movement of these terms is not a pure force of elevation (we already know that there is no pure force), but

old-fashioned term, *escarre* come from scar, means bursting, the violence of effraction by avant-garde (for beyond all the outdated uses of this password, they have never forgiven me for being the most advanced eschatologist, the last avant-garde to count, for the *escart,* another word, says the advance of the schoolboy over his adversary in prisoner's base), if I die before my mother, or G., *nam et si descendero in infernum, ades,*** will I have got ahead by dying or surviving, always leaving in the lurch for "*I no longer belonged to them from the day of my birth, that linked with this double sentiment that has always preceded me: I was both excluded and infinitely, secretly preferred by my family who had*

always in tension with a force of re-attachment to the given context (for it is still context we are speaking of here): we lower these terms which aspire to metalinguistic height, by folding them back onto their origin-text, which is however legible only insofar as there is such an aspiration. In a context of decapitation, we shall say (more or less metalinguistically) that we decapitate metalanguage (D, 178; GL, 12–13b, 71–2b, 115b; POS, 45); in a context of liaison or striction, we shall speak of band and contraband (GL passim; LOB, 172 [in the lower band]; PC, 349; SI, 148–52); in a context of supplementation, of supplementarity (GR, 141ff.), etc. There is, by definition, no end to such a list. Through the same "meta-" tendency, each term in this list has a vocation (a disappointed one: *l'érection tombe,* as *Glas* will say, among other texts [GL, 157bff.; S, 105; SI, 56; WD, 123]) to dominate and name the whole list, into which it will return, fatally. One can always make a list of examples of this structure or these events and try to find a supreme name for the whole: later we shall try the name "quasi-transcendentality," which, through the effects of a logic we shall name

lost me, from the beginning, through love, whence a series of ruptures without rupture with that family, impossibility, insured from the start, of an endogamous marriage and finally, after the debate I shall have to recount, the noncircumcision of my sons. The prophet Elijah is nonetheless the guardian of circumcision" (12–23–76)?

*"Rhétorique de la drogue," in *Autrement, L'Esprit des drogues,* no. 106 (April 1989), p. 213.

**"Because, 'even if I descend into hell, Thou art present' " (I, ii, 2).

"plus de," will not however dominate the others, but will add itself to the list thus adorned with a supplementary supplement, etc. ("Etc." here should not mislead: we are not here dealing with Wittgenstein's "and so on" in the context of the elucidation of the concept of the rule and its mastery: let us try to say for the moment that the series is produced in a machine-like but not mechanical way, that we are certainly dealing with the law but not simply with the rule.)

One might suspect here a sort of fetishism of the signifier: there is a collection, let's say, of all the occurrences of the signifier "supplement" in Rousseau, and then they are made to say the same thing each time in spite of the context and its manifest sense. But, as we shall see, what is happening here is more powerful than the received logic of the fetish, which is elaborated only in relation to the dream of a thing in itself (here, of a meaning, a signified, if need be determined by the context), which we have already placed in doubt. Moreover, that there is no signified does not imply that we place all the signifiers on the same level—we must respect the effects of signifieds, of what gives itself out as

19 "*So I have borne, without bearing, without its ever being written*" (12–23–76) the name of the prophet Élie, Elijah in English, who carries the newborn on his knees, before the still unnamable sacrifice, and I must have carried myself and the impossible port without bank and without head of this porterage is written everywhere for anyone who knows how to read and is interested in the behavior of a ference, in what precedes and circumvents in preference, reference, transference, *différance,* so I took myself toward the hidden name without its ever being written on the official records, the same name as that of the paternal uncle Eugène Eliahou Derrida who must have carried me in his arms at the moment of the event without memory

a signified (GR, 159): and as we have already shaken the limits that separate a text from its context, the presence of this or that signifier "in" a text is not a determining criterion for this type of reading, to the extent that the opposition presence/absence has been suspended by what we have said of the trace. The place of a certain signifier can be silhouetted in a text without figuring in it explicitly (D, 129–30), and the local absence of such and such a signifier (for example, the word "hymen" in a text by Mallarmé) would not disturb the reading (D, 220): everything we have seen of the sign implies that if this reading depended on the presence of this or that signifier we would not have escaped logocentrism—such signifiers would have become so many signifieds. No more are we seeking any semantic wealth or ambiguity in the terms thus privileged, but an economic access to a work of syntax—which is already implied in the refusal of a linguistics of the word (cf. D, 251). It will be said that we are opening the door to the possibilities of arbitrary readings, of just anything at all; we have already sketched the reply to these fears, and we shall add here that a reading totally programmed

of me for they are the memories of an amnesia about which you wonder why "*I'm getting ready to write them, in this book of 'circumcision' dreamed of after the death of my father (1970) and certain events that followed, deliberately projected after* Glas *but never undertaken, no doubt carried since ever in this netherworld of scars,* escarres, *scarifications and cannibalism, of alliance through the blood that flows and that the* mohel, *sometimes charged with sacrificial slaughter, sometimes sucks, like the mother here or there eats the foreskin and elsewhere the boy that of excision*" (12–23–76), and now today (6–29–89) I telephone myself today to G. as to God, an hour before sliding my body stretched out on its back into the tomblike capsule of a scanner in Neuilly to tell him what I'm writing right up against

against the risk of arbitrariness would not be a reading, and that the point is also to remark that fact. But also, much more simply, that the readings carried out by Derrida never give the impression of being arbitrary, and we need to wonder why (cf. GR, 158; PS, 188; S, 73–5).

BEYOND

We are running the risk, but it is an inevitable risk, of reinforcing the received idea which sees in Derrida a philosopher of language, one who has, moreover, the immodest pretension of absorbing everything into language. The place given to language in modern philosophy will be accepted without much trouble: it will be said, for example, that there is no thought without language, that our perception of the world would not be what it is without language, that there would not really be any desire without language, etc. But in order to say this, we must accept that language has an outside, that it is faced with a world which it fashions to some ex-

him and tell him that for several days now my face has been disfigured by a facial paralysis holding my left eye fixed open like a glass-eyed cyclops, imperturbable vigilance of the dead man, eyelid stretched by the vertical bar of an inner scar, *an invisible scar,* I tell him, and my twisted mouth from which water falls a little onto my chin when I drink, recalling me to my mother each time that, one hand holding up her head, I pour water into her mouth rather than her drinking it, *ecce ubi sum! flete mecum, et pro me flete,** for like SA I love only tears, I only love and speak through them, even if one must deny it, he commands, on the death of a mother, it's about them that I would telephone rather *restat uoluptas oculorum istorum carnis meae, de qua*

tent, but which is nonetheless there, opposite us, real, etc. But now here is Derrida, enthused by the importance of language, denying just this situation by making of this world (which in itself must be silent) into part of language, part of the text; we are, improbably enough, sent back to the great medieval book of the world which must presuppose a writer God. How could we agree to remain shut up in a library poring over old philosophers, who, for the most part, moreover, encourage us to put the books away and to go out and do something?

This type of objection habitually takes two complementary forms, the one more epistemological, the other more political.

In its first form, Derrida is accused of reinforcing Saussure's fundamental error, which supposedly consists, once the arbitrariness of the sign has been noted, in letting the referent drop in the interests of a closed system of signs which only refer to other signs without ever meeting up again with that referent. It is thought to be only one step from this position to idealism, a step taken by Saussure when he concentrates on *langue*

loquor confessiones, quas audiant aures templi tui, what SA never says about *concupiscentia oculorum,*** not counting the supplement of pleasure, the addition of the optical machine that comes to "scan" the beyond of a sensory immediacy, as I should like to brush away all the perjuries of my memory ("Dear Madam, I ask you for a scan of the trajectory of the left facial nerve"), tears, think credulous humanists, remaining impossible for machines, try to make a scanner weep, *How wisely Nature did decree, With the same eyes to weep and see!* [...] *For others too can see, or sleep, But only human eyes can weep,**** what stupidity (rictus on the right).

rather than on *parole,* the only place of concrete exchange between language and world, and on synchrony rather than diachrony. He thus abstracts the sign from its concrete usage in concrete dialogic interlocution, its only reality (summarizing Volosinov's critique, which we accept up to a point). What is more, such a theory would prevent us ever stating a truth about the world, for any statement, according to Saussure's doctrine, depends on infinite referrals to other statements, which themselves only refer to other statements still. Without being able to stop somewhere, it is hard to see how there could be sense or truth. Where a Fregean-type thinking, with its fruitful distinction between sense and reference, allows a rich analysis of meaning which is neither naive nor positivist, without for all that losing the possibility of an objective reference to the world, a thought of the Saussurian type, enclosing us in the circle of signs, inevitably leads to a sterility which is distressing for philosophy, and translates as irresponsible literary games.

Second form of the objection: in this impossibility of having any hold over the world, how could we pro-

* "See my position! Weep with me and weep for me" (X, xxxiii, 50).

** "There remains the pleasure of these eyes of my flesh. I speak of it in the form of confessions which the ears of Thy temple may hear, [brotherly and pious ears]..." (X, xxxiv, 51).

*** Marvell, "Eyes and Tears."

20 The doctor says: facial paralysis of "peripheral" origin, *period,* electromyogram and scanner, the cruel specter of this left eye that no longer blinks, I see it dissymetrizing my faces, it is looking at me from my mother like one of a pair of

ject a politics taking account of truth? A political project must be rooted in a description of the world which claims to speak its truth, and foresee or prescribe the coming of a more just world, in which we should have to be in a position to judge the truth of the statement declaring that world to be more just than the previous one. Believing in the possibility of speaking the truth about "how it is" does not of course guarantee the right politics, but without such a belief it is hard to see how a bad politics could be resisted. To the extent that Derrida, radicalizes Saussure's doctrine in its most dubious aspects, deprives himself of the means to ground a truth, and thus any knowledge, he can only encourage skepticism, relativism, and quietism, and apparently does not see that the very statement of his position falls into immediate contradiction, given that this statement claims to be a truth.

Let us note first of all that Derrida explicitly denies charges of skepticism or relativism (LI, 137), is happy to talk about responsibility (DP, 397–438, PR passim; WD, 80), and denies charges of linguisticism too, to the point of doubting that all thought is linguistic

china dogs, as though to anesthetize the view of the horror, for without weakness I must describe the *escarre* of my life, more irremediable still than those of Ester (which can also be written without an *h* like *escarre*) and if hers give us back hope these days, the fatality of mine, blasphemy on God's name, single eye or the sole witness of my crimes or perjuries, their cause, I perjure like I breathe, whose multitude runs in the tears, the love and the prayer I address each time to the unique, and the blood, *amore amoris tui facio istuc,* as might a little SA sinning the more securely after conversion, the god of love, the One, who has always been more intimate to Jackelie than myself, gathering me

(WD, 33n.4). Of course, it is not enough to invoke these passages, which might always be simple denials rather than refutations: but, as we shall show, although Saussure's thinking undeniably gives an initial impetus to the thought of difference, that thought is in no way bound to Saussure, to the point that Derrida in fact privileges language less than those who reproach him for remaining enclosed in it. We have already seen how the motif of difference in Saussure tends to ruin the fundamental distinctions proposed by his doctrine: this ruin, which carries everything including the sign with it, and therefore also its distinction from the referent, makes it quite plausible that Derrida might be closer to Frege (about whom he almost never speaks) than to Saussure. But a rapid examination would show that the basic distinction suggested by Frege between sense and reference is equally deconstructed in Derrida's thought by a generalization and reinscription, not of sense as one might be tempted to believe, but of reference (LI, 137ff.) in the generalized form of *referral* (*renvoi*) (a little later we shall see what to make of the sending [*envoi*]

in the multiplicity of loves without division, sharing the shareless of the absolute fidelities, desires subjected to betrayal through respect for the categorical empire, so that before god or before the law which summons me to appear, I return to dust through love, I only know how to deceive, deceive myself, deceive you, and you and you again, my *escarre* jealous of itself without it being any use that I tell you the truth in order to avow, for one can always describe or note the true without avowal, nothing to do with it, without public confession or repentance, but so long as I have not exhibited the grain of the content of the detail of each of the perjuries, without being con-

that perhaps precedes this *renvoi* [EN passim]). This referral, which is only a consequence of what we announced earlier about the trace, is the common root of the intra-linguistic referrals which make sense, and of reference "properly so called" supposed to cross the abyss between language and world. We can announce already that any philosophy which gives itself world and language as two separate realms separated by an abyss that has to be crossed remains caught, at the very point of the supposed crossing, in the circle of dogmatism and relativism that it is unable to break: there will follow from this at least:

—that we have to rethink all the oppositions which come down to the subject/object couple, on the basis of a more radical *-ject;*

—that all the determinations of language (or even of the symbolic) are delimited (if not transgressed);

—that the definition of humanity (with respect to animality and/or divinity) is cast into doubt, as well as that of the animate in relation to the inanimate, and especially to machines, to *tekhnè* in general;

tent to say "I say that I lie permanently to everybody, I admit it," no, so long as I do not give to be seen and heard the detail of each of the transgressions, and I'll never do so, each of those that your curiosity wants to see, know, archive, *alia forma temptationis multiplicius periculosa* [...] *curiosa cupiditas nomine cognitionis et scientiae palliata,** I am dying a counterfeiter in the depths of the blood of the four-time *escarre* of god, *Es war Blut, es war, was du vergossen, Herr,*** his eye and his act, the infinite corpus, my skizzolatry in notebooks, the wound of circumcision in which I return to myself, gather myself, cultivate and colonize hell, this *escarre* is the sponge, G., listen, it sponges endlessly the blood it

—that there is nothing outside the text.

THE PROPER NAME

—The proper name ought to insure a certain passage between language and world, in that it ought to indicate a concrete individual, without ambiguity, without having to pass through the circuits of meaning. Even if we accept that the system of *langue* is constituted by differences and therefore of traces, it would appear that the proper name, which is part of language, points directly toward the individual it names. This possibility of proper nomination ought to be the very prototype of language, and as such it can prescribe language its *telos:* however complicated our linguistic needs have become, the regulating ideal can and must remain that of a proper nomination, possibly of truth itself (M, 232ff.). Frege, for example, since you invoke him, resolves his distinction between sense and reference by thinking of sentences as proper names of propositions which all have as their reference an object called "the

expresses, and when SA tracks the origin of evil, accusing himself of not seeing it *in ipsa inquisitione,* he accuses and praises god for being that monster mother, the infinite sea containing an immense but finite sponge, measure the difference, G., and for what sponge these tears weep, *tamquam si mare esset ubique et undique per inmensa infinitum solum mare et haberet intra se spongiam quamlibet magnam, sed finitam tamen, plena esset utique spongia illa ex omni sua parte ex inmenso mari: sic creaturam tuam finitam...,*★★★ you diagnose: *scarface,* the perjurer witness of God on trial, the monocular warning light of his evil, the chosen virus of his sponge.

true" or else an object called "the false." Even if we had to accept what Derrida says about language, here is a moment that escapes his famous textuality, and which gives that textuality a grounding which limits the excessive importance he attempts to give to *différance*.

—It is not false to see something of major importance in the proper name. It is precisely the keystone of logocentrism. But there is no proper name. What is called by the generic common noun "proper name" must function, it too, in a system of differences: this or that proper name rather than another designates this or that individual rather than another and thus is marked by the trace of these others, in a classification (GL, 86b, 137a), if only a two-term classification. We are already in writing with proper names. For there to be a truly proper name, there would have to be only one proper name, which would then not even be a name, but pure appellation of the pure other, absolute vocative (cf. EO, 107–8; GR, 110–1; WD, 105) which would not even call, for calling implies distance and *différance,* but would be proffered in the presence of the other, who would in that case not even be other, etc. What we call

*"... another kind of temptation... dangerous in many ways. [...] a certain vain and curious desire—cloaked under the name of knowledge and science" (X, xxxv, 54).

**"It was blood, it was, that you shed, Lord," Celan, *Tenebrae*.

***"[I sought the source of evil and my way of searching was evil, yet I did not see the evil] in my very searching. [...] It was like a sea, everywhere and in all directions spreading through immense space, simply an infinite sea. And it had in it a great sponge, which was finite, however, and this sponge was filled, of course, in every part with the immense sea. In this way, I

"proper name" is thus always already improper, and the act of nomination that is looked for as origin and prototype of language presupposes writing in the extended sense Derrida gives to the word. Naming does violence to the supposed unicity it is supposed to respect, it gives existence and withdraws it at the same time (WD, 70), the proper name effaces the proper it promises (PC, 360), breaks (GL, 336) or falls into ruin (GL, 207b), it is the chance of language, immediately destroyed (GL, 236b): naming un-names (PAR, 99), the proper name depropriates, exappropriates (PC, 357, 359–60) in what might be called the abyss of the proper or of the unique (LOB, 171–2; S, 117–8; SI, 28); and if one wishes to call this origin by the name of God, the best proper name, the most proper name (DI, 12), then one draws God into the violence of difference (WD, 67–8), one makes of "God" the name of what dispossesses me of myself (WD, 180–2), the name of the originary confusion of names, Babel (EO, 100ff.; TB, 166ff., 183–5; TW, 153–5), *Folies* (PF, 7). There is no proper name that is not thus already worked on by the common noun (EO, 108), that does not begin to

conceived of Thy finite creation as finite [yet full of Thy infinity]" (VII, v, 7).

21 If I had the time and space in my own way, I would expound this sublime chapter on the origin of evil. SA's immense and finite sponge pregnant like a memory with all the abandoned or held back tears of the *Confessions,* on the death of the friend, his friend, Paul or Koitchi, on the death of the mother, his mother, not only all the seascapes like that in Ostia before which he stands *ad quandam fenestram* with her before her

insinuate itself into the language system: what will be called literature. As we shall see in a moment, the proper name bears the death of its bearer in securing his life and insuring his life (NA, 30).

—In a moment: there are moments, though, here-and-now's before the great machine of *différance* gets moving, absolute origin-points where truth appears. Let's accept that the so-called proper name is already drawn into a system of differences, let's call it writing if you like, and even, to anticipate on what you won't fail to do around metaphor, let's accept that proper name and proper meaning are only distinguished in secondary fashion against a background of originary improprietary or metaphoricity. But what causes proper names to be said to be proper must depend on an element or moment of propriety, if only for the blink of an eye, that these names mark or in some sense commemorate. Does it not remain the case that "I think, I am" is true every time I conceive it or proffer it to myself in a here and now, and that, beyond or before all the names that might be given to me, and which we will no longer say are properly proper, it is the punc-

death, *illic apud Ostia Tiberina,*★ ecstasy between the inside and the outside, of house and country, of source and mouth, of river and our Mediterranean, on this shore of introjection and incorporation from which even God, on the day of his death, will not be able to deliver us, but I would also show, at the end of the discourse on the sponge, in the same state as I, half his face on the other side of life, hoping to die before the mother, my obsequent, dreading it too and weeping for the unavowable truth, in other words, you will have understood in the end, that a confession has nothing to do with truth, *talia uoluebam pectore misero, ingrauidato curis mordacissimis de timore mortis, et non inuenta ueri-*

tuality of this truth which attaches language and even writing to a founding moment which precedes your famous text? My so-called proper name marks my identity with myself which is grounded in the last analysis in these moments of irrefutable certainty. Or else we can ground language on an indubitable "stimulus-meaning" (Quine) which will not prevent all sorts of vaguenesses and ambiguities in that limit-situation we'll call a situation of "radical translation" but which is in some sense the truth of language. To avoid the chaos that you merrily call dissemination, we must recognize that these moments, marked by deictics in general, pin the tissue of language to its other, without reducing that other to language...

—Let's take those deictics, then. They have no particular privilege in this respect. As for the *Cogito* version of the objection, which wants to mark and withdraw a subjective origin from the general drift, we come back to Husserl. We have already seen all the problems posed by his distinction between expression and indication: Husserl is obliged to recognize that a term such as "I" functions as an indication in interlo-

*tate,*** then I would follow the traces of blood, the first I remember having seen with my own eyes, outside, since I was and remain blind to that of my seventh or eighth day, which happens to be the day of my mother's birth, July 23, that first blood that came to me from the sex of a cousin, Simone, 7 or 8 years old, the day when the pedal of a toy scooter penetrated her by accident, *Verfall,* with the first phantom sensation, that algic sympathy around my sex which leads me to the towels my mother left lying around, "marked" from red to brown, in the bidet, when, as I understood so late, she was having her own "period," but I must synchronize the four times in the same periphrasis, a

B. Gozzoli, *The Ecstasy of Saint Augustine*, San Gimignano, church of Saint Augustine.

cution, but he, like you, wants to save the purity of expression in soliloquy. But it can be shown (SP, 94–7) that, like any other term, "I" must be able to function in the absence of its object, and, like any other statement (this is the measure of its necessary ideality), "I am" must be understandable in my absence and after my death. It is moreover only in this way that a discourse on a transcendental ego is possible, which again shows the link between transcendentality and finitude. The meaning, even of a statement like "I am," is perfectly indifferent to the fact that I be living or dead, human or robot. The possibility that I be dead is necessary to the statement. And if we link this a little brutally with Quine (but we should not perhaps be surprised to find a residue of unthought phenomenology in so-called analytic philosophy [LI, 38, 130]), we can say that the self-identity of the "stimulus" in its meaning, before we have to decide, in Quine's example, whether "Gavagai" is to be translated as "passing rabbit" or "rabbit passage," must presuppose the possibility of repetition, and therefore the possibility of an

necessity which came close to me so many times, such as this one, at the beginning of the eighties: "*In relation with the singular score of these four epitomes, unrational enough to have to be denied or complicated, cut into, I discover the quaternary model of a paradisiac discourse of Jewish 'rationality,' to be specified, etc.:* 1. Pshat, *literality denuded like a glans,* 2. R'Emez, *crypt, allegory, secret, diverted word,* 3. Drash, *morality, homily, persuasive and pulpit eloquence,* 4. Soud, *profound, cabbalistic ..., although I've got the* PaRDeS *of this partition 'in my blood,' it does not correspond exactly to the one imposing itself on me, some laborious translation of it is not forbidden.* [...] *it was the last time, the mirror on my right, her left, sudden terror faced*

ideality, and therefore also of differences, traces, and *différance,* which alone could justify the assumption that two interlocutors (native and ethnographer in the fable of radical translation) receive the same "stimulus," marked by the deictic in the ethnographer's question, "What do you call *that?*"

Whether we try to secure it on the side of the subject or on that of the object, the passage to language presupposes not a prior meaning that signs would then only have to express, but a certain continuity that we are here calling "the same" (and which is none other than *différance* [M, 17]). Which means that in referring to a stimulus or a self-presence of the subject, we are not finally referring to a fundamental presence with respect to which we might then comfortably envisage all the ambiguity one might wish, but still to a network of traces. This "continuity" (which is made up only of difference and caesuras) forbids us from accrediting the idea of an abyss between language and world or experience, but also, for example, between readable space and visible space (PS, 106). Which does not prevent us

with the secret to be kept, of no longer being able to form the letters and words, fear of absolute inhibition through fear of betraying oneself. [...] it was like a beehive sponge of secrets, the buzzing rumor, the mixed-up noises of each bee, and yet the cells near to bursting, infinite number of walls, internal telephone."

*"[She and I were standing alone, leaning] on a window [from which the garden inside the house we occupied could be viewed.] It was at Ostia on the Tiber [where... we were resting in preparation for the sea voyage]" (IX, x, 23).

from recognizing all sorts of differences between these domains, but obliges us to think of the trace as their common possibility.

Given that the ground promised by proper names and deictics is thus divided and complicated, one might be surprised to see Derrida, in the text on Descartes which takes its distances from Foucault's analyses, evoking, "before" the statement of the *cogito,* an instantaneous experience, a "point" (WD, 58–9) before any sentence. Is this not precisely the type of foundation we have just cast into doubt by extending our earlier exposition?

Let us note first of all that the objector provisionally accepted the necessity of presenting language in terms of difference, and sought in language traces which would not simply be traces of traces, but would refer finally to an origin escaping the text in the act of grounding it. Such an origin would secure the system against the madness of permanent dissemination. Now in the presentation of Descartes, it is precisely the point of the experience which is "mad," because it is anterior to the metaphysical distinction between reason and

**"Such thoughts I turned over within my wretched breast which was overburdened with the most biting concern about the fear of death and my failure to discover truth" (VII, v, 7).

22 Quick may I die, I am fighting against so many antibodies, the race against death has started up again the more vigorously between Esther and me, how I love her, and the *différance* is that if I go before her she will know nothing of it, she got me going again yesterday at the Salpetrière in the Charcot lecture theater, an easy-diagnosis neurologist, his of me, mine

madness, and the statement which inscribes it in language (even if this is only to address it to the subject himself) which brings it back to *logos* and reason. The moment of this "point" should not delude us (any more than a reference to "the living energy of meaning" in a text of the same period [WD, 5]): in spite of certain appearances, this is precisely not an origin in the metaphysical sense. Where Descartes insures the self-presence of the subject via the unexplained intermediary of the deferred action of the sentence *saying* the *cogito,* Derrida (and this is why, as we announced, he would not simply accept the common idea whereby thought and language are coterminous) shows that the *cogito* is valid in a sense even if I am mad (we should have to say, too, even if I am dead, or a machine), and therefore cannot provide the grounding certainty we were looking for. It is certain that what is here thought of as the point or even the "experience" of the *cogito* before its sentence must be questioned further, which we shall do further on in terms of the gift, but we see that even here this reading of the *cogito* does not give a more simple or secure foundation than *différance,* but

of him, who tried to insinuate, as though I did not know, that this "viral" "facial paralysis" *a frigore "peripheral"* (!) was my fault, as though I were seeking anything other, before him and so much better, than my faults, without my daring to ask him if he had heard of a certain Charcot from before scanners, or of those cultures in which F.P.'s, Jean tells me, are said to be "self"-punishments for the transgression of certain interdicts, notably around funeral sites, what I do all day long, without mentioning other perjuries that twist up my face, divide it into two, squint me with an evil eye which is painful to see for a man who accuses himself so much of lying must be madly in love with the

extends that *différance* well beyond language. All experience is made up only of traces, and whether we look to the side of the subject or to that of the object, we will find nothing preceding the trace (M, 317–8). It is not simply that proper names and deictics do not manage properly to name or indicate something that escapes language while anchoring it somewhere, but that "reality" thus improperly designated is present nowhere else. But saying that nothing precedes the trace is an apparently impossible proposition: it makes the trace into an origin, whereas by definition the trace, always being trace of a trace, cannot be one. We need to understand the necessity of thinking an origin which cannot be originary, and to do so we must try to understand time.

TIME AND FINITUDE

A note to the text on Foucault and Descartes evokes the God of classical rationalisms as the name of what alone can reconcile truth and temporality in the positive in-

truth to the point of weeping for it, but don't rely on it, *non te amabam et* fornicabar abs te... "euge,"* one cannot *do* without truth but it's not the one they think they're confessing, they still haven't understood anything about it, especially those I see queuing up, *too late,* to get themselves circumcised and authorize themselves to speak for the "Jews," this "for" which makes you burst out laughing, obscene though it remains, either *in favor* or *in place* of the "Jews," Jews "themselves" knowing that they must not speak "for" them, do I do that, "*now delicately detach the ring of flesh around my foreskin and put it on the lady's finger, you know the iconography of Catherine of Siena, and if I graft, will it be a naturalization of the symbolic seal or the condition of an*

finity of Reason. If one is seeking a secure foundation in the sense of subjective certainty, one must recognize that any such certainty is threatened at any moment by forgetting. Finitude condemns us to time.

—Let us accept your description so far. You're simply trying to redo Kant, by formulating the conditions of possibility of any experience for a finite consciousness. Your *différance* is just our finitude under another name, and you can't help projecting a compensatory infinite or absolute, which you call text, or *différance* again, the better to lead us astray.

—It is true that the terms "finite" and "infinite" function in a disturbing way in Derrida's texts. It is difficult for example not to think *différance* spontaneously as a *de jure* infinite movement, whether this infinite be thought of as "bad" ("and so on..."), or as the good totalization of equivocality in a sort of negative image of Hegel's absolute knowledge. And yet we find that this infinite *différance* is finite (SP, 102), that its essence excludes a priori that it become infinite (GR, 131, cf. 143), that it is the possibility of an experience of finitude (HAS, 29), but that nonetheless *différance* is not to

ineffaceable pact for the only philosopher to my knowledge who, accepted—more or less—into the academic institution, author of more or less legitimate writings on Plato, Augustine, Descartes, Rousseau, Kant, Hegel, Husserl, Heidegger, Benjamin, Austin, will have dared describe his penis, as promised, in concise and detailed fashion, and as no one dared, in the Renaissance, paint the circumcised penis of Christ on the incredible pretext that there was no model for it, come off it, now if I do not invent a new language (through simplicity rediscovered) another fluid, a new SENTENCE, *I will have failed in this book, which does not mean that that's the place to start, on the contrary, you have to drag on in the old syntax, train oneself with you, dear reader, toward an idiom which in the end would be untranslatable in return into*

be reduced to finitude, and does not, for example, amount to announcing once again the death of God (GR, 68).

Let us rapidly resume the demonstration around Husserl. The presence of the ideal object and the ideal self-presence of the transcendental ego in the present depend, through their very ideality, on the possibility of repetition. This repetition necessarily involves the possibility of my death, and therefore of finitude. But ideality is pure only if it allows a repetition to infinity: *in fact* we are in finitude, but *de jure* ideality implies infinity. This infinite only appears in the finite: we have seen that "I am" is understood on the basis of "I am dead." This finitude is marked in the very statement of the "I," which, ideally, at an infinite distance, ought to be replaceable by an objective expression: this is also what the so-called "philosophical" "I" tries to do, and this is why we have seen Derrida insisting unexpectedly on a moment "before" the statement of the *cogito* which already operates, in the use of the sign "I," the transmutation of the concrete subject into a transcendental subject, profiting from my finitude to speak it-

the language of the beginnings, learn an unknown language, Elie, I call you, break down the wall, intercede for the intercessor that I am, you, for the third circumcision before the first, not the second, that of Easter in the plains of Jericho, 'Make stone knives and circumcise them again" (12–24–76).

* "I was not in love with Thee and I was unfaithful to Thee, [and during my unfaithfulness the shout went up on all sides: 'Well done,] well done.' [For, the friendship of this world is unfaithfulness to Thee, and 'Well done, well done' is shouted so that one may be ashamed unless he show himself a man in this way. I did not weep over these things]" (I, xiii, 21).

self and immediately reducing my death to the level of an empirical accident. But as infinite here implies repetition, which cannot be thought outside finitude, we see the inextricable complication of the finite and the infinite that *différance* gives us to think. The point of insisting on finitude is not simply to recall philosophy to a concrete here and now—that is rather the gesture of the human sciences; the movement that philosophy carries to infinity to reach the ideal is not disallowed by the demonstration of its spiriting away of the originary finitude that alone makes it possible: for we were only able to demonstrate that finitude by recognizing the rights of this same movement under the name of repetition and necessary possibility. But recognizing "the rights" here precisely renders impossible the habitual distinction between fact and right which is none other than that between finite and infinite. So we cannot simply bring the infinite back to the finite without recognizing a movement of departure in the finite, in its very finitude. In the text on Descartes, this is what Derrida calls the (mad) project of exceeding the totality in order to think it: but as soon as we have shown that

23 Well, I'm remembering God this morning, the name, a quotation, something my mother said, not that I'm looking for you, my God, in a determinable place and to reply to the question, *Sed ubi manes in memoria mea, domine, ubi illic manes? quale cubile fabricasti tibi?* [...] *tu dedisti hanc dignationem memoriae meae, ut maneas in ea, sed in qua eius parte maneas, hoc considero,** etc., and neither my will nor my power is today to "go beyond," as SA wanted, *istam uim meam, quae memoria uocatur,*** but to quote the name of God as I heard it perhaps the first time, no doubt in my mother's mouth when she was praying, each time she saw me ill, no doubt dying like her son before me, like her son after me, and it was almost always otitis, the

the infinite is projected in the same movement as finitude, one can no longer really think of it as the *telos,* even an infinitely distant one, of this movement, and the word "project" becomes unsatisfactory. (Whence too Derrida's caution around the "Idea in the Kantian sense" [OG, 137ff.; SP, 9, 100ff.].) This "movement" of *différance* is therefore no longer simple and smooth, but constantly folds the infinite back onto the finite without ever being able to immobilize itself (for there is nothing without this movement, which "constitutes" the finite in going beyond it), and has no longer strictly speaking a direction (a sense), for there can no longer be anything beyond this movement to orient it. This cannot fail to upset our common representations of history and time. In spite of its obvious difficulty, this argument is not essentially different from the one bearing on context and metalanguage, and can only repeat more or less explicitly the reasons which prevent us from giving our exposition a simple linear organization, and the reasons which oblige us to go in for all these returns and repetitions.

tympanum, I hear her say, "thanks to God, thank you God" when the temperature goes down, weeping in pronouncing your name, on a road in the "little wood," one summer, when a doctor had threatened me with a violent and dangerous operation, that serious operation that in those days left you with a hole behind your ear, and I'm mingling the name of God here with the origin of tears, the always puerile, weepy and pusillanimous son that I was, the adolescent who basically only liked reading writers quick to tears, Rousseau, Nietzsche, Ponge, SA, and a few others, that child whom the grown-ups amused themselves by making cry for nothing, who was always to weep

METAPHOR

If Derrida's writing is difficult to insert into the genre of philosophy, this is because he appears to play metaphor against concept. Not that metaphor is unphilosophical in itself, but the concept of metaphor deployed by philosophy (for "metaphor" is the name of a philosophical concept) is concerned to give it a secondary place which it obviously does not have in Derrida's writing. One can, classically, illustrate conceptual propositions by metaphors, but in principle one ought to be able to say what is to be said in philosophy without using them. Whence for example, in part, the philosophical *topos* of the imperfection of "natural" languages and the need for a clearer and less ambiguous language, and if needs be an "artificial" logical notation. It is not difficult to see why a tradition ordered around the value of presence would be wary of metaphor, which speaks obliquely, exploits lateral connotations, insinuates things without really saying them, suggests ideas without making them explicit. And if

over himself with the tears of his mother: "I'm sorry for myself," "I make myself unhappy," "I'm crying for myself," "I'm crying over myself"—but like another, another wept over by another weeper, I weep from my mother over the child whose substitute I am, whence the other, nongrammatical syntax that remains to be invented to speak of the name of God which is here neither that of the father nor that of the mother, nor of the son nor of the brother nor of the sister, and of that syntax coming slowly to me like the hope of a threat, I'm more and more scared, like the scared child who up until puberty cried out "Mummy I'm scared" every night until they let him sleep on a

we do indeed find many metaphors in the texts of philosophy, in principle they are reducible to the status of inessential ornamentation which helps the reader to traverse the hard pages of conceptual argumentation, a slightly risky detour the better to recuperate meaning in the end. (Thus, for example, Quine's *Word and Object* is written in a dense and passably "literary" style, full of recherché metaphors: but the same book proposes means to reduce all philosophical propositions to the most formalized logical notations.) This secondary position of metaphor with respect to a conceptual propriety is linked just as obviously to the value of seriousness (cf. LI passim), responsibility and truth established against seductive and hence irresponsible games, the fictioning of artists. So long as artistic writing remains in its place, in literature, philosophy admires it and draws examples from it, even recognizing that poetic intuition can give a visionary access to a truth the philosopher would need much work to achieve: but as soon as it appears to demand an *essential* privilege, as such, in thought, then the danger of irrationalism is denounced and the frontiers are tightened.

divan near his parents, fear today of what has just happened to me halfway through, just before I'm 59, with this facial paralysis or Lyme's disease which, gone now without leaving any visible trace, will have changed my face from the inside, for henceforth I have changed faces and my mother is not for nothing in this, not the eternal visage of my young mother but hers today, especially near the lips, that's the event, unpredictable both for G. and for me, in the writing of a circumfession for the death agony of my mother, not readable here but the first event to write itself right on my body, the exemplary counterscar that we have to learn to read without seeing, "*Kar: to do in Sanskrit, the thing*

There is, however, a whole tradition which would like to recall philosophy to its forgotten truth in metaphor. It is important not to go wrong here, for Derrida himself has very often been assimilated to this ("artistic") tradition, and this is false. Clarifying this point is a condition of our hoping to grasp the relationship Derrida's texts entertain with literary works, and to see why his readings of Blanchot, Celan, Genet, Mallarmé, and Ponge answer to *none* of the current models of exegesis, commentary, or interpretation, and especially not to the (essentially philosophical [cf. WD, 28]) model of literary criticism, and to understand that he is not looking simply for confirmation or illustration of theses developed more properly elsewhere.

This other tradition not only demands the right to metaphor, but recalls the austere conceptual tradition to *its* own metaphorical truth. Thus it is argued that all philosophical concepts have etymological roots in the sensory world, and that their use as concepts is possible only on condition of forgetting the metaphorical movement which distanced them from the original meaning, and forgetting that forgetting. The intelli-

done as sacred thing, what happens in circumcision, what is done, outside language, without sentence, the time of a proper name, the rest is literature..." (8–1–81).

*"But where dost Thou dwell in my memory, O Lord; where dost thou dwell there? What resting place hast Thou fashioned for Thyself? [What sanctuary hast Thou built for thyself?] Thou has granted this favor to my memory, to dwell in it, but in which part of it Thou dost dwell, this I now consider" (X, xxxv, 36).

gible world of metaphysics would on this account be merely an analogical transfer of the sensory world of physics. Transcribing a philosophical sentence into its "true" meaning, one can thus, for example, transform the sentence "The soul possesses God to the extent that it participates in the Absolute" into "Breath sits on he who shines in the bush of the gift he receives in what is entirely unbound" (quoted in M, 212–3). This transcription makes philosophical discourse look like an oriental myth, unmasks the philosophical imposture which fails to understand that its *logos* is only a *mythos* ("the white mythology") among others, but which it arbitrarily and violently attempts to impose as Reason itself. Philosophical discourse, in its apparent seriousness, would then be merely forgotten or worn-out metaphors, a particularly gray and sad fable, mystified in proposing itself as the very truth. One can see how tempting such a reading can be for a critique of philosophy from the human sciences or from literature.

Derrida also very often invokes the etymology of the terms he reads or uses; he writes, sometimes at least, in a language which exploits turns which are un-

**"[I shall even pass over] this power of mine which is called memory, [desiring to attain Thee where Thou canst be attained]" (X, xvii, 26).

24 "Quid ergo amo, cum Deum meum amo? *Can I do anything other than translate this question by SA into my language, into the same sentence, totally empty and huge at the same time, the change of meaning, or rather reference, defining the only difference of the* 'meum'*: what do I love, whom do I love, that I love above all?* [...] *I am the end of Judaism*" (1981), of a certain Judaism, they

acceptable to philosophy, if only because they defy any attempt at translation, whereas philosophy ought in principle to be absolutely translatable. And if the current of thought we have just invoked calls on an essentially symbolic conception of language (isolated words are picked out and taken back to their original sense, considered as their true natural meaning), have we not seen Derrida talk of a becoming-sign of the symbol (rather than just an arbitrariness of the sign [GR, 47]), which would seem to join with the artistic transcription of philosophy? Is it anything other than denial when Derrida, replying to Ricoeur in "Le retrait de la métaphore," refuses the latter's assimilation of his description of metaphor to this artistic tradition (RM, 11–16), or when, anticipating this assimilation in "La mythologie blanche" itself, he claims to be de-limiting rather than sharing the presuppositions of that tradition (M, 215)? This question becomes even more complicated when we see Derrida, after replying quite severely to Ricoeur, say that the point is not to defend a proper, literal, and correct reading of his text against too "metaphorical" a reading like Ricoeur's, and that

will understand it as they like, the fire I'm here playing with is playing with me again, I am no longer the same since the FP, whose signs seem to have been effaced though I know I'm not the same face, the same *persona,* I seem to have seen myself near to losing my face, incapable of looking in the mirror at the fright of truth, the dissymmetry of a life in caricature, left eye no longer blinking and stares at you, insensitive, without the respite of *Augenblick,* the mouth speaks the truth sideways, defying the diagnostics or prognostics, the disfiguration reminds you that you do not inhabit your face because you have too many places, you take place in more places than you should, and

moreover there is no such thing as a literal reading, only differences of "tropic capacity" (RM, 16). We cannot avoid seeing a problem here, as we appear to be striving to provide as literal a reading of Derrida as possible

> Derrida's point is not to criticize philosophy for its use of metaphors, nor to criticize the critics who do go in for such a criticism, but, as always, to show the fundamental complicity linking the two camps here. "La mythologie blanche" has misled its readers because not enough attention has been paid to its argumentative structure: in short, it has not been read philosophically enough, and this is the matrix of all poor readings of Derrida (whether they are presented as pro- or anti-)—it is decided in advance that he is *against* philosophy or reason or meaning or the concept or Hegel and then only what can comfort this initial hypothesis is read. In fact, the greater part of "La mythologie blanche" is qualified by an "as if" (something like a metaphorical turn, then) produced by a formal argument near the beginning: it is rapidly established that it is impossible to dominate philosophy or tell its truth on the basis of

transgression itself always violates a place, an uncrossable line, it seizes itself, punishes, paralyzes immediately, topology here both being and not being a figure, and if it is a disfiguration, that's the trope I've just been hit right in the face with for having violated the places, all of them, the sacred places, the places of worship, the places of the dead, the places of rhetoric, the places of habitation, everything I venerate, not the unpredictable event I have supposedly written, myself, namely sentences fit to crack open the geologic program, no, that took place outside the writing that you're reading, in my body if you prefer, this conversion ought to be the surprise of an event happening to "myself," who am therefore no longer myself, from the wood I

metaphor, but the rest of the essay takes this formal law (which we shall reconstruct in a moment) as a provisional hypothesis, the better to track its historical destiny. This structure, whereby a law deduced a priori, and which has every appearance of being a *thesis* (there is nothing outside the text, the proper name is not proper, at the beginning is repetition, the thing itself always escapes, etc.), is surrounded by long "historical" readings, is not peculiar to this essay, but constitutes the movement of deconstruction itself (cf. too LG, 206; 0S, 9): the relation between "thesis" and "reading" does not answer to a model of illustration or exemplification for reasons which we shall approach slowly—but our own reading, which began with a representation of apparent theses, will itself have to espouse this movement and incline increasingly toward the historical. Let this movement here surround the following pseudo-thesis (the athesis, according to *La carte postale* [PC, 259–73]): there is (only) deconstruction.

Here then is the formal deduction, already announced under the title "Plus de..." Any attempt to ex-

warm myself with, that's the "conversion" I was calling with my wishes or avowals, they were heard even if you remain deaf, even if I could not foresee what the vows of avowal destined me to, but the fact that it is not decipherable here on the page does not signify in any way the illegibility of the said "conversion," I have to learn to read it while my mother is still alive, today is July 23, her 88th birthday, I must teach you to teach me to read myself from the compulsions, there will have been 59 of them, that make us act together, we the chosen of unhappiness, *non enim tantum auditoribus eorum, quorum e numero erat etiam is, in cuius domo aegrotaueram et conualueram, sed eis etiam, quos electos uocant,*★ even if a circumfession is always simulated, the symp-

ceed metaphysics which appeals to the concept of metaphor to do so can only fail, because this concept is an essentially metaphysical concept (M, 219, cf. 230). If all philosophy is explained on the basis of this concept, one has not explained all of philosophy, for the concept of metaphor has been withdrawn from the object to be explained, precisely to do the explaining, and thus escapes the explanation it seemed to allow. But, according to the very criteria of this type of explanation, it would have to be admitted that "metaphor" is itself a metaphor (whose "real meaning" would be, for example, "transport"), which cannot be done without depriving oneself of the promised explanation, plunging back into the field to be explained the concept supposed to provide the explanation. One "metaphor" less, then, in the field, one more with respect to that field. Supplement, quasi-transcendental. *Plus de métaphore.* And if we accept that the thought of the trace makes it impossible to claim to withdraw in this way a concept on its own without its pulling others with it (the concept of "concept," for example), we see that any attempt of this type must remain futile. This is

tom said figuratively to be "real," the conversion *which happens* ought no longer to cause any fear, as though she had said to me: "I know you are innocent right up to the most extreme of your perjuries, perhaps because I am a woman, I do not know if what I am saying to you does good or harm, you cannot save on your torment, your angel protects you, Elie."

* "[I was associating even then, in Rome, with those false and fallacious 'saints']: not just with their auditors, to which rank belonged the man in whose home I recuperated and regained my health, but even with those whom they call the 'elect' " (V, x,18).

also, in passing, why the human sciences always run the risk of being more bound up with metaphysics than any philosophy, but this is also the constitutive double bind of philosophy itself, which cannot be comprehended by anything other than itself, but cannot comprehend itself either, although it just is the effort to do this.

So we behave as if this formal law (which is valid for any philosopheme: philosophy cannot understand the totality of its field with the help of one of the concepts of that field—one sees the relationship with Gödel's theorem about undecidables) were simply a hypothesis, and we set off on a long detour through the texts of the tradition to confirm it. This is why Derrida writes long texts in which one learns a lot about the history of philosophy, rather than short logical demonstrations. Is this simply a question of taste? Of disciplinary formation? Why not simply accept the logical demonstration and try to formulate new, less vulnerable concepts?

But this is exactly what is done: do not forget what we have already said of the impossibility of inventing a

25 *Sed excusare me amabam et accusare nescio quid aliud, quod mecum esset et ego non essem,** the question remains, after months of interruption, we are in November now, it's almost a year since my mother went into her lethargy, her *escarres* are closing, what health, she still does not recognize me but she smiled at me the other day, at least she smiled at someone, replying, when I said, "You see, I'm here," "Ah, you're here," it remains to be known who will be there, if she will still be alive if I arrive, before the end of this year if I survive it, at the end of my 59 periods, 59 respirations, 59 commotions, 59 four-stroke compulsions, each an Augustinian *cogito* which says *I am* on the

new conventionalist terminology, and the necessity of paleonymy. We *must* go through the history of philosophy just because concepts are not pure arbitrarily named "X's"—the "becoming-sign of the symbol" says this sufficiently clearly. We cannot simply stipulate a content for a concept, if it is true that we receive language like the law, and if it is true that there is never "one" concept. The point, then, is not to choose between a concept of philosophy as a perfectly synchronic system, its own contemporary, and a historicist conception which would take each term separately and lead it back to its roots in order to show, triumphantly, its metaphorical origin: we have already sufficiently complicated the synchronic/diachronic opposition to forbid any such choice. We must attempt to respect *both* the systematicity of a network of concepts (Derrida does so here for what Aristotle says of metaphor) *and* the historical imprint which can mark each of these concepts. Passing through the history of philosophy becomes as necessary, in its very "as if," as the formal demonstration it appeared to illustrate: what Aristotle says about metaphor, for example, is not simply an *ex-*

basis of a *manduco bibo, already I am dead,* that's the origin of tears, I weep for myself, I feel sorry for myself from my mother feeling sorry for me, I complain of my mother, I make myself unhappy, she weeps over me, who weeps over me, syntax to be invented, neither the father's nor the mother's nor mine but what trinity's, if not a compulsion grenade for I promised to God never to write anything more except on the most irrepressible of drives, the double condition, no?, of the worst and the best in literature, but that's what you have always done, answers God, I'll answer for it, yes, but all the same, more or less, my father would specify who must for his part have seen the thing

ample of the formal law, but, in its apparent contingency, an integral part of what confers truth on that law, which it thus affects with an "as if," a "quasi-," in its turn. We thus trouble the relationship between the contingent and the necessary, the transcendental and the empirical, in a non-historicist fashion.

Metaphor is conceived by metaphysics as a detour, a passage of meaning via the risk of nonmeaning to recover itself in the concept. The schema of this secondarization is not essentially different from that which works on the sign, a provisional passage of the *logos* outside itself in view of its return. Just as we were able to say that the metaphysical concept of the sign effaces the sign, we shall say the same thing of the metaphysical concept of metaphor: if the point again is in some sense to efface that effacement, then we must *maintain* sign and metaphor against the effacement inscribed in their very concept. So we keep the old name, insisting on an apparently secondary predicate which in fact turns out to describe the general structure—writing in the case of the sign. And for metaphor? This would be *catachresis,* the name of a figure which cannot be re-

when his brother Eugène Eliahou held me on his knees, his brother Elie, i.e. me, already, "*holding myself on his knees, in my arms, I am sitting on the high chair and am holding the velvet cushion, little Jackie is howling, his hands in the air, hallucination, I am uncle Eugène Eliahou and I see Jackie, he already bears this name, not the other, he was born one 15th of July in this house,*" not in the rue Saint-Augustin, in town, where I lived with my parents until I was 4 except in the summer, I remembered a few months ago, in the middle of my facial paralysis, I was driving in Paris near the Opéra and I discovered that other rue Saint-Augustin, homonym of the one in Algiers where my parents lived for 9 years

placed by a more proper term, and which is thus a sort of not very proper proper meaning: and we find that in this sense all the founding concepts of philosophy would be catachreses (including "term" and "foundation"): the concept "concept" would be a catachresis, for example. Which implies the possibility of a non-propriety no longer thinkable according to the ideas of substitution that rule the concept of metaphor.

Donald Davidson's theory of metaphor could appear to escape this characterization. According to Davidson, there is no "metaphorical meaning" to oppose to a "proper meaning." Where there is meaning, one can by definition say it properly, propositionally. Metaphors have no meaning *other* than the literal meaning (the only meaning) of the statement, but the incongruity, contradictoriness or obvious falsity of reference in the *use* of these statements signal the fact that they are not to be taken in the sense of their meaning. To the extent that there is something other than formulatable propositions in metaphorical statements, then we are not dealing with meaning at all, but with something else, which could be called "tone," for example. Tone is not

after their marriage, my elder brother René was born there, Paul-Moïse, whom I replaced, was born and then died there before me, a few months old, I remembered this when all that precedes this had already been written on the trace of SA, the only "images," very vague ones, that I still have of my early childhood coming from the rue Saint-Augustin, a dark hallway, a grocer's down from the house, we had returned there after the summer of the "*poker game, hot holiday night, I am also the* mochel, *my sacrificer, I write with a sharpened blade, if it doesn't bleed the book will be a failure, not necessarily the book produced, evaluable by others in the marketplace, but the self-surgery, my father is looking,*

to be understood, by definition, but we should be sensitive to it: literary criticism can help us to be so, but this does not belong to philosophy. Beyond a still expressivist side to Davidson's description of meaning in general (which is perhaps not essential), we should note that the simplicity of his solution to the problem of metaphor does not give an inch on the traditional demand of philosophy, but singularly restricts the terrain of meaning, and thereby of philosophical concern, to simply propositional meaning. Within a huge linguistic domain, philosophy has retrenched itself in a little logical fortress, abandoning its traditional jurisdiction over the domain as a whole to the various disciplines that might take it on. From this point of view, Derrida's enterprise might appear still too attached to the classical philosophical foundations and demands, even if he works interminably to show their impossibility. Davidson could pride himself on having better than Derrida escaped from philosophy, done his mourning for it: it would remain to be shown that doing one's mourning just is the philosophical operation *par excellence*.

but where is my brother, and my mother? no doubt in the next room with the women, she lost a son less than two years previously, scarcely older than myself" (12–24–76).

*"[For, up to that time, it seemed to me that it is not we who sin, but some other unknown nature within us which sins...] but I loved rather to excuse myself and accuse some other unknown being which existed with me and yet was not I... [Thou hadst not yet set a watch upon my heart and a door of safekeeping about my lips (*custodiam ori meo et ostium continentiae circum labia mea*) [...] So, until then, I associated with their elect]" (V, x,18).

If, then, the metaphysical concept of metaphor destroys itself by sublating into the proper and the concept, there must be another way of thinking its secondariness or its effacement. This time we generalize it in the other direction: if metaphysics says that all metaphors are sublatable into concepts, we shall say that all concepts are only "metaphors," pushing to the limit marked by catachresis. Just as the generalization of the term "writing" obliged us to reinscribe its concept beyond its opposition with voice, the generalization of metaphor outplays its opposition with the proper, and so we can no longer claim to name properly the result of this operation, even with the name "metaphor." We will, then, have an originary "(quasi-)metaphoricity" which would give rise to effects of propriety and effects of metaphor. This is not other than writing, which helps us to explain the paradox whereby it is in its *proper* sense that writing is systematically belittled by the tradition, and in its metaphorical sense that it can be praised: but now that we have complicated the supposed "proper meaning" of writing by lifting its opposition with voice, we can understand that this

26 If one more circumcision (M/L) delimited my lips, if my confession sucked at the truth that appeases and reassures, even without redemption, I would put an end to the being in perdition that I am, although I feel myself to be still kept in the prayer of my living mother, *"Vade" inquit "a me; ita uiuas, fieri non potest, ut filius istarum lacrimarum pereat." quod illa ita se accepisse inter conloquia sua mecum saepe recordabatur, ac si de caelo sonuisset,** I would escape this whirlpool, the experience of a confession which no longer has anything to do with truth, like a circumcision susceptible to all figures and features, old names or catachreses, but a confession or a circumcision, rites, aren't

"proper" meaning is none other than metaphoricity itself (GR, 15–17; cf. MEM, 104–5).

THE UNCONSCIOUS

We started from the linguistic sign in order to deploy a thinking which will increasingly overrun the frame of linguistics. If linguistics appeared a good means of questioning the metaphysics of presence, this is for reasons that we can formulate quite rapidly. To the extent that, according to Heidegger's suggestion, metaphysics remains subject to the—forgotten—question of the meaning of Being, and thus in part to the precomprehension of the *word* "being," and to the extent that linguistics, at least in some of its currents, questions the unity of the word in general, including that of the word "being," then in principle it ought to be able to escape from a regional position, subject to a fundamental ontology, and exceed everything that is commanded by this precomprehension, thus indicating a certain exit from metaphysics (GR, 21; cf. M, 203–5). Not that lin-

they, owe it to themselves to resemble, belonging to the family, the genre, where one must confess that, and I wanted it this way, this story doesn't look like anything, nothing has shifted since the first morning on the threshold of the garden, and my circumfession inaugurates instead of stratifying in the Macintosh pad, with the amnesiac, reiterable and vulnerable structure of the double-sided/double-density, double track, micro floppy disks MF2-DD, for example, made by Sony, a word which reminds me of the dream in Turin, between Rousseau and Nietzsche, my two positive heroes, in which I was saying in English of Pierre my elder, "*He doesn't even identify with the sun,*

guistics escapes without more ado, and any attempt to reduce philosophical problems to problems of language always runs the risk, as Derrida shows with reference to Benveniste, of falling back into metaphysics through its very haste to escape from it (M, 177–205).

In the *Grammatology,* Derrida indicates that we can expect the possibility of such a "breakthrough" from psychoanalysis too. In truth, such an assertion is less surprising at first sight, for we have rather got into the habit of seeing in the hypothesis of the Freudian unconscious an immediate and irreversible questioning of any self-presence of reflective consciousness, as Cartesian or Husserlian philosophy would like to establish it. It is not by chance that, at a decisive moment of the reading of Husserl, Freud's *Nachträglichkeit*—his true discovery (WD, 203, 211–2)—should come to support a thinking of time no longer dominated by the privilege of the present (GR, 67; M, 21; SP, 63). And it must also be said that in Derrida's texts as a whole there is much more discussion of psychoanalysis than of linguistics properly speaking. However, Derrida's relationship with psychoanalysis is complicated, to say the

how do you want me to give him anything?", and if the story doesn't look like anything, this is also by way of a challenge thrown out to those idiots who think that computers are harmful to writing, to the good old Sergeant-Major pen, parental writing, *la plume de mon père, la plume de ma mère,* and finally sorts out the problem of doubles or the archive, what naiveté, it's because they don't write on a computer, I've nicknamed mine *subjectile,* like I'd baptized my attic, where I stock the skizzes of my circumcision, *my sublime,* my upside downs, for I have neither up nor down, like the squirrel climbing up and down horizontally, the form of my world, a literature that is

least, and has never taken the form of an alliance. And if we expected that Lacan (who in some sense wants to reunite the two "sciences" which according to Derrida have the best chance of shaking up metaphysics) would represent the successful escape, then we will be disappointed. Beginning of "Freud and the Scene of Writing" (WD, 196–7): beware, deconstruction might look just like a psychoanalysis of philosophy, but is not at all. It is not what Freud says about repression that is going to help us to understand the metaphysical repression of writing, but rather the opposite (see too PC, 288). *All* Freud's concepts belong to the history of metaphysics, and therefore to logocentrism. Of course, these concepts are deployed in an original discourse (syntax, work), which cannot be entirely reduced to the conceptuality which is to be displaced, but Freud does not reflect the necessity of this work and this displacement. Forewarning, in *Positions,* of what "The Purveyor of Truth" will be: no, Lacan does not succeed in performing the breakthrough expected of linguistics and psychoanalysis—what he takes from Saussure remains massively dominated by a phono-

apparently, like the very look of my writing, cosmonautical, floating in weightlessness, marine and *high-tech,* more naked, whatever they say, thanks to the simulacrum, "*the circumcised Jew: more naked, perhaps, and therefore more modest, under the excess of clothes, cleaner, dirtier, where the foreskin no longer covers, protects itself the better for being more exposed, through interiority, pseudonymy, irony, hypocrisy, detour and derelay, whence my theme, foreskin and truth, the question of knowing by whom by what the violence of circumcision was imposed, if it is a traumatic wound and if there are others, symbolic or not, where the debate fixed around the figures of the father (Freud) or mother (Bettelheim) no longer satisfies me, or only as*

centrism; his "full speech" remains caught in a metaphysical determination of presence and truth; his textual attention to Freud does not thematize the written as such; what he calls "return to Freud" also repeats Hegel's phenemonology of consciousness (POS 84n.44)—and his way of privileging the signifier in the determination of meaning and the psychic simply inverts the metaphysical opposition, and moreover sets up a transcendental signifier (the phallus), which communicates straightforwardly with the most traditional phallocentrism.

And yet, on another side and in another tone, the reading of Freud gives rise to some of the most difficult and surprising texts, around what will be called the postal or "tele-" motif, and which implies a whole reflection that it would have been difficult to predict (it is also a question of prediction) about the postal service, the telephone, and even—what will we be able to say about this?—telepathy.

Derrida shows that Freud's efforts to think the psychic lead him to have massive recourse to scriptural metaphors, which lead eventually to the representation

a relay in view of another etiotopotomology, another stratagem of the heteronomic alliance, in the 'es gibt' *of the stroke of the gift with which to sew up the chain of all my texts*" (12–24–76).

*" 'Leave me now; as I hope for your salvation, it is impossible for the son of these tears to perish.' And she often recalled in her conversation with me that she took this as a message from heaven" (III, xii, 12).

of the psyche as a writing machine. The psychic apparatus writes, and the psychic content is a text: Freud's "mystic pad" united better than other models (but no doubt less well than the computer I am writing on [cf. MEM, 107]) the coexistence of an always fresh receptivity and a capacity for retention that characterizes the psyche while defying representation up to that point. Before reaching this representation, a language of force, resistance, and path-breaking communicates with all we have said up until now, and shows that life (which we have already seen essentially defined by a relation to finitude) lives only in a relation to death, an "economy of death" which is originary and constitutive.

> Pure life would be death. The absolute exposition of an inside to the outside destroys it immediately. But it cannot be absolutely shut away safely either. Every inside exposes a face to danger, without which it would be already dead. During one of the first American expeditions to the moon, a careless astronaut pointed his camera at the sun, which immediately burned out its cells. The camera cannot tolerate the source or purity

27 *This* time for a singular period, yes, here I am, since always here he is in alliance with death, with the living death of the mother, *quoniam sponsionem uolebat facere cum morte,* I still love this *facere,* like when SA talks of *making* truth, *et* qui amat periculum, *incidet in illud,** the mother to whom here I am giving things to eat and drink like a baby, again in Nice for the 19th anniversary of the death of my father whose death notice I find rummaging in the cupboard, a death notice he carefully composed for himself and that I read holding my mother's hand or caressing her forehead for we will have had to wait for her to be 88 and me 59 for this living death liturgy to become possible, and I'll never know if I was alone in it with myself, for my

> of what its only *raison d'être* is to capture and relay. This lunar drama of reflected light, of a burning that leaves only ash, of the sun and death that cannot be looked at directly, haunts all of Derrida's thought. We should follow all the suns that figure this blinding source of what allows us to see (AT, 15ff.; D, 166; HAS, 33; M, 218–9, 242ff., 250).

Here is the most complex formulation, derived from *Beyond the Pleasure Principle*. The primary processes seek discharge, pleasure, at whatever cost, scorning any consideration of the system's survival. The secondary processes bind them. Discharge, absolute unbinding, would be immediate death, but total binding, nonmobility, asphyxiating compression, would be death too. So the apparatus must protect itself against its own life pleasure (die a little) and protect itself against too much protection too to live (a little). There is no life before this compromise (WD, 203). (This is also why Derrida says that there is no writing or supplementarity which does not also involve a protection against itself [EO, 7; cf. GL, 53–4a, 61; GR, 154–5, 179–80; M, 285–6; WD, 224], why it is part of

mother is still talking, she who was playing poker and swimming three years ago, she tries again to reply to this question whose syntax suddenly appears to me to be incredibly difficult to understand in a mirror, when cerebral circulation took a blow from it, "who am I?", and I imagine her protesting in silence, impotent, impatient faced with the incorrigible narcissism of a son who seems to be interested only in his own identification, but no, that of his double, alas, the dead brother, "*revise the whole thematics of the twin, for example, in* The Postcard, *put it into relation with* Envy and Gratitude, *i.e. that the desire to understand oneself is linked to the need to be understood by the internalized good object, as aspiration that expresses itself in a universal fantasy, that of*

the game to appear to come to an end [cf. D, 156–8], why, in short, there are effects of meaning—which are not illusions to be measured against a truth present elsewhere—or why the trace appears as signifier and signified.) The pleasure-principle here names this setup in which the reality-principle serves it by putting obstacles in its way which oblige it to seek its goal via the detour of *différance*. Pure pleasure and pure reality would be equally mortal. Life is in their *différance*. It follows that the reality-principle is not in opposition to the pleasure-principle, but that it is the same thing, in *différance*, the detour via which the pleasure-principle rules and rules itself. But even this detour cannot be absolute (we know that *différance* cannot be absolute)—for it is nothing other than the passage of pleasure through the constraints of reality. The pleasure-principle is thus not *other* than the reality-principle, which it would become absolutely if the detour did not finally return to pleasure. Pleasure is in the end nothing other than the passage of its own detour through reality, and it thus never arrives at its purity, which would again be death. We are still in a structure of

having a twin whose image represents all the parts of the ego separated by splitting, and not understood, that the subject desires to understand by reconstituting himself in them, and sometimes the twin represents an internal object [just now, July 17, 198?, Jean has woken up and said to Marguerite that he has 'just dreamed he had a double,' and that 'it was grammatical'] to which one could accord absolute confidence, in other words an idealized internal object. 'Now I am here as though in a family. Outside, it is raining, the mother is doing the cards, the son is writing. There is no one else in the room. As she is deaf, I too could call her Mother' (Kafka), the mother does not reply, dissymmetry, she lets herself be called, it suffices that, essentially deaf, she allow herself to be represented by someone who lets themselves be called in her place,

the nonidentical same, which Derrida here calls "life-death."

This is a way of deducing repression and showing that it is *différance* which allows it to be thought, and not the other way around. Repression makes it possible for pleasure to be experienced as unpleasure, in a formulation which is obviously unacceptable to a philosophy of consciousness, and which, to avoid this being a logical scandal too, necessitates the topical differentiation which means that unconscious pleasure can be conscious unpleasure. Now the structure of the same in *différance* welcomes this possibility and even produces it, for it says that pleasure is only produced in a necessary tension with unpleasure, that the two imply each other necessarily without being opposed to each other, that pleasure is bound as unpleasure in order be the pleasure that it is. If consciousness does not accept this stricture, we have thus produced a becoming-unconscious at the same stroke (cf. GR, 69): it is not that there would be two different places, but a *différance* of places, a spacing, precisely, still within the same.

deafness becoming essential in order to constitute the family 'play,' and that she 'do' the cards appears as necessary" (7–17–8?), perhaps this will surprise no one, but to know if there is a commotion, if there will have been a surprise and therefore an event, you have to wait, general truth that remains to be *made* and will no doubt surprise those who have confidence in that so indispensable but so deficient grammatical category of the future perfect, the last ruse of presentations, confessions, conversions and other peripheral contortions.

* "Since he wanted to make a pact with death and 'he who loves danger shall perish in it' " (VI, xii, 22).

However, this structure, still that of the mastery of the pleasure-principle and not its beyond, takes place in a vaster *différance* or detour which sends the living being (which only lives already in life-death) toward its own death. According to Freud, life (thus complicated) is a detour of the inorganic toward itself: the pleasure-principle defers the mortal cathexis or decathexis in the service of a movement, insured by the partial drives, toward a death which would be proper to the living being, the proper of the living being thus being to reappropriate to itself the very thing (death) which disappropriates it. Abyss of the proper. The self of the living being is constituted as this detour toward its proper, its death.

The pleasure-principle binds the freely circulating energy of the primary processes. For there to be pleasure, the pleasure-principle must limit pleasure, which would otherwise be absolute unpleasure and short-circuit in the burnout of an im-proper death. Pleasure begins by binding *itself* or limiting *itself* in order to be what it is. There is no (absolute) pleasure, but by the

28 I'm having a great time, I will have had such a great time, but it costs a crazy price, that's at least what they would like to tell themselves about me, hoping for the crazy price, precisely, over the top, the bad calculation at a loss, and I reply that I don't know, I'm one of those smokers who now carry their ashtray on them, no one knows where and when they empty it, and this nonknowledge is the only interesting thing, the best condition for having a great time like a lunatic, that's the happening I oppose or reveal to G.'s absolute theologic program, not that I love nonknowledge for itself, on the contrary, I

same token there is no (absolute) unpleasure. This band and contraband, this stricture of the pleasure-principle constitutes reality as the very tension of self-binding pleasure. No pleasure without stricture (TP, 43). There is no lack or opposition in this logic (cf. DIA, 83), desire is here, "productive," certainly, but only in limiting its "production"—we cannot say that the more it binds, the more pleasure there is, nor the opposite, we're always dealing with more and less, and this is also why we have insisted on the fact that it is each time singular, an event.

This is also the place to talk about mastery. The whole discussion of the pleasure-principle turns around its mastery in the negotiation between primary processes and reality. Freud also talks, in passing, of a drive to mastery, or, as Derrida translates it into French, of *emprise*. "Quasi-transcendental" privilege of this drive: one drive in the series of the drives, it also says the being-drive of drives, the driveness of the drive. Every drive must retain a relation to itself (as other) which binds it to itself, if it is to be the drive it

am even ready to think like certain Muslims that "the ink of the learned is more sacred than the blood of the martyrs," but sacred, precisely, through something other than knowledge, sacred truth of this nonknowledge, *et cum amant beatam uitam, quod non est aliud quam de ueritate guadium, utique amant etiam ueritatem nec amarent, nisi esset aliqua notitia eius in memoria eorum,** for in drawing nonknowledge from the future of what happens, I find it nowhere other than in the confession of my memory, when for example I do not know if I will begin or give up writing *on* the death of my mother, with this writing thus *promised unto*

is—this is how deconstruction formulates the law of identity in general (PC, 403). And psychic life in general is described as a power game between drives, and between the drives and the pleasure-principle (PP, the supposed master). (In French, "PP" is pronounced "pépé," slang for "grandfather," and Derrida plays extensively on this in *The Post Card*.) This question of mastery thus logically precedes the question of pleasure and unpleasure: *différance* of power, of forces still.

> Somewhere mastery no longer masters, encounters its limit. Fails. *Il faut* mastery, you would say, perhaps. My own: *ci falt*. And yours.

Mastery/*emprise* speaks of a relation to the other, who can also be oneself. This is one of the most constant themes: in order to be itself, a subject must already relate to itself as to an other. Identity comes only from alterity, called by the other (cf. F, xxii). This is what we shall be following more obviously from now on. This structure is what gives rise to the fundamental mistake with respect to Derrida, namely that his thought is just a thought of reflection which never gets

death, whereas the desire to speak, a fortiori and a priori to write, would come to an end, that's my absolute knowledge, if one of my uncircumcised sons left me, the remaining, and luminous, fact that my first publication followed the first of them, as though addressee meant for me the son, the dreamed of daughter, any possible reader becoming the uncircumcised to be confessed, line thrown for all the girl-martyrs who will ask the question of what they're *doing* here, with or without excision, "*in this place which perhaps situates the absolute lure: take this* affair *(thing, cause,* Sache, *trial) of circumcision as determining in my*

outside its specular referrals, which gets caught up in the games of a narcissistic writing, etc. But everything Derrida has written says that the relation to self is precisely not specular, that there is always alterity before (any) self, primary telephone call (AL, 265–75). Other "in" the same, calling it up by contaminating it. This is why Derrida likes placing things in an abyss while being wary of what can be too enclosing in the *mise-en-abyme* (PC, 304; TP, 33–4). We can sense that this alterity cannot simply be stated in the form of theses, that it is not really thematizable, not a phenomenon, that it does not exist.

This is why psychoanalysis cannot fail to interest us, but also why we are wary of its conception of the unconscious: this is still "metaphysical" because the term is only defined with respect to consciousness, itself thought in terms of presence. (And a doctrine of the unconscious always runs the risk of reinforcing the [deep] identity of a subject whose conscious discontinuities are accepted the better to link them to a more secure substratum or sub-ject.) Whereas for Derrida

case...*whereas from all the nonidiomatic necessities I would give myself the booby-trapped hope of getting close to the proper language of my life on the screen of circumcision that would then have to be traversed, which is here the trial, even if the screen can reflect interesting things, me and the others, during a projection the richer for being well placed to dissimulate, the others then having to read me* on the screen *at the very moment I am telling them how little I believe for example in the psychoanalytic metaphor of the screen-memory, its topic or its dynamic, whereas the operation—without an operating-operated subject—named circumcision retains an essential relation to the production of a*

this "presence" is an effect produced by a relation to alterity in the binding to itself of all identity and therefore all presence. Generalization and radicalization of the unconscious (which can thus be invoked strategically, for example against John Searle [LI, 73ff.]). The unconscious for Derrida would be the reserve of repetition—iterability—which means that an event arrives in its singularity only if the possibility of a certain repetition prepares its coming and its identification, memory of the future (PMW, 593, 595). And as, in the generalization of writing, it is voice with its effects of presence that becomes mysterious, here it is consciousness which becomes enigmatic (HAS, 17), more infiltrated or lined with alterity than the unconscious supposedly in a different "place." (This is a permanent and misunderstood structure of deconstruction: because it is thought that Derrida is carrying out a critique, it is imagined that he detests voice, presence, sincerity, etc., whereas that is the only thing that interests him [PC, 14–15].) And primary narcissism becomes something quite different from a self-absorption or an inability to

screen (scribe or chrism as I was saying)..." (12–27–76), the screen that I believe I see my mother holding out to me today when the living dead woman pretends to say nothing, know nothing, understand nothing, "what are you thinking about?" I asked her on May 16, 1989, no reply, "who are you thinking about?", no reply, "nobody?", reply: "nobody," then "what do you want to talk about?", no reply, "about the past?", reply: "yes, about the past."

*"[For they love (truth), also, since they do not wish to be de-

welcome the outside. We shall not cease to verify that it is on condition of a folding back on oneself that there is communication with a radical "outside" which can no longer be thought of as a world over against a consciousness or an object over against a subject. This other in the relation to self is not the Lacanian Symbolic, for it already intervenes in what ought to be the Imaginary, and cannot be assimilated to the Real: Derrida does not accept this distinction, which presupposes a linguisticism which we have already answered in principle, and does not accept either what it can support in the area of sexual difference (PC, 492; POS 84ff.).

But Derrida finds the means to think this complication or implication of outside on the inside, here nicknamed the crypt, in Nicolas Abraham and Maria Torok. This is the same thing as is developed around mourning (and friendship) in what he writes after the death of Paul de Man. The dead friend only now exists in us or between us, we who have his memory and guardianship: but in welcoming the other in this way,

ceived.] And, when they love the happy life, which is nothing other than joy arising from truth, they certainly love truth, also. Nor would they love it, unless some knowledge of it were in their memory" (X, xxiii, 33).

are we assimilating him to ourselves, which annuls him as other, or are we keeping him *as* other, interiorizing him still outside? In the first case, we have "successful" mourning, in which I eat the other who dies to become part of me (of my Ego)—"introjection." In the second case, we have melancholy, incomplete mourning, the other remaining in me like a foreign body, living dead—"incorporation" (F, xivff.; MEM, 21–28ff.; and, on the foreign body, TEL, 33–4). Incorporation forms the crypt: hidden under the inside which it thus supports, outside without really being outside. Who will say that "successful" mourning is the best mourning: how could one know this? The crypt would be a space foreign to the Ego, a space of the foreigner thus introduced, but the better to be kept outside, exclusionary inclusion, not the unconscious but a false unconscious. I am here, in the crypt.

> Could one say that Derrida's relation to metaphysics is to be thought of in terms of incorporation rather than introjection? In that case there would be a certain truth in saying that Derrida has not accomplished his

29 Quick, memories, before the thing arrives, *multa praetereo, quia multum festino. accipe confessiones meas et gratiarum actiones, deus meus, de rebus innumerabilibus etiam in silentio. sed non praeteribo quidquid mihi anima parturit de illa famula tua, quae me parturiuit et carne, ut in hanc temporalem, et corde, ut in aeternam lucem nascerer,** and like him, in great haste, I confess my mother, one always confesses the other, I confess (myself) means I confess my mother means I own up to making my mother own up, I make her speak in me, before me, whence all the questions at her bedside as though I were hoping to hear

mourning for metaphysics, that he is keen not to do so. Half-mourning, rather (GL passim; PC, 335). And therefore *neither* incorporation *nor* introjection.

THE SIGNATURE

My proper name outlives me. After my death, it will still be possible to name me and speak of me. Like every sign, including "I," the proper name involves the necessary possibility of functioning in my absence, of detaching itself from its bearer: and according to the logic we have already seen at work, one must be able to take this absence to a certain absolute, which we call death. So we shall say that even while I am alive, my name marks my death. It already bears the death of its bearer. It is already the name of the dead person, the anticipated memory of a departure (EO, 7; FC, 22; MEM, 62–4). The mark which identifies me, which makes me me rather than anyone else, depropriates me immediately by announcing my death, separating me a priori from the same self it constitutes or secures.

from her mouth the revelation of the sin at last, without believing that everything here comes down to turning around a fault of the mother carried in me, about which one might expect me to say however little, as SA did about the "surreptitious" taste of Monica, never, you hear, never, the fault will remain as mythical as my circumcision, do I have to draw you a picture, this December 2, 1989, in Madrid, when it's a year ago, to the day, that I thought my mother was already dead from her fall and that I know her to be alive without knowing what I know in this way, about she who is all over me, whom as regards the

El Greco, *The Burial of Count Orgaz* (Toledo, Church of Saint Thomas; detail: on the right, Saint Augustine; on the left, the page, the painter's son). The allusion to J.-C. in *Circumfession* 29 refers to a reading of this work by Jean-Claude Lebensztejn, in *Zigzag* (Paris: Aubier-Flammarion, 1980)

Romeo is the separable bearer of the name "Romeo" only thus de-nominated (AL, 426–7). The signature, and this is precisely what distinguishes it from the proper name in general, attempts to catch up again the proper we have seen depropriate itself immediately in the name.

In speech, what is called the enunciation marks the presence of the present moment in which I speak. The signature ought to be its equivalent in writing (M, 328). The I-here-now implied in every enunciation and lost in writing is in principle recuperated in the signature appended to the text. The act of signing, which is not to be reduced to the simple inscription of one's proper name (EO, 52; LI, 33; SI, 54) attempts, via a supplementary turn, to reappropriate the propriety always already lost in the name itself. Which implies that the signature, in order to mark a here-and-now, is always accompanied de jure by the mark of a place and a date (cf. AL, 387). *In fact,* this is not always the case, which can give rise to all sorts of legal problems around wills and other documents, problems produced by the ability of writing to separate itself from its place of

eyes and lips I resemble more and more, as I see her for example today at Toledo, this Saturday afternoon, with her ancestors, Saint Augustine as an extra returned at the moment of the burial of the Conde de Orgaz to place his remains in the tomb, and here I am stopped with her, in the corner of the picture, I am the son of the painter, his signature in my pocket, *domenikos theotokopolis epioei,* and on my return to Barcelona, where I lived in the *via Augusta,* I reread "The Burial of the Conde de Orgaz" signed by J.-C., I re-comma and underline "(burial is a reverse birth, return to the womb), by assimilating the picture and the child indicating the miracle, the anachronism *spreads* the pres-

emission. There is much to be said, within the framework of a quite simple phenomenology of writing, about different modalities and forces of signatures on different types of documents, manuscript or other. For example, one does not often see a author's manuscript signature on a printed book such as this. But it is presupposed, and the whole code of authors' rights depends on this in its aberrant and fascinating complexity (TB, 197–200), that there is somewhere a true manuscript signature (on a publishers' contract, for example) which can be linked in a continuous and secure way to the author's name printed on the cover of the book. Such a signature is supposed to guarantee the enunciation of the text by tying it to a unified agency of emission, and, what is more, to guarantee what is called, in a very vague way, the originality of the text. If we enlarge this classical acceptation of the word "text" to include in it, for example, computer software or telecommunications signals, we shall see problems of this sort multiply.

We shall not delay here around the details of this description: we can see that we should have to specify

ent, by presenting simultaneously in one single place *four* distinct epochs, the old date of the count's death and the miracle, the inscribed date of birth (legitimation of the bastard son?) the date at which the canvas was painted, with the portraits of the Toledans at that date, and the fleeting, indeterminate epoch at which the spectator is watching, outside the picture but attracted toward its space by the look and gesture of the son, anticipated metaphor of the canvas... without counting ethernity," and I wonder why SA returns at the moment of the burial, hers, mine, and all the characters in the picture, the contemporaries in fact, are looking in different directions, never crossing a glance,

all sorts of exceptions and problems; for example, it is enough to invoke the quotation, in a text, of the text of another author, and the practice of quotation marks (cf. LI, 29ff.; OS, 31, 65–7) which mark off part of the text as non-signed, or at least as signed in a different way from the text without quotation marks for which the author is supposed to take responsibility. We see immediately that these quotation marks are not sufficient to account for the difficulties which go with quotation and the respect of the other's signature it ought to imply. This respect ought to involve a respect for the context in which the quoted passage has been taken, and we have already said that insofar as one quotes by definition out of context, such a respect could never be total. And one can always quote without marks, or practice other methods of not entirely assuming what one writes and signs. The case of a fictional text is different again, in spite of all the temptations the reader may feel to refer the text to the person of the author via the signature.

Further on, for these same reasons, what is called literature will appear inseparable from these problems of

like my readers, the condition for there to be, or not, a world, like the obstinate deformation of a gaze, as the sustained hallucination of El Greco produces a work, "*for centuries, the* mohel *sucked the glans of so many little Jews: give to the hallucinating repetition of this enlarged gesture its duration, its acceleration too, mechanical, compulsive, describe the inspiration*" (12–30–76), the orgy.

*"I pass over many things, for I am in a great hurry. Receive my confessions and my thanks, O my God, for numberless things, even when I am silent. But, I shall not pass over whatever my soul brings forth concerning that servant of Thine who brought

law: but law, which loses itself in these questions (in the very simple sense that in order to have force of law a text must be signed by a legitimate agency, and that law—positive law at least—must presuppose an understanding of the signature in order to be the law it wants to be), is also inseparable from what is called literature.

Without following these complications any further, let us return to the idea that the signature marks in writing what is marked in speech by enunciation itself. It is obvious, and this is the root of the traditional description of writing and its dangers, that this mark is very poor security for the authenticity of writing. We can already note, without feeling unduly concerned by it, a division in the signature of a book. First because there is no real present moment of writing: one writes over a period which is more or less long, more or less interrupted, one rarely writes in the order in which the finished book is presented, one revises one's text at several different moments. All this highly complex temporality of writing is in principle gathered up, not into a single signature (for example that of the contract),

me forth in the flesh, so that I was born into the light of time—and in the heart, so that I was born into the light of eternity. [I would speak not of her gifts, but of Thine in her]" (IX, viii, 17).

30 "*. . . the mixture on this incredible supper of the wine and blood, let people see it how I see it on my sex each time blood is mixed with sperm or the saliva of fellatio, describe my sex throughout thousands of years of Judaism, describe it (microscopy, photography, stereophototypy) until the paper breaks, make all the readers drool, wet lips, high and low, stretched out in their turn on the cushions, right on the*

but into what must be considered as a countersignature added to that on the contract: for example, the moment when, having finished the text, one adds after the event an introduction or a preface (D, 7–59) to which will be appended, with a solemnity which is never questioned, a date and perhaps an indication of the place of composition. This signature, which is already a countersignature, pretends to gather up all the moments of the "enunciation" of the text into this single moment of meta-enunciation which closes the already written book for the writer and opens it for the reader. Where the signature on the contract promises the writing of a book that one day I shall be able to sign as my own, the countersignature at the end of the preface replies proudly to this promise by assuming as my own, here and now, what has been written in the meantime. But it goes without saying that the text of the preface, however minimal, is also worked on by the temporality that the countersignature will never reduce: even if one signs a single sentence or a single word, the signature does not accompany this text like the enunciation that is the lining of the speech, but follows it: and we

knees of 'godfather' Elie—high mourning—leave nothing, if possible, in the dark of what related me to Judaism, alliance broken in every aspect (Karet), with perhaps a gluttonous interiorization, and in heterogeneous modes: last of the Jews, what am I [...] *the circumcised is* the proper" (12-30-76), that's what my readers won't have known about me, the comma of my breathing henceforward, without continuity but without a break, the changed time of my writing, graphic writing, through having lost its interrupted verticality, almost with every letter, to be bound better and better but be read less and less well over almost twenty years, like my religion about which nobody understands anything, any

have to say that the signature itself takes time to be written, does not quite accompany itself, is never a pure present.

What makes all this complexity around the written signature possible? If we go back to the good old manuscript signature on the publisher's contract which appeared to serve as a guarantee for the proper name printed on the cover of the book, thus marking an origin-point for writing, we see that this signature is already not simple. This contract exists in several copies, and the signature must be appended to each of these copies. The text of the contract itself is mechanically reproduced, with special conditions typed in carbon, but the signature must be written by hand separately on each copy. It must be the *same* signature, but this same signature is written on three *different* sheets. The signature, which functions and has force of law only on condition that it mark a present moment (which also has the force of a promise—we have already promised several times to come back to this), exists as signature only on condition that it be repeatable as the same signature, in several copies. After every-

more than does my mother who asked other people a while ago, not daring to talk to me about it, if I still believed in God, *nutrierat filios totiens eos parturiens, quotiens abs te deuiare cernebat,** but she must have known that the constancy of God in my life is called by other names, so that I quite rightly pass for an atheist, the omnipresence to me of what I call God in my absolved, absolutely private language being neither that of an eyewitness nor that of a voice doing anything other than talking to me without saying anything, nor a transcendent law or an immanent *schechina,* that feminine figure of a Yahweh who remains so strange and so familiar to me, but the secret I am excluded from,

thing we have seen around repetition, no one will be surprised to see machines and death loom up again here. Indeed, this necessary repeatability of the signature simultaneously makes possible its mechanical reproduction: for example, there are signature machines designed to save overworked company directors from the fatigue of constantly having to sign documents; and the fact that the use of these machines is regulated by all sorts of codes which are somewhere guaranteed by a "true" signature in no way prevents one noting that the present marked by a signature is immediately divided by the necessary possibility of its repetition, if needs be its mechanical repetition. And as one cannot touch machines without playing with death (WD, 227), we must note that such a signature machine remains in principle perfectly indifferent as to whether the signatory whose careful paraph is being imitated is still alive or not. Bank notes bear the printed reproduction of the signature of a designated official (in England, this signature explicitly signs a promise to pay the bearer the sum indicated on the note), and remain valid after the latter's death. Through a necessity the

when the secret consists in the fact that you are held to secrecy by those who know your secret, how many are there, and do not dare admit to you that this is no longer a secret for them, that they share with you the open secret, letting you reckon that they know without saying, and, from that point on, what you have neither the right nor the strength to confess, it is just as useless to make it known, to hand it over to this public notoriety you are the first and only one to be excluded from, properly theological hypothesis of a blank sacrifice sending the bidding up to infinity, God coming to circulate among the unavowables, unavowable as he remains himself, like a son not bearing my

measure of which we are far from having taken, these possibilities, which can look like subjects for a bad film, are not simply accidental, but constitute an integral part of the structure of the signature.

It follows that any signature is a signature only on condition that it call or promise a countersignature. Derrida invokes the example of travelers' checks, which one signs first before departure, but which have to be countersigned on arrival if one is to get one's money, the validity of this countersignature being guaranteed by its resemblance to the "original" signature. To accelerate the demonstration, let us say immediately that any signature is no more than a promise of a countersignature, but that every countersignature remains subject to the same structure of principle. Whence the relationship with death, which we shall here describe as the interruption of an ability to sign, which confers on the last signature a capital importance in all the scenes of inheritance and tradition we shall follow later on. As the possibility of the interruption of an ability to sign forms part of what we call a signature, we see that the signature, which, as we said, attempts

name, like a son not bearing his name, like a son not bearing a name, and if, to give rise to this beyond of the name, in view and by reason of this unacceptable appellation of self for my mother has become silenced without dying, I write that there is *too much* love in my life, emphasizing *too much,* the better and the worse, that would be true, love will have got the better of me, my faithfulness stands any test, I am faithful even to the test that does harm, to my euthanasias.

*"She had brought up her children, being in labor with them each time she saw them wandering away from Thee" (IX, ix, 22).

to deal with the power of death at work in the proper name, only moves this power to a different level.

We have already disturbed the usual distinction between speech and writing: but one would be tempted to believe that this distinction turns out to be necessary here. Perhaps this is where we shall find the resources to safeguard speech against the encroachment of writing. Our description of the signature will be accepted without difficulty, but it will be said that it is precisely because it is written that it participates in the dangers of writing in general, and that therefore there is nothing to be surprised about if it is threatened by repetition, simulacrum, and falsity. On the other hand, the I-here-now of oral enunciation, which the signature does not manage to reproduce, would mark a temporality safe from these doublings and repetitions.

Nothing could be further from the truth. Naturally, we are not attempting to deny the effects of presence linked to living speech. But everything we have seen of the blink of self-presence in Husserl, that moment divided against itself to constitute itself, even in soliloquy, forbids us from making it into a secure foun-

31 *"Her love has the better of me, did I write this sentence for its value, its meaning, its truth, its actuality, or because, in its syntactic and lexical powers, it comprises a formidably formalized economic potential, rendered in advance to the place where it bleeds, and how many statements of this type have I allowed to be lost, for want of an immediately available surface of inscription, without knowing if they were being inscribed elsewhere, nor what remains once the surface of inscription has been buried, like foreskin or moleskin... coin of a new concept* [in English in original], *fellocircumcision, autofellocircumcision, one's own* mohel *doubled up, of my laughter, having taken and kept a swig of wine from her mouth, very cold Algerian rosé, we used*

dation, safe from the effects of what we are here expounding about the signature. Insist as one might on the unique character of the instant of living speech and defend as one might its efficacy against all the *hommes au magnétophone* you like, the fact remains that in order to be memorable, even recognizable, such moments must precisely carry within themselves a power of repetition or memory which divides them while constituting their finitude or their death. Without which there would be no time at all. However truly subtle and ungraspable the components of these instants (such as tone [AT, passim]) may be, their very identity as graspable-as-ungraspable is made possible only through the very repetition they are supposed to disallow. Derrida shows with reference to Artaud the aporias of any attempt at an absolute reduction of the text, or even of articulated language, in a quest for something absolutely nonrepeatable (WD, 245:ff.): which, let it be said in passing for those who see in Derrida a nihilistic troublemaker, in no way diminishes the dignity or pathos of such a quest. The point is not at all to disapprove of or attempt to destroy this type of desire,

to drink it at the fishing ground, he circumcises himself, the 'lyre' in one hand, the knife in the other, and drinks his own blood, to make himself even cleaner, i.e. circumcised, he then says to himself I love you and in drunkenness begins to lament his solitude, my love will have got the better of me" (12–31–76), according to what must be declared, like in the customs, my impossible homosexuality, the one I shall always associate with the name of Claude, the male and female cousins of my childhood, they overflow my corpus, the syllable CL, in *Glas* and elsewhere, admitting to a stolen pleasure, for example those grapes from the vineyard of the Arab landowner, one of those rare Algerian bourgeois in El-Biar,

which we cannot but share (PC, 194), for it is desire itself, but to show how this desire is possible only to the extent of the radical impossibility of its accomplishment (GR, 143). Just as the signature is constituted only as a promise of countersignature, the present moment of voice, or of any experience at all, exists only as a function of a "promise" of memory, and thus of repetition.

We see that this is not without its links to Nietzsche's Eternal Recurrence. And perhaps above all as it appears in Heidegger's reading of Nietzsche, to which Derrida does not however entirely subscribe (GR, 18–20; S, 79ff, 108ff). This improbable analysis of the experience of the signature would no doubt be impossible without reference to Heidegger's reading of time in *Kant and the Problem of Metaphysics.* And if we looked back toward Freud, remembering that the "invention" of psychoanalysis hangs on a desire to account for memory, we should see immediately what links this structure to what we have said about the memory trace which only breaches its path (its signature) through the network of neurons by inscribing in them the possibility of re-

who threatened to hand us, Claude and me, we were eight or nine, over to the police after his warden had caught us with our hands on the grapes, and there was a nervous burst of laughter when he let us run off, since then I have followed the confessions of theft at the heart of autobiographies, homosexual ventriloquy, the untranslatable debt, Rousseau's ribbon, SA's pears, *nam id furatus sum, quod mihi abundabat et multo melius, nec ea re uolebam frui, quam furto appetebam, sed ipso furto et peccato. arbor erat pirus in uicinia nostrae uineae pomis onusta nec forma nec sapore inlecebrosis* [...] *non ad nostras epulas, sed uel proicienda porcis, etiamsi aliquid*

peated passages along the same road (cf. WD, 202). And it will be remembered that the question of writing was inseparable from memory, *mneme* and *hypomneme* in Plato, *Erinnerung* and *Gedächtnis* in Hegel read by de Man (MEM passim). This inscription of a memory to-come in the present moment condenses what could look like a general problem, or even a contradiction, in Derrida's texts, which appear both to valorize the event as absolute unpredictability and pure expense while insisting on the impossibility of any such event, which is produced only by opening itself to a possibility of repetition. Whence too the possibility of believing that Derrida remains unduly attached to the metaphysical tradition that he also seems to want to transgress. Later we shall see the reason for this apparent duplicity.

What was said above about the relations between writing and reading ought to complicate further this description of the signature. Writing, as we were saying, already, always already, has a reading relationship with itself, which divides its act, forbidding any pure inspiration while explaining it. If we return to the signature with the memory of that complication, we

*inde comedimus, dum tamen fieret a nobis quod eo liberet, quo non liceret. ecce cor meum, deus, ecce cor meum, quod miseratus es in imo abyssi,** as though beyond need, but still bowed over it, the circumcised one were caressing himself on the theft of what he addresses to his mother, I tell you, o *mohel,* rummaging in the cupboard in her bedroom, before her eyes which no longer see me, each time I am in Nice with her to note that she has kept almost nothing, a few at most of the cards and letters I wrote her over nearly thirty years, twice a week, not to speak of the two telephone calls whose ghosts still scan my Thursday and

ought no longer to be able to presuppose a given identity of the signatory through the acts of signature (and indeed the extension of the properties of the signature in the narrow sense to the presence of the enunciation which it is supposed to supplement, and even beyond the enunciation, right up to perception itself, supposes a still more radical questioning of identity) because such an identity would still be the subject we are attempted to delimit here. And we must add, in the logic of what we have seen so far, that there is no valid reason to presuppose that the countersignature—already at work, as we have seen, in the "first" signature—must necessarily be carried out by the first signatory. The fact that my signature, if it is to be a signature, must be repeatable or imitable by myself entails just as necessarily the possibility that it can be imitated by another, for example a counterfeiter. The logical form of the reasoning by "necessary possibility" authorizes us to say that my signature is *already* contaminated by this alterity, already in some sense the other's signature.

We must then rethink reading as a relation of signature and countersignature, which allows us to think

Sunday mornings, at the time when for twelve months now I have no longer been calling her, she will no longer reply, nor soon to the eye at the end of blind fingers, 16, raucous tone, 93–84–13–32, nor all these forgotten call numbers of my life.

*"For I stole what I already possessed in abundance and of much better quality. Nor did I desire to enjoy the thing itself which was the object of my inclination to steal, but the very act of stealing, the sin itself. There was a pear tree near our vineyard which was laden with fruit that was attractive neither in appear-

in what way a text remains *essentially* open to the other (to reading). The text's signature calls up the reader's countersignature, as is the case with all signatures: we can now see more clearly that the countersignature it calls up is essentially the countersignature of the other, be that other myself. And if we fold this consequence back onto the beginning of the demonstration, we notice again the alterity which alone makes possible the constitution of anything like a subject. What we were thinking of above as a reading which accompanied all writing and even preceded it, *soufflé*'d it (WD, 169–95), we are now thinking of as a play of signatures countersigning each other, and thus committing each other.

This is why a text is never closed upon itself, in spite of the effort of the signatory who wants to appropriate it. This desire is also paradoxical: for to make one's text absolutely proper to oneself, absolutely idiomatic, would be to bar all reading of it, even by oneself, and so the totally signed text, proper to its signatory, appropriated by him, would no longer be a text (this is an argument, in our opinion a more rigorous one than Wittgenstein's, against the possibility of a

ance nor in taste [...] not as a treat for ourselves, but just to throw to the pigs. Of course, we did eat a few, but we did so only to be doing something which would be pleasant because forbidden. Look at my heart, O God, look at my heart, which Thou hast pitied in the depths of the abyss" (II, iv, 9).

"private language"). Better, because of the fact that any signature is only a memory and promise of a countersignature, no signature is really complete before the (counter) signature of the other, and Plato's signature, for example, is thus not yet finished (EO, 87). Whence a far from neutral relation to the other's signature, both on the side of the "original" text and on that of the text of the "reading," or the inheritor of the original. Traditionality, which we have seen in the reading of Husserl to rest *essentially* on writing, here takes on a more complicated and almost *ethical* dimension in these signature relations—but as we have been unable to limit this logic to the domain of writing, or even of language, this dimension will unfailingly open up too in the very heart of "experience" itself. This dimension can also be that of an extreme violence: if the signature (Plato's, for example, but also Derrida's, of course) calls for our countersignature, this call and our reply to it are not necessarily situated in (filial or other) piety, supposing that we know what such a piety would be outside the play of signatures: just as we have in some sense taken on, in generalization, the traditional description of

32 And mourning capitalizes, it accumulates, it stocks up, saving loves me, a work that no longer has to work, like what I am staking here and meaning is working all alone at my reserve, simultaneously put ahead and put to one side, a stake in any case, a stake in itself, but in me of she who is eating less and less, they tell me, almost nothing, it's the end and I wonder, each time I feed her with a spoon, a baby, sure that this image will never leave me, why I chose "eating the other" or "loving-eating-the other" for this year's seminar, *ipsam memoriam uocantes animum* [...] *nimirum ergo memoria quasi uenter est animi, laetitia uero atque tristitia quasi cibus dulcis et amarus: cum memoriae conmen-*

writing as bastard son and parricide, inscribing the concepts of bastardy and parricide *in* that of writing, so here we should have to think these signature relations before posing questions of fidelity or piety. And as there could be no reading absolutely respectful of a text, for a total respect would forbid one from even touching the text, opening the book, so there could be no countersignature absolutely respectful of the signature it countersigns, for in that case it would become confused with that first signature and would not longer sign at all. The prefix "counter" must also mark this contestatory value which in principle inhabits every reading, even this one. To collapse a chain of deductions once more, let us say that we always remain indebted to the first signature which calls us before we have any choice in the matter. But by the same token, this first signature remains in our debt too, depending on our response to that call, to the very extent that it indebts us. Following the generalization we have attempted toward experience in general, we should also be able to say thus that any experience of the other must be engaged, however minimally, in this reciprocal

dantur, quasi traiecta in ventrem recondi illic possunt, sapere non possunt, ridiculum est haec illis similia putare, nec tamen sunt omni modo dissimilia [...] *cur igitur in ore cogitationis non sentitur...*,* failing this nourishment, and more and more guilty for counting these blood compulsions, the 28 of this patience before the end, what end, I am waiting for the interruption of a race against time between writing and her life, hers, hers, hers alone, the one I'm getting away from as I speak about it, in betraying or slandering it with every word, even when I address myself to her without her hearing to tell her that I am betraying you, I ask your pardon, I admit to you, I ask your pardon for admitting to you,

indebtedness produced by the relation to death inscribed by a signature: we shall say that this indebtedness (let's call it friendship) is grounded in a certainty underlying any encounter, namely that one of us will die before the other, will in some sense see the other die, will survive the other, and will therefore live *in memory of the other*, wearing the other's mourning (AL, 422), like it or not.

TRANSLATION

We can perhaps clarify these very complex relations by examining the question of translation. Derrida gives this problem an importance which is again quite unusual in the philosophical tradition, and even goes to far as to say that translation involves everything that is at stake in the passage to philosophy (D, 72; EO, 120). In the simple case of a translation by someone of someone else's text, we have a very clear, if not very simple, relation between two texts and two signatures. In a long commentary on Benjamin's famous text on trans-

who represent everything, in this duel, all my addresses, would you believe it, pardon for confessing you where you hear me no longer, where you perhaps never heard yourself, neither in me nor with me, nor even in you, I am content to turn around you in this silence in which you stand in for anybody, my god, I ask your pardon for not addressing myself to you, for still addressing myself to you to tell you so even if you don't hear me, you never heard me, nor read me, nor perhaps saw me, you do not even know that you are wearing mourning for me, and therefore this half mourning that I have been ruminating in my mouth for so long, "*high mourning, if mourning is (structurally)*

lation, Derrida describes the mutually indebting relations between original and translation. According to Benjamin, the translator is indebted with respect to the original, in the sense that the original imposes upon him the task, the duty, that he will have to try to fulfill. Like a son or at least an inheritor, the translator comes into a responsibility for the survival of an original; but to the extent that the original depends on the translator for this same survival, it is indebted in advance to any translator who will take on the task thus prescribed. We can say the same thing for reading in general, of which translation here is just a special case. Every text is indebted toward its future readers while remaining, as we have seen, indifferent to the death of any empirical addressee in general: indebted, then, in its very destinerrancy, open to the chance of indebting. But every reading is also indebted to the text read (cf. PS, 175). This law imposed by the text in its event is thus not a pure constraint (no text, not even the text of the law, which dreams of doing so, prescribes an inevitable reading; but no text authorizes just anything at all, which would not be a reading either), but also the prescription of a

half mourning, if full mourning is half mourning, what follows for the mourning of mourning? 'In botany and entomology, "mourning" is used of beings that in their colorings have a mixture of white and black. High mourning, half mourning, butterflies. Half mourning, popular name for the argé galatée *(diurnal lepidoptera), called galatée, satyr galatée; whereas others call it half mourning satyr* [...] *In Old French, in the nominative,* li dels, li dex, li diaux, *in the oblique case,* le duel.' '*The marks of mourning, among the Israelites, were to tear one's clothes...*' Deuil du elle, *tear one's suit, clothing, veil, a covering skin, the operation that does not circumcise with a blade but with the fingers*

certain liberty (TB, 204–5). We are here speaking as much about the law itself, the being-law of the law, as about the text in the narrow sense, and we must therefore recognize the duty to return to it.

Benjamin distinguishes between original and translation: the original allows itself to be translated and retranslated an indefinite number of times, whereas the translation does not let itself be translated in its turn (TB, 193). We must follow Derrida's implicit advice here and recognize that such a criterion only functions after the event: something is original if it will have let itself be translated and retranslated, and thus read and re-read. Some translations or readings will let themselves be retranslated: Derrida himself invokes the Sophocles translations by Hölderlin which get retranslated in turn, thus becoming originals (EO, 148; cf. PS, 271–2). We can say too, generalizing a little the meaning of the word "translation," that all of Derrida's own texts are (only) readings or translations of "originals," but we shall assert the originality of these readings by recognizing that in turn they demand translation—this is notably the case with the term

by twisting the skin, criticized method, the button that, on the death of my father, the Rabbi with his hand pulls off my shirt" (12–31–76).

* "We call the memory itself, mind [...] Without doubt, memory is something like a stomach for the mind; so, joy and sorrow are like sweet and bitter food. When they are committed to memory, conveyed down, as it were, into the stomach where they come to be stored, they cannot be tasted. It is ridiculous to consider these things similar, yet they are not entirely dissimilar [...] But why does one not perceive in the mouth in cogitation...?" (X, xiv, 21, 22).

"deconstruction," proposed as a translation of Heidegger's *Destruktion,* but also naming, in the fold which makes it an original, a certain supplementary work of translation.

But let us not hasten to generalize translation to the point of making it no more than a particular case of reading. Before reaching that point (and we already know that deconstruction happens more in the journey than the arrival), there are specific problems which we shall do well to approach directly via translation itself. We started with the proper name to find ourselves arriving very quickly at the question of the signature. Now, if there is something that seems in some sense to resist translation, it is precisely the proper name. A proper name cannot be translated into another language—one would not say that "James" *translates* "Jacques," nor that "Paris" pronounced in the English way *translates* "Paris" pronounced in the French way (cf. TB, 172–3). Indeed this is what made us think for a moment that the proper name escaped the language system, and that one could therefore seek in it a fixed point that would resist *différance* by attaching the tissue

33 The satyr galatea that I am, a half-mourning satyr without confession which begins by getting lost in seduction, at the very moment it admits in me the dissidence of the true, "*the splitting of the ego, in me at least, is no transcendental claptrap,nor the double focus with-without monocular vision, I am, like, he who, returning, from a long voyage, out of everything, the earth, the world, men and their languages, tries to keep after the event a logbook, with the forgotten fragmentary rudimentary instruments of a prehistoric language and writing, tries to understand what happened, to explain it with pebbles bits of wood deaf and dumb gestures from before the institution of the deaf and dumb, a blind groping before Braille and*

of language to a solid place in the world. Yet we were obliged to see that such a proper name would not be one, and that in order to be "proper" or give the impression of being proper, the proper had immediately to be depropriated in a *différance*-affected classification in which its finitude was inscribed. Which brings the proper name back within the sphere of influence of *différance,* without for all that integrating it in the language system strictly so called—but this just is what prevents us from speaking the language system properly, and in the situation of impropriety that results from this, we shall have to say that the proper name *belongs without belonging* to the language system. Derrida will also ask (ibid.), to point up what is at stake, what a language would be that did not allow someone or something to be called by a proper name (cf. too, F, xlvii-xlviii). Proper names are necessary for a language which does not tolerate them as such, and which nonetheless holds onto them jealously enough to refuse that they be translated into another language. This means first that we have been wrong to speak up until now of *language* in the singular, as we are from the first faced

they are going to try to reconstitute all that, but if they knew they would be scared and wouldn't even try..." (12–31–76), there will be neither monogram nor monograph of me, not only because I will always be too young for the contemporaries, then what G., the one or the other, will perhaps never have heard, I confided it to myself the other day in Toledo, is that if I am a sort of *marrane* of French Catholic culture, and I also have my Christian body, inherited from SA in a more or less twisted line, *condiebar eius sale,*★ I am one of those *marranes* who no longer say they are Jews even in the secret of their own hearts, not so as to be authenti-

with a multiplicity of languages in a situation of reciprocal translation: but what each language keeps as most proper, and therefore as untranslatable, are precisely proper names which do not even belong to it as such, and which can thus appear to do quite simply without translation, being already in a domain of universal absolute reference. Which would come back to the claim that what is absolutely untranslatable is absolutely translatable, or else always already translated.

We cannot be satisfied with that, but, following a movement of thought that is beginning to be familiar to us, must seek out, not the *end* in this type of situation (we have seen in relation to Freud that death is at the end), but the "differantial" tension of the *middle*. Deconstruction is not an extremism, although it can look just like one when it is viewed from the vantage point of a mode of thought which always wants pure and clear concepts. For such a thinking, the propositions that we have just formulated are unacceptable, although they are the rigorous product of that same thinking, if we insist on its demands. The production of this type of proposition is thus not due to any per-

cated *marranes* on both sides of the public frontier, but because they doubt everything, never go to confession or give up enlightenment, whatever the cost, ready to have themselves burned, almost, at the only moment they write under the monstrous law of an impossible face-to-face, *tu... qui mecum es et priusquam tecum sim* [...] sed neque me ipsum diiudico, *Sic itaque audiar* [...] *ego uero quamuis prae tuo conspectu me despiciam et aestimem me* terram et cinerem, *tamen aliquid de te scio, quod de me nescio. Et certe* uidemus nunc per speculum in aenigmate, *nondum facie ad faciem* [...] *confitear ergo quid de me sciam, confitear et quid de*

versity on the part of the "deconstructor" pleased to push paradoxes (cf. AP, 22–57n.6), but it remains an indispensable lever of intervention: deconstruction cannot propose a language that is simply *other* than that of metaphysics (and our discussion of the signature will have perhaps helped us to understand how deconstruction must remain in debt, and in mourning, with respect to metaphysics).

It is also in a relation of *translation* with respect to metaphysics, and what we have called "torsion" or "reinscription" of metaphysical terms, the strategy of placing "under erasure," can in fact be descriptions of so many translations. Translations in a bizarre sense, of course, for if translation implies that we keep the same signified that we adorn with other signifiers (POS, 20), here it appears that we keep the same signifier and attach it to other signifieds: in this way we will already have translated the "metaphysical" concept of translation before justifying our procedure in doing so. This is an inevitable risk of deconstruction, which anticipates upon itself by definition. Derrida finds in Nicolas Abraham the means with which to think this

---

*me nesciam,*** at the moment of writing, neither before nor after but otherwise, I have the vision of SA, too, as a little homosexual Jew (from Algiers or New York), he has repressed everything, basically converts himself quite early on into a Christian Don Juan for fear of Aids, which he could see coming like me, from so far off, and, very well turned, very dignified, he does not recount his death, it is still too near, the only ally, the most secure, it's to death that already I owe everything I earn, I have succeeded in making of it, as I have with god, it's the same thing, my most difficult ally, impossible but unfailingly faithful

operation as an "anasemic translation": in the discourse of psychoanalysis, for example, the word "pleasure" would be "translated" into something quite different, to the point that it becomes possible to speak of a pleasure felt as unpleasure (MP, 7–8). This is not an exchange of signifieds (we have already warned against this way of putting it), but a passage toward a "before" or a "back of" meaning—in Derrida, "trace" and "supplement" state the possibility of meaning, its condition or its element, and therefore have strictly speaking no meaning.

So we are not obliged purely and simply to reject these apparently contradictory propositions: in a deconstructive movement, we shall take seriously the idea whereby proper names belong without belonging to the language system, and we shall do so by saying that the idea of an essential depropriation of the proper name ought to be complicated by the idea of a *becoming-common* of the proper name. Once more, without this becoming-common and the attachment of reattachment to the language system it allows, there would not be what is called by the common noun

once you've got him in your game, it costs a great deal, believe me, a great deal of love, you have to forgive yourself the hurt you do yourself, and the grace of the child is not certain, when I was a child they said I was "gracious" rather than "pretty," but my mother used to pass salt over my head of an evening in the kitchen to ward off the evil eye.

*"[Fresh from the womb of my mother, who put much hope in Thee, I was marked with the sign of His cross and] seasoned with His salt" (I, xi, 17).

"proper name," but pure vocative, non-iterable prayer (HAS, xxx-xxxi).

BABEL

To serve as a sort of emblem of this situation, Derrida chooses the "example" of Babel, which ties together the themes of translation and the proper name. The book of Genesis recounts how the tribe of the Shem (the word Shem means "name" in Hebrew) wanted to make a name for itself by building a tower and imposing its language alone on all the peoples of the earth. To punish them for this outrageous ambition, Yahweh destroyed the tower, shouting out his name "Bavel" or "Babel," which sounds (confusedly) like the Hebrew word which means "confusion," and imposed linguistic differentiation on the earth. This story, to which Derrida returns several times, fascinated (AL, 268, 405ff.; AT, 25; EO, 98ff.; PC, 240–1; TB, passim; TW, 153ff.), contains resources we shall not exhaust here. The essential fact hangs on this: by imposing his name

**"Thou Thyself [...] art with me even before I am with Thee. However, 'I do not even judge myself.' Thus, then, may I be heard [...] In fact, though I despise myself before Thy sight and consider myself but earth and ashes, yet I do know something about Thee which I do not know about myself. Truly, 'we see now through a mirror in an obscure manner,' not yet 'face to face' [...] Therefore, I will confess what I know of myself and what I do not know of myself" (X, iv, v, 6, 7).

(confusedly perceived as "confusion") against the name of name (Shem), God imposes both the necessity and the impossibility of translation. The dispersion of the tribes and languages on earth will condemn them to confusion, and therefore to the need to translate each other without ever managing to achieve the perfect translation, which would come back down to the imposition of a single language. In this milieu of relative confusion, the result of a confused translation of the name of God, we are condemned not to total incomprehension, but to a work of translation which will never be accomplished. As absolute confusion is unthinkable, just as is absolute understanding, the text is by definition "situated" in this milieu, and thus every text calls for a translation which will never be finished. Whence all we have just seen about task and indebtedness.

But if the story of Babel illustrates in some sense the problems of translation, it also gives us something to think about in the direction of the proper name and the common noun. For God's shouting out a proper name which can be heard as a common noun suggests

34 *"The 'alliance' was first of all for the 13-year-old child the name of the place one had to go to, a school really, a year after the exclusion, the numerus clausus and the other school, the Jewish one, rue Emile-Maupas, to learn and sit exams with a view to the bar mitzvah ('communion', as they called it), the word 'alliance' had no continuity with its simple homonym that [in French] designated the wedding ring, to describe the places..."* (12–31–76), and from that moment on I used to flee that Jewish school as well as the "alliance," I played truant without telling my parents for almost a year, I used to go to the rue de Chartres to the depths of the cousin's

the becoming-common of the proper we announced a moment ago. Elsewhere, there is a fascination (see Proust for example), equal to its impossibility, for what proper names "mean," whether this demand pass through an etymological or some other form of inquiry. We have seen that the idea according to which the proper name would be foreign to the economy of *langue*, of *différance*, gives rise to untenable aporias. The proper name cannot be absolutely external to *langue*, absolutely untranslatable, but at most *more or less* external and untranslatable (cf. TB, 165). Babel, proper name, name of God or the father, can be heard *in a given language,* here Hebrew, as the common noun meaning "confusion." We have to emphasize that this scene happens in a determinate language, in the contingency of an idiom, even if an analogous confusion can come about in other languages too (in English, between Babel and "babble"; in French, between Babel and "babil," but there would be a line of filiation and translation to establish here), and even if we are trying to make this into something like a general law. We have to emphasize this clearly to mark the fact that we are from

little watchmaker's to watch the soldiers, the "Allies," queuing up in front of the brothels, the Moon, the Sphinx, I knew how to "zap" even before television gave me that pleasure, as I have always zapped in writing, *Wechseln der Töne* which leaves the other rooted to the spot from one sentence to the next, in the middle of a sentence, dead or vigilant at last, ally for life or murderer, as though the reader had to wish for my death when for example I slip the *alliance* G. talks about on the other side to make it fall into the depths of my childhood, at the very surface of my tongue, reminding you that "alliance" for me will always be a Jewish building on the rue Bab Azoun, "What's new?" I

the start in a situation of multiplicity of languages, a situation which can, however, only be marked in *one* given language, even if this language can aspire to an absolute translatability, or even, like the language of the Shem, aspire to make itself a name as universal language (one thinks for example of what has been said about the privilege of such and such a natural language where philosophy is concerned [GL, 10a; OS, 68ff.]). To the extent that the so-called proper name involves something untranslatable, any such aspiration is condemned in advance—whence the inevitable violence of any attempt to put into action or works such a claimed privilege. Whence too a certain valorization in Derrida of texts which re-mark this multiplicity, and especially Joyce's text: an expression from *Finnegans Wake,* "and he war," lets several languages resound at once in its event, and this event defies any translation to preserve this effect of multiplicity (TW, 154–5).

In general (but, as we have already seen, this "in general" is always already marked by the necessary singularity of its being formulated in *one* given language, quasi-transcendentality again) the situation we are de-

asked her this 30th of December 1989, as if I were interrogating myself at every moment, that is without waiting for a reply, and indeed there was none, no more than to the question "Are you happy or sad?", not a sign of sadness when I leave without knowing whether I shall see her still living, she who wept as much as Monica at each of my departures, from the first, on the *City of Algiers* in the autumn of 1949, seasickness bad enough to make you give up the ghost, and so many times since, I lied to her all the time, as I do to all of you *sed quare hinc abirem et illuc irem, tu sciebas, deus, nec indicabas mihi nec matri, quae me profectum atrociter planxit et usque ad mare secuta est. sed fefelli eam violenter me*

> scribing here is that of a "double bind" (how will I translate this term if ever I translate my text into English?) in which what we have called the proper name calls for a translation which it simultaneously disallows. This type of defiance of the remark can also happen in simpler fashion, or at least apparently so: for example, how are we to translate into French a poem of Celan's which already includes French words (AL, 408), or a text of Borges's whose Spanish is already marked by a French inflexion (EO, 99–100); and how do we include in the Latin translation of Descartes's *Discourse on Method* the paragraph explaining why the text was written in French rather than Latin (LIP, 105)? If one cannot translate the event of a multiplicity of languages, one cannot translate either the event in which a language remarks itself or, as we shall say later, signs itself (AL, 257–8).

Shouting out his name, Babel, God demands a translation that only succeeds by producing confusion itself. Jealous of his name and his idiom to the point of wanting to stop the Shem at any price imposing theirs, God demands a respect for his singularity, for his name, by

tenetem [...] *...et mentitus sum matri, et illi matri, et euasi, quia et hoc dimisisti mihi misericorditer seruans me ab aquis maris plenum exsecrandis sordibus usque ad aquam gratiae tuae, qua me abluto siccarentur flumina maternorum oculorum quibus pro me cotidie tibi rigabat terram sub uultu suo, et tamen recusanti sine me redire vix persuasi, ut in loco, qui proximus nostrae naui erat* [...] *maneret ea nocte. sed ea nocte clangulo ego profectus sum, illa autem non; mansit orando et flendo. et quid a te petebat, deus meus, tantis lacrimis, nisi ut nauigare me non sineres?,** we euthanize ourselves in asking what a living woman would think *if* she saw death coming, whereas my mother had, when she was alive, before her lethargy, demanded from the

instigating the confusion which alone makes necessary the translation it simultaneously renders impossible. This *coup de force,* God's signature bending us to our infinite task of translation, would be that to which literature in general aspires.

LITERATURE

The story of Babel, as recounted by Derrida, is not to be taken literally, and moreover cannot be, on pain of violently resolving the *double bind* of confusion and believing that one has succeeded in the impossible translation of the name of God. It follows from this too that one should not be overawed by the appeal to the name of God, to the extent that "God" can no longer exactly be a proper name. This is, moreover, the same structure as that which made us say that God was in history and in violence. If we say now that all literature wants to repeat God's *coup,* there is, then, no fear of falling into the traditional facileness of making the writer into a (failed) figure of God the creator (cf. EC, passim). It

doctor cousin, who told us this later, that he should never let her live in this way, never practice on her what the doctor is accusing us of, therapeutic harassment, as though—

* "Thou, O God, didst know why I left here and went there, but Thou gavest no sign either to me or to my mother. She complained bitterly at the prospect of my leaving, and followed me to the seaside. But I deceived her, while she was urgently holding on to me [...] I lied to my mother, and such a mother, and I slipped away. Thou hast mercifully forgiven me even this, preserving me from the waters of the sea, though I was full of

is not on the basis of what we think we understand about God that we propose to explicate literature, but indeed on the basis of what we are here calling literature that we can hope to understand something about God.

Literature aspires to the idiomatic. The literary text, which is of course overdetermined by all sorts of things, has no noninstitutional definition (but the literary will here suspend every institution, including that of literature) other than through the idiom. As a writer, I want to write like no one else, and thus impose my proper name or rather my signature (for a writing that was absolutely proper and idiomatic to me would have to be considered as a signature). My writing is thus a demand for translation in the double bind which indebts it in advance, eternally, toward any reader or translator (whence the writer's misery and poverty), while simultaneously indebting this same reader (whence narcissism and megalomania). My desire to write like no one else is thus immediately compromised in the desire that my inimitability be recognized, or, to translate from this language which is too Hege-

abominable filth, unto the water of Thy grace, to be washed by it, when the rivers of my mother's tears might then be dried up, those with which in my behalf she daily in prayer to Thee did moisten the ground beneath her countenance. Yet, when she refused to return without me, I persuaded her with some difficulty to spend the night in a place which was near our ship [...] But on that night, I set out secretly, while she remained behind in prayer and tears. What did she ask of Thee, O my God, with so many tears, but that Thou wouldst not permit me to sail away?" (V, viii, 15–16).

lian, that my proper name be received, and therefore translated. I would like my whole text to be no more than an enormous, monumental, colossal, inimitable (therefore unreadable) signature, *stupid* (as in the case of a certain Thompson, whose name, inscribed in enormous letters on Pompey's column in Alexandria, was seen by Flaubert in admiration and derision: cf. IF, 788n.9), but this desire immediately compromises with readability and therefore imitability. To get across the idiom of my proper name, to impose my law by shouting my name, I must thus ruse with the language which just is not proper to me (that I receive like the law, as Saussure said—but I have also received my proper name, I do not baptize myself), I must attempt to mark this language surreptitiously, get a reader who thinks he is just reading literature to swallow my name.

If the story of Babel is taken as a figure of translation, a translation of translation, says Derrida (TB, 165), the works of Ponge (SI passim) and Genet (GL passim) figure in some sense that work on the proper name that is called literature (GL, 56). But it is important not to go wrong here: the fact that in Ponge one

35 February 23, 1990, under the effect of corticoids, she livens up a little, replies "yes of course" to Jacqueline's question "Are you hungry?", she takes my hand, kisses it or rather sketches, as she always has since she has been surviving, a sucking or inhaling movement with her thin lips, her mouth sunken between the two sharp points of chin and nose, almost deprived of lips by the absence of teeth, she even smiles and remains silent, her empty gaze resting on me when I ask her, how many times will I have asked her this: "who am I?", it's as though for you I had changed my name without her knowing

finds a whole thematics of the sponge, to be read as an attempt to appropriate part of language, that there are *genêts* in Genet, and even the fact that one can see in Derrida's "déjà" the more or less hidden signature of Derrida Jacques (cf. EO, 74ff.; FH, 482) (in which case the insistence on the *always* already would signal an excessive ambition with respect to language—we shall return to this to show up all its modesty too), this in no way prescribes a new reading "method" which would consist in tracking in the whole of literature the proper names of authors. It is clear, for example, that all the problems that are occupying us here are at work in acute fashion in Rousseau, but we do not believe for a moment that it suffices, nor even that it is interesting, to seek out the syllables of this proper name dispersed throughout his works. The quest or demand for the idiom does not necessarily pass through what is recognized as the proper name. It does not follow from this that one should simply extend the field of research to attempt to pick out a secret, perhaps unconscious, proper name (cf. OA, 105–6), because such work would merely repeat the after-the-event structure of

and my presence then finally becomes the absence it always was, *amabat enim secum praesentiam meam more matrum, sed multis multo amplius, et nesciebat, quid tu illi gaudiorum facturus esses de absentia mea. nesciebat, ideo flebat et eiulabat,** this looks more and more like the beginning of "*a big bio-mythography of Elie (eh! lis, et lie, élit, et lit, et l'I, elle y, L. I., l'Y at the end of the double session)*" (12–31–76) for from this 23rd of February 1990 I date the revelation of the origin of my hidden name, the name of he who on my death you will call Elie, I learned it from my brother when I told him how, during the last few weeks, receiving a card from cousin Roger ("My dear Jackie, as you may know, I asked René

The Old Jewish Cemetery in Prague.

any search for origins; the point, on the contrary, is to explain—and moreover there is no secret (F, xviii–xix, xxxvi; HAS, 16ff.; M, 315; cf. PC, 11, 46, 188). If Derrida privileges Ponge and Genet from this point of view, this is as always in part contingent, and at most motivated by concerns of strategy or economic condensation. And as is the case with all of Derrida's texts, and we have sufficiently insisted on this, while knowingly lacking respect in this matter, each of these analyses itself remains idiomatic, entering each time into a different relation with the signature of the other, a relation that we shall attempt a little later to think in the stricture of an alliance.

Let us take the analysis of Ponge. If Ponge's work has in some sense the status of an emblem (if not an example [SI, 20]), this is not because every literary text supposedly hides the author's proper name, with Ponge having the dubious advantage, in this respect, of scarcely hiding the fact. But this way of negotiating the relations between proper name and language stages the problem of the idiomatic and the literary in general. In the course of this analysis, Derrida provisionally distin-

for your address, intending to send you a surprise card from Prague where I was supposed to go on the 25th and 26th for a musical weekend. But the trip has been canceled, not for reasons of security, but because the musician's strike that has been called would have prevented the planned concerts from taking place. See the trouble friend Havel puts me through too! With all best wishes"), I had sent him in my turn, as a sign of thanks, a postcard of the old Jewish cemetery in Prague, bought just before I was arrested, then had learned from my brother in Nice that cousin Roger was dead and already cremated, perhaps before, perhaps after receiving my card, then at the Choays' house, Jan-

guishes three modalities in what is commonly understood as a signature. First, in the common sense, the signature of my proper name, the authentification that what I write is indeed by me: this is the sense we have been content to expound up until now, in which the signature consists in doubling the name with an assertion saying: this name is indeed my name. The second modality would be the one according to which what I write is obviously by me, whether or not it be explicitly signed, immediately recognizable in what is usually called style: this is what Derrida explores elsewhere under the name of *ductus* (TP, 192ff.). Thirdly, we shall say that when writing designates itself *in actu*—remarks itself, as we would have said earlier—it signs itself in a general signature which no longer depends on such and such a proper name (SI, 52–6). Ponge's work is peculiar in that it succeeds in signing in all these ways at once, in such a way that Ponge's inimitable "style" (signature 2) would hang essentially on the inscription of his proper name (signature 1) *in* his texts (and not simply at the end or in the margin) which would thus sign themselves (signature 3) and do

uary 16th, I meet Nine who, leaving the next day for Algiers, sends back, "a proof," she says, "that I thought of you," a very beautiful color photograph of the tomb of Eugène Derrida, in the cemetery of Saint-Eugène, the tomb, then, of my father's brother and the father of this Roger who had just died, but above all the uncle who held me in his arms the day of my circumcision, and who was called Elie for the secret reason that my brother told me, then, namely that he had been named thus in memory of his uncle, the brother of my grandfather Abraham, called Elie, that no one ever mentioned again in the family from the day he abandoned his wife and children to make a new life

without him at the very moment at which they inscribe his proper name within themselves. Whence Ponge's double success, making out of his signature a text which is absolutely proper to him and which nonetheless stands upright all alone without him (here's the monument again or the colossal column, *à la* Flaubert, which also occupy Derrida elsewhere [GL passim; TP, 119ff.]), hiding his name in the language. The sponge in Ponge operates this condensation, and this success is enough to outplay the old subject/object couple (and the "merry-go-round" turning between a phenomenologist Ponge and a subjectivist Ponge [SI, 12]); which will introduce us slowly to a thought of the "thing," the gift and the law.

For we must find courage to envisage literature as singular writing (the signature, then) subject to the law of the thing—but as the thing is each time singular in its event (in its signature, then) this law is not really a law, if by definition a law must be general. And we must above all try to think that the respect for the law of the thing implies that the text becomes a thing too,

for himself in mainland France, Eugène Eliahou alone of his generation having this revealed to him and confiding it to his daughter Fernande, Roger's sister, who told my brother who told me yesterday, what the devil...

* "For she loved to have me with her, as mothers do, but much more than many mothers, and she did not know what joys Thou wert to fashion for her by my absence. She did not know, and so she wept and moaned" (V, viii, 15).

dictating thus its singular law to our readings. Here again is reciprocal indebting or the alliance, and here too is the principle which explains why in literature there is a question of "ethics" (SI, 52). The thing dictates its *thou must* which is each time singular (SI, 50), and literature can give an idea of a probity or frankness in the negotiation of this singularity and the letting-be of the other thing in its alterity, which will guide us in our discussion of more immediately "ethical" or even "political" questions. Which will help us understand why a writing which is apparently completely absorbed in itself can nonetheless better open out to the singularity of the thing and the coming of the other than all the apparently more serious and referential writings that sometimes would like to condemn Derrida in the name of ethics and politics. As literature, ethics, and politics are the places *par excellence* where one measures oneself against stupidity (which is always in some sense the fact of philosophy [cf. IF, passim]), including one's own inevitable stupidity, then that is where we shall allow ourselves to raise the tone a little.

36 And you ask if I write, G., because the Jews know nothing of confession, to which I reply that I am not confessing myself, rather I'm confessing the others for the imponderable and therefore so heavy secrets I inherit unbeknownst to myself, for example Esther or the two Elie's, for there is more than one now, and I have known for a few days that the first will not have held the second in his arms at the moment of circumcision as the second will have held the third, i.e. me, but me who deliberates passively, here or elsewhere, not about what there is to be said, the content, this or that, but if one must or must not, if I can desire to resist confession or not, for example

Letting the thing be in its singularity before any objectivity (and therefore before any dialectic of subject and object) implies that in some sense one says "yes" to the law of the thing. One submits to it, inclines oneself before it. From the standpoint of its alterity, the thing, the other, dictates a law that is received in a passivity—or passibility—which stands before the active/passive distinction. But to speak of law too soon here runs the risk of leading to misunderstanding, for this law is just as much a gift. We must try to think the gift before exchange, and the law before the contract, if we want to approach the thing.

If the essence of the gift is not to be an object of exchange, then we see that strictly speaking the gift annuls itself as such. For your gratitude toward a gift I give you functions as a payment in return or in exchange, and then the gift is no longer strictly speaking a gift. If, given the extreme difficulty of being in a position to accept a gift (PS, 163) you attempt, in order to give the gift a chance, to repress any reaction, you

if I ought to tell them that I pray, and describe how that could happen, according to what idiom and what rite, on one's knees or standing up, in front of whom or what books, for if you knew, G., my experience of prayers, you would know everything, you who know everything, you would tell me whom to address them to, *et ubi essent tantae preces et tam crebrae* sine intermissione? *nusquam nisi ad te,** and you would tell me why I am interested in what at bottom, in the depths of me, precisely describes the "without-interest," what I am only, what "I" is only the misdirection, i.e. the presumed crime I am calling circumcision, and "*the role of the mother in circumcision for if she who desires,*

l'unité et le rassemblement de soi. Tendance vers le centre et l'unité, la matière n'est donc l'opposé de l'esprit qu'en tant qu'elle reste résistante à cette tendance, en tant qu'elle s'oppose à sa propre tendance. Mais pour s'opposer à sa propre tendance, à elle, matière, il faut qu'elle soit esprit. Et si elle cède à sa tendance, elle est encore esprit. Elle est esprit dans tous les cas, elle n'a d'essence que spirituelle. Il n'y a d'essence que spirituelle. La matière est donc pesanteur en tant que recherche du centre, dispersion en tant que recherche de l'unité. Son essence est sa non-essence : si elle y répond, elle rejoint le centre et l'unité, elle n'est plus la matière et commence à devenir l'esprit, car l'esprit est centre, unité liée à soi, enroulée auprès et autour de soi. Et si elle ne rejoint pas son essence, elle reste (matière) mais elle n'a plus d'essence : elle ne reste pas (ce qu'elle est).

on ne peut tenter de déplacer cette nécessité qu'à penser — mais qu'appelle-t-on penser? — le reste hors de l'horizon de l'essence, hors de la pensée de l'être. Le reste *n'este* pas, comme on traduit en s'aidant d'une béquille, d'un ersatz ou d'une prothèse (*west nicht*).
Encore faut-il franchir le pas dialectique

« Une des connaissances qu'apporte la philosophie spéculative, c'est que la liberté est l'unique vérité de l'esprit. La matière *(Materie)* est pesante dans la mesure où existe en elle une poussée *(Trieb)* vers le centre [le milieu : *Mittelpunkt*] Elle est essentiellement complexe [*zusammengesetzt*, rassemblée] et constituée de parties séparées qui toutes tendent *(streben)* vers un centre *(Mittelpunkt)*. Il n'y a donc pas d'unité dans la matière. Elle est une juxtaposition *(Aussereinander)* d'éléments et cherche *(sucht)* son unité; elle cherche donc son contraire *(Gegenteil)* et s'efforce de se relever elle-même *(sich selbst aufzuheben)*. Si elle y parvenait, elle ne serait plus matière; elle aurait sombré comme telle *(untergegangen als solche)*. Elle tend vers l'idéalité, car dans l'unité elle est idéelle. L'esprit au contraire a justement son centre en lui-même; il tend *(strebt)* lui aussi vers le centre — mais il est lui-même ce centre. Il n'a pas son unité hors de lui, mais la trouve en lui-même.

se confirme ici l'affinité essentielle — et non seulement figurative — entre le mouvement de relève (*Aufhebung*) et l'élève en général : élévation, élèvement, élevage. Ascension aérienne du concept. Le *Begriff* saisit et emporte vers le haut, oppose sa force à tout ce qui tombe. Il est nécessairement victorieux. La victoire ne lui échoit pas, il est ce qui gagne. D'où son caractère impérial. Il gagne contre la matière qui ne peut lui tenir tête qu'à se relever elle-même, à se nier en s'élevant à l'esprit. Il gagne aussi contre la mort : en érigeant jusqu'à la tombe. La sépulture s'élève.
Ne nous approchons pas trop vite de la sépulture de Hegel autour de laquelle il faudra s'affairer plus tard

La fleur épanouit, achève, consacre le phénomène de la mort dans un instant de *transe*. La transe est cette sorte de limite (transe/partition), de cas unique, d'expérience singulière où rien n'advient, où ce qui surgit s'effondre « en même temps », où l'on ne peut pas trancher entre le plus et le moins. La fleur, la transe : le *simul* de l'érection et de la castration. Où l'on bande pour rien, où rien ne bande, où le rien « bande ».

Non que le rien soit.

Peut-être peut-on dire qu'*il y a* le rien (qui bande).

« *Transe*. s.f. Grande appréhension d'un mal qu'on croit prochain. [...] E. Wallon, *transs*, glas qu'on sonne pour la mort; espagn. et portug. *trance*, heure de la mort, moment décisif; ital. *transito*, passage de vie à trépas; du lat. *transitus*, passage. En français, *transe*, qui a voulu dire toute vive émotion pénible, tient à *transir* (voy. ce mot). » *Littré*

Plus tôt qu'*il n'y a*, il y bande (régime impersonnel) dans un passé qui ne fut jamais présent (la signature — déjà — le nia toujours) : *il banda* (régime

bander, c'est toujours serrer, ceindre (bandé : ceint), tendre, avec une bande, une gaine, une corde, dans un lien (liane, lierre ou lanière). « *Bande*. sf. [...] E. Wallon, *baine*; namurois, *bainde*; rouchi, *béne*: provinç. et ital. *benda*; espagnol, *venda*; de l'anc. haut. allem, *binda*; allem, mod, *binden*, lier; sanscrit, *bandh*, lier. Comparez le gaélique *bann*, une bande, un lien. » Plus haut : « Elles nourrissaient leurs enfants, sans les emmailloter, ni lier de bandes, ni de langes », *Amyot*. *Littré*, dont il faut lire tout l'article, pour y relever au moins que les bandes sont en termes d'imprimerie, des « pièces de fer attachées aux deux langues du milieu du berceau de la presse, sur lesquelles roule le train ». Double contre sens, au moins, du mot *bandé*. Qu'appelle-t-on panser

impersonnel) égale *il lia*. Serrure.

Un certain rien, un certain vide, donc, érige.

30

Glas (p. 30 of the French edition [pp. 22–3]), which later treats of circumcision according to Hegel and Genet (pp. 41–7): "He [Hegel] had, in passing, situated circumcision and the sacrifice of Isaac" (p. 45); "... through the privilege it has, in one word, of giving rise to decollation, of assigning to the executioner the dividing line (circumcision or castration)..." (p. 62); "These cloths that bind the angel resemble those with which babies are swathed after circumcision" (p. 239).

nevertheless inscribe the gift in the possibility of exchange by receiving or recognizing it as a gift, consciously or unconsciously. For the gift to be pure of any movement of exchange, it would have to go unperceived by the donatee, not be received as a gift, not be a gift at all. The gift only "exists" or gives in an exchange in which it already gives no longer. It is recognized only by being lost in indebtedness or exchange (GL, 242a; MEM, 149; TW, 146–7). What is commonly called a gift or present is therefore only the trace of a pre-archaic event of donation which can never have taken place as such. The gift has always already compromised itself with exchange, which, however, never manages to measure up to the gift which "precedes" it. There is a whole complication of temporality implied here: the gift is never (a) *present* (cf. GL, 80b; MEM, 147); it is given in a past which has never been present and will be received in a future which will never be present either.

This gift which does not present itself as such precedes any exchange and therefore any dialectic. In the long reading of Hegel that constitutes the left-hand col-

sometimes commits circumcision, compromises with the inhibited desire for child-murder, she is indeed in the position of obsequence (Glas, *with its circumcisions, guillotines, incisions, still illegible tattoos), figure without figure, armed extra who is no longer present among us at the operation she now delegates after having previously performed it herself,*" (7–1–77), and I am trying to disinterest myself from myself to withdraw from death by making the "I," to whom death is supposed to happen, gradually go away, no, be destroyed before death come to meet it, so that at the end already there should be no one left to be scared of losing the world in losing himself in it, and the last of the Jews that I still am is doing nothing here

umn in *Glas,* and which we shall soon be reading as an effort to follow, in Hegel's own text, the tracks of what withdraws from the speculative dialectic, this gift can, for example, be the light of the sun (GL 241–2aff., where we also find striction and the ring, and the column). We cannot prevent dialectical thinking from drawing on this, but the fact remains that the dialectico-ontological circle must open onto this pre-ontological gift that it cannot receive as such but must constantly presuppose (AL, 302).

If one cannot receive this gift as such, no more can one refuse it—the gift is thus always poisoned (*gift, Gift,* as Derrida reminds us, playing on English and German [TB, 167; cf. S, 121]). Whence too its character as imperious law. We can push this correspondence between gift and law a long way: for example, we have recalled on several occasions Saussure's assertion that language cannot be the result of a convention, but is always received like the law—this law is none other than the gift of languages, which is in turn the imposition of the name of God as a common name, and of the multiplicity of languages in the story of Babel. One re-

other than destroying the world on the pretext of making truth, but just as well the intense relation to survival that writing is, is not driven by the desire that something remain after me, since I shall not be *there* to enjoy it in a word, *there* where the point is, rather, in producing these remains and therefore the witnesses of my radical absence, to live today, here and now, this death of me, for example, the very counterexample which finally reveals the truth of the world such as it is, itself, i.e. without me, and all the more intensely to enjoy this light I am producing through the present experimentation of my possible survival, i.e. of absolute death, I tell myself this every time that I am walking in

ceives the gift of language like the law, and everything that one says in that language, even to protest against that law and demand the institution of a new law by free convention, must, in the protest itself, have accepted that law or that gift. Even if one open one's mouth only to say "no" to language, one has already said "yes," just as silence says "yes" too.

It will come as no surprise that silence should constitute a reply or a sentence, to speak like Lyotard. But what we have seen of the signature obliges us to say that one signs this silence in spite of one's will not to do so. Rousseau would again give us something to analyze in this respect (see for example the end of the preface to the *Letter to d'Alembert*). In order really to say nothing, one must open one's mouth and say something (see Beckett), and this desire to say nothing leaves a deep mark on Derrida's writing. That whereof one cannot speak, thereof one cannot be silent—one must write it.

Every metalanguage presupposes this "yes" that it can never dominate, and which could thus never become the object of a knowledge: double bind again, of the

the streets of a city I love, in which I love, on whose walls I weep myself and was weeping myself again yesterday in the night of the rue de l'Abbé de l'Epée not long after leaving you, G., at Gatwick.

* "And where would then have been such great, such frequent, and uninterrupted prayers? Nowhere but with Thee" (V, ix, 17).

writer who tries to sign an event of language against the language he has received, already, from the other: jealousy of this *déjà* (which also bespeaks my finitude: GL 79b, and 134b for jealousy) to which one says "yes" like it or not, before trying one's luck at writing a new law and new gift that will indebt posterity and oblige it to live in one's memory, after one's death, which is inscribed in all writing. But before (any) self, there is already the other (AL, 299), *coup* of a gift demanding my assent in spite of myself.

This affirmation demanded by the gift or the law (the gift of the law, the law of the gift) chimes with Heidegger's *Schuldigsein* from *Sein und Zeit,* but more profoundly perhaps with a later Heidegger who displaces the *question* from the dominant place it had at the beginning of *Sein und Zeit*, in order to become attentive to this affirmation and indebtedness with respect to language, to the "engage" (OS, 94n.5, in a note of fundamental importance for everything we are developing here; the term "engage" already appears in GL, 241a). It sounds too with a Nietzschean reference which leads from the beginning to the claim to an affirmative and

37 They are going to think that my mother's metaphasic chaos is becoming my sentence, as though through an ultimate confusion with "the last loved face" in *L'Amour fou,* at the moment when I have not even had the good luck to have the contemplation of Ostia, only of teaching it, of seeing it in San Geminiano, when Augustine can speak with *his* mother in the imminence of her death, *Impendente autem die, quo ex hac uita erat exitura—quem diem tu noueras ignorantibus nobis* [...] *conloquebamur ergo soli ualde dulciter et* praeterita obliuiscentes in ea quae ante sunt extenti *quaerebamus inter nos apud praesentem ueritatem, quod*

not critical or destructive status for deconstruction (POS, 96; WD, 233, 246, 297). It is not foreign to the "privilege" we have recognized to a certain "literature" in Derrida's thought (AL, 257, 297; cf. DIA, 79–80). And this is where we shall encounter the most serious ("ethical-and-political") questions: for if the law, given, demands that one say "yes" to it, and if one says "yes" even when saying "no," then how could one resist or rise up against an iniquitous law?

We must also beware of this gravity of the ethical and the political, which seems to go without saying to such a point that any displacement can appear irresponsible or dangerous. But if gravity has always been associated with writing by Derrida (WD, 29–30), laughter is perhaps necessary too (cf. OS, 68, 72n.8). One cannot simply demand of deconstruction that it present its ethical and political titles without presupposing that one already knows what ethics and politics are, whereas that is just what we are trying to interrogate here, laughing at the edifying naiveté informing such a demand.

tu es, qualis futura esset uita aeterna sanctorum [...] *et uenimus in mentes nostras et transcendimus eas, ut attingeremus regionem ubertatis indeficientis, ubi pascis Israel in aeternum ueritate pabulo* [...],* I gave in to the counterexemplary thing—"*only write here what is impossible, that* ought *to be the impossible-rule*" (10–11–77), of everything G. can be expecting of me, a supposedly idiomatic, unbroachable, unreadable, uncircumcised piece of writing, held not to the assistance of its father, as Socrates would say, but to my assistance at the death of a mother about whom I ask *to ti en einai* before witnesses, for if G. contests me, it is in the sense of

Maillart, *The Death of Saint Monica* (Paris: Petit Palais):
"I pressed her eyes closed … yet at the same time my
eyes, under the forceful command of the mind,
repressed their flow until they were quite dry.
In such a struggle, I felt very bad"
(*Confessions,* IX, xii, 29).

In the Anglo-American reception of Derrida's work, the suspicion with respect to this "yes" has above all borne on an established order which might be capitalism, but also the literary or philosophical canon: people have wanted to seek a political efficacy for deconstruction, and as "political efficacy" is often thought of in terms of refusal, of "no," people have been disconcerted by this "yes." More recently and more dramatically, it is around Nazism that such questions have been posed more acutely still: are we not here condemned to accept even Nazism, to say "yes" to it, like it or not, either as to necessity itself or even, worse still, as to a sort of literature? Is it by chance that this thought of deconstruction is associated with those of Nietzsche and Heidegger, and that it therefore inherits a relationship with Nazism that is to say the least unclear? We see how easy it is to panic faced with this "yes" and how a sort of overbidding in the "political" reactions to Derrida's work could come about.

This overbidding showed up especially around the Heidegger and de Man "affairs" in 1987–88, but its possibility was inscribed from the beginning: every-

the witness who, through countersigning attestation, confirms the logic of the counterexample, by daring to kill the quotation marks, without quoting me, calling me back to the moment when, like twelve years ago, I did not yet know what circumcision means, "*is there* one? *for the moment it is just a word with which I want, in a more or less continuous way, but why, to do things, to tell stories, to interest a male or female reader (the furthest away possible), to please myself* [with what I can't manage to get interested in, but why?] *to stitch myself up again at this time of my life when I have never been more undone, bloody and bleeding: I no longer even have to sustain me through the operation the arms of Elie who at the worst*

thing said in the third interview of *Positions*, for example, can be read, beneath the politely epistemological appearances, as driven by this political concern, and this is also the case in very many Anglo-American reactions. As early as 1969, J-P. Faye had suspected fascist resonances in Derrida's thought, naively thinking that he could read in Derrida an effort to save a *mythos* repressed by the *logos*: Derrida replies indirectly in "Plato's Pharmacy" (D, 167–8, cf. 102; cf. also CH, 266, 273ff.). That there is political concern among Derrida's readers does not worry us, on the contrary: but it could easily be shown that this "worry" claims in fact to resolve politics in such a way that one should no longer have to worry about it, so that nothing should happen in it, so that there should be no more politics. According to a law which we are formalizing little by little, it is precisely where one protests most against a supposed lack of political reflection that such reflection is most sorely lacking. In fact, Derrida addressed these questions long before the "recent affairs" (cf. "Restitutions" [EO, 23ff.; TP, 255–382]): and it must be recalled that *Of Spirit* was written and published before

moment stays there... if I wanted to be moving, I would describe a child incapable of articulating what is going on, even if it sees and knows everything and talks interminably round it, better than anyone, at the moment when it is happening, and that Elie will have let drop during the operation, describe in detail this appalling scene, the 'godfather' drops the nameless child during the circumcision, the blood, the instruments, the terror of the participants who flee or finish off the child, then the intolerable foreclosure, there is in what I write something that calls: *foreclosure: the intolerable, loved, already known, which cannot be quoted, only incorporated"* (Ibid.), I would like to gather myself in the circle of the *cum*, the circus of the *circum*, in front of him

the book by Farias which set off the recent Heidegger "affair."

This is where we are in stupidity, as the very milieu of our judgments, and the fact that this is where we are cannot fail to confirm the accuracy of this description of gift and law: for the thing that dictates this law and prescribes us an infinite task (of translation, of thought) condemns us structurally to a certain stupidity. In this situation the worst stupidity certainly consists in declaring oneself to be intelligent, in claiming simply to have received the gift and to have acquitted oneself of one's debts, as do those who claim to understand everything about Nazism, for example.

Let us first take the measure of what is played out in this description and this staging of the "yes" which we have deduced from the gift and the law. This "yes" is not simple, which will appear to make our case worse still: we cannot be content simply to note it down as the slightly bizarre name of some condition of possibility, then to forget it and begin just as simply to say "no." We cannot be content with this on pain of making this thought once more into a banal transcen-

whom I have always sought by fleeing, the constituting witness who will put an end to the illness of Proteus, as I confided in my adolescent diary in the mirror of Gide who said he was deprived of any nonproteiform identity.

* "When the day on which she was to depart this life was near at hand (Thou knewest the day; we did not) [...] We were talking to each other alone, very sweetly, 'forgetting what is behind, straining forward to what is before.' Between us, 'in the present truth,' which Thou art, we tried to find out what the eternal life of the saints would be [...] We came to our own minds. Then,

dental philosophy, whereas it is at the price of not having this status that it can precisely lay claim to a political relevance. If the "yes" is not simple, this is because it is not a simple punctual affirmation, but *already* a promise of its own repetition, in anticipated memory of itself, divided in its act just as was the signature (itself a way of saying "yes" to what one signs and to the fact of appending one's name to it [AL, 279]). "Yes" opens a future in which one will again say "yes." Eternal return, in Blanchot as much as in Nietzsche: in affirming, I commit myself to the repeated affirmation of this event of affirmation; or rather this "en-gage" has already taken place whether I like it or not, before any explicit speech act of a "yes" or a "no," *quasi*-transcendental condition of any such act (AL, 298; EO, 14, 20; GL, 228b; LOB, 132, 273ff.; 185; NY passim; OS, 94n.5; PAR, 23ff., 116), Only this element of repetition can ground for example the questions of historical responsibility or even culpability (of Heidegger [or de Man] with respect to Nazism [OS, 38ff.; PMW passim], for example, but also of Nietzsche, however bizarre that may appear).

we transcended them, so that we might touch that realm of unfailing abundance in which Thou feedest Israel eternally on the food of truth" (IX, ix, 23–4).

38 As Montaigne said, "I constantly disavow myself," it is impossible to follow my trace, like that of Aids, I never write or produce anything other than this destinerrancy of desire, the unassignable trajectories and the unfindable subjects but also the only sign of love, the one gaged on this bet (rather Aids than lose you) and you try to calculate the itinerary of texts

It is not enough to say that Nietzsche was dead before the arrival of Nazism and that he would certainly have refused the Nazi interpretation of his texts. Everything we have said about the proper name and the signature ought to suspend such a short understanding of chronology and death. The point here is never to re-establish against "false" interpretations a truth conceived as that of a (conscious or unconscious) meaning-intention attributed to a text: our explanation of the Husserlian doctrine of the sign ought to disallow any such approach. From the moment that reading does not proceed according to hermeneutics, one will no longer be able simply to condemn or simply to excuse on the basis of appeal to what the signatory of a given text "meant": to the extent that a text is not closed and a signature never finished, any announcement of a meaning-intention is only ever a countersigned rewriting which tries to erase the singularity and historicity of its act according to the after-the-event structure of any identification of an origin. That there can be a "Nazi" reading of Nietzsche or Heidegger (and that the latter can on occasion read, counter-

which do not explode immediately, being basically nothing but fuse, intermittently you see the flame running without knowing where nor when the explosion will come, whence the trance, anguish and desire of the reader, quick let's be done with it, *I beheld the Angel who stretched out his arms embracing the flame of fire and he was consumed and arose as Elijah. This Angel, who is now become a devil, is my particular friend,* but I give up neither water nor blood, *et eum texendi sermonis modum, ut neque illi* [...] *dicta recusarent* [...]. *Sicut enim fons in paruo loco uberior est pluribusque riuis in ampliora spatia fluxum ministrat quam quilibet eorum riuorum, qui per multa locorum ab eodem fonte deducitur, ita narratio*

sign, his own writing in these terms) must be explained otherwise than by an attempt to find in their texts a nucleus or an essence that Nazism would have done no more than repeat. If deconstruction refers happily to Nietzsche and Heidegger, this is because it finds in their texts resources which allow one to understand this general structure, this "destinerrancy" which we assert to be necessary, and which implies responsibility as being held to an earlier appeal ("Come") to which one must respond (EO, 31–8; DP, 397; PMW passim). We have already sufficiently complicated the notion of "necessity" by inscribing chance (and therefore freedom) in it for this assertion not to be understood as the surreptitious conversion of a prescription into a constative. Such a conversion, as we shall show, takes place in traditional political thought, and this is precisely what the "yes, yes" is going to deconstruct. Which is not at all a way of whitewashing Nietzsche or Heidegger, does not at all prevent one condemning Nazism, but certainly disallows the self-righteousness which thinks that it has acquitted itself of the task of thinking when it has condemned

dispensatoris tui sermocinaturis pluribus profutura paruo sermonis modulo scatet fluenta liquidae ueritatis, unde sibi quisque uerum, quod de his rebus potest, hic illud, ille illud, per longiores loquellarum anfractus trahat, "always the question of the continuum, I write in Latin because the* uum *mimes the fluid and slowly stretched substance, the one that I desire to keep, desire* as *what is kept, keeping not being the object but the continuum of desire, a writing without interruption which has been looking for itself forever, looking for me across the cut and only forces me to state it in 'depression,' with narcissistic self-involvement, return upon itself of the libido at the moment of loss (approximative and false jargon) but why the desire to name New York, where 21 years*

Nazism, and which represses all the more dangerously the necessary complicity called history. It goes without saying that these remarks also apply to our own reading or repetition of Derrida, as well as to his own reading of his own texts.

This apparently simple structure of the "yes" in fact engages with everything we have developed thus far, to the point that the little text "Nombre de oui" (NY passim) can appear to contain *the whole of Derrida* (if only you have read the rest) in a condensation that would demand hundreds of pages of commentary. This originary "yes," another nickname for what escapes the question "What is . . . ?" (AL, 296; PS, 163), replies to the pre-originary gift (cf. AL, 297, where the "yes" replies to the "primal telephonic 'hello' "), countersigns it in opening itself to the repetition whose trace is already inscribed in its "first" time, thus inaugurating time in finitude—for "yes," as archi-signature, cannot withdraw from the possibility of its "mechanical" repetition which marks its finitude while remaining indifferent to it. Repetition, without which the "first" time would not have been able to take place, opens

ago, on notebooks lost in Algeria in '62 unless they're hidden here, I had begun again, at the Hotel Martinique, to write 'for myself'—follow the New York thread, from trip to trip, up to this one, the Kippours of N.Y., the cut with Kippour, the noncircumcision of the sons—up to that year when, coming out of a restaurant near the MOMA I enter a 'reformed' synagogue... circumcision remains the threat of what is making me write here, even if what hangs on it only hangs by a thread and threatens to be lost—double syntax of perdre *in French ('je te perds': I no longer have you but also I push you to your doom, I compromise your salvation)—and if I say that I am losing life at this moment, that curiously comes down to the same thing, my life is that*

memory, in mourning for this impossible "first" time. But it also opens, immediately, the domain of the simulacrum: the "yes" immediately parasites itself, mimes itself, fictionalizes itself in the possibility of its repetition (AL, 279). This is why Zarathustra's "yes" can always be doubled by the ass's "yes" to the point of being mistaken for it. This is also why, in insisting on the *quasi*-transcendental privilege of this "yes" with respect to any "no," we are not promoting any quietism, but opening to the recognition of a *certain* inevitable complicity (see again WD, 282) which ought to call any political self-righteousness into question: for example, it is in no way to reduce Heidegger's responsibility with respect to Nazism to bring out what he can share or exchange with Husserl or Valéry (OS, 60n.1; 110). A conception of ethics which immediately places itself, as we have seen, in an "economy of violence" will never give in to the ethical demand to *decide* once and for all between good and evil, and this is a rigorous consequence of the thought of writing, which is indeed beyond good and evil (GR, 314–5). But that in no way prevents judgment.

other that 'I lose'... I have just killed an insect fallen on to this page, I draw a tomb for him (drawing): the fact that he doesn't give a damn and that this, which endures after him, does not return to him, that's the real with which it is necessary to stop rusing (necessary?): what covers this real over is not a mirage but all that is left of a language, culture itself" (10–12–77): in a word circumcision.

*"... and such a method of fashioning my speech that those [who are as yet unable to understand how God creates] would not reject my statements [as things exceeding their powers] [...] Just as a spring, within its small space, supplies a more abundant

SEXUAL DIFFERENCE

This repeated "yes" is linked, if only by the reference to Molly Bloom's "monologue" in *Ulysses*, to femininity. In the Blanchot readings gathered in *Parages*, the association of affirmation and woman is constant (see especially PAR, 278ff.). We have already seen that in *Spurs*, "woman" is one of the names of what escapes the metaphysical question "What is . . . ?" Elsewhere, a "female" voice intervenes in dialogues or polylogues such as "Restitutions" (cf. TP, 256), "Pas" (PAR, 21–116), the "reading" of *Droits de regards*, or *Feu la cendre*. In *Glas*, the "déjà" (but also the signature and the countersignature) is associated with the mother (GL, 117b, 134b). The second text on Levinas ("En ce moment même dans cet ouvrage me voici" [ATM passim]), a dialogue also involving a female voice, suspects Levinas of still secondarizing sexual difference by posing a neutral alterity before sexual distinction (PS, 194; cf. also OS, 107 and n.7). "Nombre de oui" recalls some of these references (PS, 643n). One can easily, too easily, talk of a "feminism" of Derrida's by basing oneself

flow over wider areas by virtue of the many streams which it feeds than do any one of these streams which lead away from this spring through many regions, so, too, does the story told by the original dispenser of Thine, which was to supply many who would speak of it in the future, cause to bubble forth, by the tiny flow of Thy word, floods of clear truth, from which each man may draw the truth that he is able to get concerning these things—one man one truth, another man another—through the longer windings of their discussions" (XII, xxvi, 36–7).

on such texts (and some others, more discreet ones, that we will pick out later), and on a remark, consigned in the proceedings of a colloquium, on the desire to write like a woman (cf. *Nietzsche, aujourd'hui?*, collection 10/18, 1973, vol. 1, p. 299). It would be too easy to speak of feminism (cf. EO, 38) until we have made this association explicit. The essential point here does not rest on a sociological or anthropological hypothesis according to which women would in fact hold the privilege of affirmation: such a hypothesis is not for all that simply excluded, but it goes along too easily with a transcendental privilege of a "femininity" still present to itself in the form of an essence. What is called "feminism" is no doubt marked in its very "-ism" by the turnstile of these mutually dependent positions of the empirical and the transcendental. This is why, seeing Blanchot attribute a privilege to women when it comes to affirmation, Derrida will insist on an "almost always" in which the *almost* still allows the workings of an uncertainty and simple probability between women who say "yes, yes" and a transcendental femininity that they would supposedly express or represent in so

39 When 85 years old, not long before her fall, but her fall then multiplies as she falls every year, she goes swimming at Villefranche between two poker games, goes cautiously into the water, hands joined in front, less for enjoyment no doubt than to give herself the proof or the sign of an enjoyment still possible, up to the last moment, striving, like the lure itself, to live and pray in a naive faith, in truth a puerile and naked faith whose tribute God was supposed to pay in the coin of sensory pleasure, *absit, ut tu falleres eam in illis uisionibus et responsis tuis* [...] *quae illa fideli pectore tenebat et semper orans tamquam chirografa tua ingerabat tibi. dignaris enim, quoniam* in saeculum misericordia

doing (LG, 222ff.). This element of probability, of chance and devilishness, for it is the devil, probably (cf. PAR, 86; PC, 271, 379–80; SI, 118), which is still the mark of the "quasi-" affecting the transcendental, is also Derrida's object in the text on Levinas we have just cited, in which it is linked to the question of responsibility toward the other which led us, precisely, to sexual difference, and which will lead to the questions addressed to Levinas as to his way of thinking it (PS, 173–4).

This complication of the empirical and the transcendental marked by the prefix "quasi-"—which would perhaps, if such a formulation were still possible, be Derrida's contribution to the history of philosophy, what would make him a "contemporary"—disallows *on the one hand* that philosophy relegate sexual difference to the status of an object of a regional science on the pretext of a transcendental neutrality which in fact has always veiled a privilege of the masculine (whence "phallogocentrism"), and *on the other hand* that we attempt simply to unseat this masculine transcendental to replace it with a feminine. We will show for

tua, *eis quibus omnia debita dimittis, etiam promissionibus debitor fieri,** I see her naked all the time now, the bedsores opening afresh, both hips, the sacrum, and the sullen guilty aggressivity of the "how long?", "what's she waiting for?", that everyone is accusing themselves of while asking pardon from her, from God, the one and the other coming to be inscribed in the hand held out to feed, to give to drink, to turn the body onto the other side, to caress even, and then to write for never will the man flayed alive that I am have written like this, knowing in advance the nonknowledge into which the imminent but unpredictable coming of an event, the death of my mother, Sultana

example that the "phallogocentric" tradition rises only by compromising, in spite of itself, with the conditions of its own downfall, which will prevent by the same token any attempt at a simple erection of the feminine. The nicknames "woman" and "mother" would name in Derrida this whole situation which, in its complication, is unmasterable (by a mastery which would still be masculine), rather than one of its terms.

THE MOTHER: *CHORA*

We have already seen that the names put forward to say what precedes the ontological question cannot be proper names. They form a nonfinite series constituted in part by the chance of Derrida's encounters with the texts that he reads. If therefore *Glas* can seem to put forward the name "mother" in place of "already" or "text," we know a priori that this name cannot be the first or last name finally discovered. Taking the risk of saying that it's called "mother" is also to recognize that one no longer has a very clear idea of what a mother is.

Esther Georgette Safar Derrida, would come to sculpt the writing from the outside, give it its form and its rhythm from an incalculable interruption, never will any of my texts have depended in its most essential inside on such a cutting, accidental and contingent outside, as though each syllable, and the very milieu of each periphrasis were preparing itself to receive a telephone call, the news of the death of one dying, "*and today when the event which marked the interruption in February has happened (again), confirms itself after the event as though it had not yet taken place but needed time to intersect with itself, no one will ever know from what secret I am writing and the fact that I say so changes noth-*

No more than any other term can "mother" be a transcendental signified (GL, 116–7b) nor can it be proper (GL, 133–4b): this mother is neither good or bad, before sexual *opposition* if not before sexual *difference.* All our difficulties are going to be concentrated on understanding this *différance* between difference and opposition: we would need to try to understand why this depropriation of the mother (still following the "anasemic translation") respects a sexual difference that oppositional thought, which would like the mother to retain her feminine properties, must allow to dissolve in a homogeneity always violently reappropriated by the masculine.

Let us again go quickly through the family scenes described in "Plato's Pharmacy," already invoked around writing in its status as bastard or parricide son. In Plato's description, the *logos* needs the assistance of its father, which in principle it has in speech, whereas writing exists only in the absence of a father to reply for it. This threat against the power of the father (whose effect is not to kill the father to the profit of the son—and we can in any case suspect that such a way of

ing" (10–12–77), dying is the word I discover at the age of 59, a sort of verbal adjective whose tense I had not yet known how to read, which says neither the mortal nor the moribund nor the agonizing but that other present from which I demonstrated yesterday to some students that only an immortal can die, beyond or short of a being-toward-death, the time of the orchestra, for I admit, G., that when I am not dreaming of making love, of being a resistance fighter in the last war blowing up bridges or trains, I want one thing only, and that is to lose myself in the orchestra I would form with my sons, heal, bless and seduce the whole world by playing divinely with my sons, pro-

killing him would preserve his power all the better [DL, 138]—but to mean that we no longer have a very clear idea of what a father is [cf. D, 80–1]), this threat could invite us to look for confirmation of our description of the mother: and it is indeed toward the end of the same text that Derrida speaks for the first time of the *chora* in Plato's *Timaeus*. In a brief listing of the scriptural "metaphors" that come in when Plato wants to think an irreducible difference, we indeed find the *chora* as the place of the originary inscription of the forms. This "place" of a "third kind," before the distinction between the real (illusory) world and the world of the (real) Ideas, which Plato can only think in an unfurling of metaphors, is described among other things as nurse, matrix, receptacle, mother (D, 160–1). A thinking of the originarity of the trace, which is thus already to be found in Plato, even if it is repressed by "Platonism" (CH, 287–8), can indeed appear to contest the father on the basis of the mother. And it is certainly not by chance that Plato's *chora* has been the object of commentaries and appropriations by Kristeva and Irigaray, for example.

duce with them the world's ecstasy, *their* creation, I will accept dying if dying is to sink slowly, yes, into the bottom of this beloved music.

*"Perish the thought that Thou wouldst have deceived her in those visions and in Thy answers [...] These she kept in her faithful breast and, unceasing in her prayers, she would urge them upon Thee as if they had been Thy own signed pledges. Since Thy mercy endureth forever, Thou dost vouchsafe to become, by Thy promises, a debtor to those whose entire debt Thou hast forgiven" (V, ix, 17).

And yet we must take many precautions here to avoid confusion. For example, we must not attempt to *identify* (the) *chora* and the mother, for fear of giving back a propriety to what cannot have one, because it is the prior, quasi-metaphorical, condition of any proper at all. Nor must we think what can be thought of as "mother" here in *opposition* with the father, just as earlier we had not to think writing as being in opposition with voice (for all those problems form a series which we shall endeavor to describe for itself later). What was at stake in the thought of writing was not to rehabilitate writing in the common sense, but to see writing already at work in the voice: so the point is not to promote a matriarchal power against a patriarchy, but to show that what has always been understood by "father" (or even by "power") is constituted only on the basis of an anteriority which can be called "mother" solely on condition of not confusing it with the habitual concept of mother. If we *sometimes* keep this name (which we shall also make fun of a little, because of the piety it can provoke [cf. TP, 353–4]), this will be because the thought of this anteriority communicates

40 Commotion of writing, give in only to it, do not make oneself interesting by promised avowal or refused secret, so no literature if literature, the institution of "saying everything" breathes to the hope of seeing the other confess and thereby you, yourself, confess *yourself,* admit *yourself,* you my fall, in an effusion of recognition, whereas I have *put,* staked this word for "word," "for" her, my mother, who would be the last, and my family, to find her bearings in what I am writing *here,* me, always less recognizable in my family than in my country, in my country than in Europe, in Europe than anywhere else, so that I do not deprive myself, me whom they called "the sav-

with the common concept of "mother," just as the enlarged concept of writing elaborated in *Of Grammatology* kept the name "writing" because it communicated with the common concept, which was, however, generalized beyond all its traditional limits.

> This strategy of paleonymy (D, 5; DR, 275; POS, 71, cf. SP, 77, 103), as we are beginning to realize more clearly, produces, along with the chance of intervening *now*, all the risks of misunderstanding which seem so acute in these "political" domains where danger and terror surround everything that is said: the affirmation we are expounding here is *also* an affirmation of these risks, without which there would be no politics at all.

There is, then, some mother in the father, which means that the father also begins to escape from the question "What is . . . ?", whereas everything gave us leave to think that the father just was what is (D, 80ff.). In order to avoid confusion, one always produces a certain confusion, the necessity of which is *also* what we are concerned to affirm here, in its political dimension too. As the text entitled simply "Chora" will show much later, the "third kind" thus named can shake up

age" or "square-head", to speak Latin, to oblige you to learn Latin again to read SA, me, at work, the little Latin I know through having begun to learn it when Vichy had made it, I believe, obligatory in the first form just before booting me out of the school in the Latin name of the *numerus clausus* by withdrawing our French citizenship, I have no memory that my mother noticed anything, any more than she will ever have known that my fear of death will only have reflected her own, I mean my death *for her* whose anxiety I perceived each time I was ill, and doubtless more subterraneously all the time, *non itaque uideo, quomodo sanaretur, si mea talis illa mors transuerberasset uiscera*

all the constitutive oppositions of metaphysics, and especially those attributed to Platonism: this demonstration passes somewhere *between* Plato and Derrida, i.e. across the whole of metaphysics. It confirms what we have said above about the essential incompletion of Plato's signature (and therefore, we might add now, of metaphysics "itself"), and implies at the same stroke a certain indeterminacy of the signature of Derrida "himself": trying perhaps to sign everything, Derrida perhaps signs nothing. If these possibilities did not *already* inhabit metaphysics, there would be no chance of thinking its closure: what some have seen as a nostalgic attachment on Derrida's part to the texts and terms of the tradition is an absolute necessity from which no thinking escapes and which can only be negotiated. It is also this structure that is here called the mother.

FEMININITY

But this leaves us still in difficulties for understanding the place of sexual difference in Derrida's thought.

*dilectionis eius,** and if my mother thus carried my fear of death, I fear dying from no longer being scared of death after her death, as perhaps happened to M.P. in 1962 and B. in 1980, that is no doubt what is meant by: "put Ça to work, 'my' *circumcision, enormous narcissistic monument with* ceci, ci *becoming the abbreviation,* ciseaux, scie, si *(if),* si *(but yes, no not no)*, s'il, cil [...] *put to work* ça, ci, *Sassi the Jewish singer who used to haunt all the religious festivals in Algiers, the narcissistic monument of my last child, the third one, the one I will not have had, the daughter,* c'est s'il, *in the depths of despair, blasphemy and perjury, immense upsurge of sublime desire for Ci again, in the evening when every other path is*

Everything that we have said implies that the mother is not a woman (GL, 134b). We have seen on the one hand an explicit link between the redoubled affirmation (a singular figure of *différance* that we are following here) and femininity, but when we followed a little way down the path suggested by the no less explicit link between the *already* and the mother, we found what runs the risk of looking quite simply like an attempt to erase the question of sexual difference. Which, according to the arguments of Derrida himself, would run the risk of immediately reinstating the metaphysical privilege of the masculine (PS, 194; S, 109–15).

It is unsatisfactory, for example, to map the "strategic" justification for the retention of the word "mother" onto a classical (Leninist, for example) idea of political strategy, on pain of mistaking the dimension of necessity that we have invoked, which is not a necessity of supposed "laws of history," grounding a supposed "objective interest" of women or others. It is not satisfactory to say, for example, that the pre-ontological *déjà* that we are trying to think would in truth be in a pre-sexual neutrality that one would as-

blocked to me, reflect on the fact that even in case of failure, which is more than probable, since I shall not live much longer in any case, it is on this ci, *the 'my' circumcision, that is gathered the interrupted autobiothanatoheterographical opus, the only confidence that has ever interested me, but for whom? a question to which my inability to respond gives the measure of what divides me and will have prevented me up to this point from loving, for in spite of so many overflowings, too many, in spite of everything I (appear to) give, I have no doubt never known how to love, other than in the place (double place, with internal partition and essential replaceability, referral toward the absence of the other) of a figure unknown to me, harassing the miserable but inexhaustible*

sign to the feminine—knowing that it is not true but pretending it is for the good of the cause—to react against a tradition which would systematically have appropriated it under the authority of the masculine. Naturally this is not nothing, but would turn every feminism into an opportunism, or into an "interest" which has to fight against other interests for its share of available resources, according to the common representation of politics. As always, deconstruction is going to find itself *between*, not in the middle but in the *milieu*, and will think politics neither as the objective product of an ontological ground, nor, in the absence of such a grounding, as a simple competition of more or less antagonistic (individual or collective) subjectivities: meaning that deconstruction is not one new thought (here a political one) to be added to the list of philosophies or systems provided by the tradition, nor a "postmodernism" defined as a pure and simple refusal of tradition and foundation.

For the double science plays here too. Above, we had to distinguish between two heterogeneous ways of questioning the relation between signifier and signified

filial narcissism of what is given in me, but whom will I have loved, who is loved, by me?" (10–13–77).

* "Thus, I do not see how she would have been made well again, had such a death of mine blasted the vitals of her love" (V, ix, 17).

or writing and voice, of which the first, the classical one, consisted in deriving the first term from the second so as to subordinate it to it, to produce the concept of writing only in its erasure, to *secondarize* it, as we said, and of which the other, through the movements of reversal and reinscription constitutive of deconstruction, consisted in displacing the general system of this secondarization without claiming to install signifier or writing in the place of signified or voice, for fear of secondarizing them again, of losing the trace in trying to make it present (cf. PS, 190). Here, we must distinguish between two ways of thinking the feminine, the first of which consists in deriving it from an earlier neutrality which in fact will always have been marked as masculine and which is thus determined after the fact by what it is supposed to explain, and the second in marking how the "qualities" traditionally attributed to women outplay the very opposition in which they have been caught up. If, on the basis of the notoriously "misogynistic" reflections of Nietzsche, for example, it is possible to show that woman escapes the true/false opposition (S, 107), then we lead ourselves back to a "be-

41 No longer even the right to make them admit the violence by which they still try to extort writing, to confess, to "confess me," pretending to believe in order, in truth, in reconciliation, in repentance or expiation, in short in this justice that is panting and finally appeased by guilt assumed, exposed, shouted out, before them or before God, "ah, if at least he'd owned up!", as though this economy were not to my eyes the worst, shameless forgetting of the fault, lack of respect for evil, as though anyone in the world could be more severe and pitiless toward me than myself, as though I needed someone to hurt me more with the hurt I have caused, as though someone had the right or the power to deliver me from it or to withdraw me

fore" of metaphysical oppositions which will certainly not be feminine in itself, but which will no longer allow itself calmly to be marked as masculine. What will be "masculine" will therefore no longer be a term in an opposition, but the very *position* of the opposition: and what will be "feminine" will be to show how this op-position depends on what it devalorizes (as logocentrism depends on an opposition subordinating the signifier, and therefore also depends on what it calls the signifier in order to reduce it [WD, 281]) for what is no longer any more than a parade or fiction of mastery.

So it follows neither that sexual difference is denied, nor that it is derived from an earlier (anthropological) unity. Like Derrida defending Heidegger against Levinas, who understands Being in the latter's thought as a neutrality (WD, 136ff.), we must say that what is diversely named *already, différance, trace,* etc., cannot be neutral. This is implied again by the impossibility of naming "it" other than by these singular contextual nicknames which cannot be reduced to any conventional "X" (and this is why they are not synonyms). And in fact it is by returning to Heidegger and

through some judgment, *taking* knowledge or *taking* note of my crimes, perjuries, blasphemies, what am I meddling with, as though the other me, the other in me, the atheist God, infinitely smaller and bigger than I, left the slightest chance for the guilty party ever to save himself, even if it were by the ruse of avowal or asked-for pardon, but who do they take themselves for, what they don't know is the conversion in me, *adhuc enim mihi uidebatur non esse nos, qui peccamus, sed nescio quam aliam in nobis peccare naturam et delectabat superbiam meam extra culpam esse et, cum aliquid mali fecissem, non confiteri me fecisse, ut sanares* animam meam, quoniam peccabat tibi, *sed excusare me amabam et accusare nescio quid aluid, quod mecum esset et ego non essem. uerum autem*

Levinas (a little later we shall wonder why this question is worked out between these two names) that Derrida begins to explicate a little more this formidably difficult question.

We have already sketched several times—with a view to a more rigorous formalization that still awaits us—the logic according to which binary thought depends more or less secretly on the terms it subordinates in its foundational oppositions. Thus, the signifier/signified opposition lives only off the signifier it nonetheless attempts to erase, and the speech/writing opposition off the writing it denounces. What one tries to keep outside inhabits the inside and there would be no inside without that fact. There is in this situation an irreducible duplicity which above allowed us to say that writing is beyond good and evil (GR, 314), ultra-ethical (ALT, 74), the nonethical opening of ethics (GR, 140). We could say, for example, that the term excluded by the binary divide *returns* in some sense (let us also hear the ghost in this returning) to sign the act of its own exclusion: but that this apparent complicity (which alone explains the fact that in general people

totum ego eram et aduersus me inpietas mea diuiserat [...] *nondum ergo posueras* custodiam ori meo et ostium continentiae circum labia mea, *ut non declinaret* cor meum in verba mala ad excusandas excusationes in peccatis,* I shall never know the whole of me, nor you, i.e. with whom I have lived, and primarily what "with" means, before "whom," this remains hidden from myself, more secret than all the secrets with which I know that I shall die without knowing if I shall know how to die, "*here: order never to show these exercise books, never to publish them, narrative, recircumcision here now, paint, in all colors, the cries, innards out, the operation, as the immense, insolvent pain and* also *the supreme enjoyment for all, first of all for him, me, the nursling, imagine the loved*

were able to *write* condemnations of writing, without this "performative contradition" seeming very serious to all those who have gone in for it) is also what outplays the legality of the decision to exclude. This is beginning to exploit the ambivalence of the prefix "counter" in "countersignature," and it will also contaminate the "yes, yes" in that aspect of it that may so far have seemed most troublesome.

This logic plays in extremely refined fashion in the part of the second reading of Levinas devoted to sexual difference. Derrida recalls from "Violence and Metaphysics" the observation in the last note of that text, that Levinas in some sense explicitly assumes his own sexual position, instead of masking that masculinity behind supposedly neutral marks (WD, 153n.92); PS, 194). Contrary to normal philosophical usage, Levinas's signature marks a sexual identity. This is already an equivocal gesture, of course, but one that is striking enough to suspend any hasty suspicion that it might merely confirm the traditional distributions. If the tradition, massively masculine in its supposed neutrality, erases such a mark, reinscribing it can just as well con-

woman herself circumcising (me), as the mother did in the biblical narrative, slowly provoking ejaculation in her mouth just as she swallows the crown of bleeding skin with the sperm as a sign of exultant alliance, her legs open, her breasts between my legs, laughing, both of us laughing, passing skins from mouth to mouth like a ring, the pendant on the necklace round her neck" (10–13–77), I was already replacing the dead one, and the fear that kills me in face of death, "my" death, is not the fear of dying, how simple that would be, but the fear of replacing one more dead one before being able to die myself, myself, you hear—no.

test that tradition by betraying its secret as reinforce it by letting one assume that there is no longer any reason to keep the secret secret.

And yet it is this second possibility that would be encouraged by what can appear to be a new secondarization of woman, figure of alterity with respect to the male philosopher, but subordinated to a more radical alterity, the entirely other, and which, situated in principle *before* sexual difference, nonetheless is attributed a certain masculinity according to the metaphysical schema we have already described. Which would mean, via a movement which doubles again the haunting we have just recalled, that sexual alterity thus subordinated returns in fact against all expectations to haunt the alterity of the entirely other with a supplementary and excessive alterity. *This* alterity, which Levinas attempted to circumscribe in the sphere of the same, as a merely relative alterity with respect to the *entirely* other, would in fact be, in encrypted form, the alterity of that alterity, which by the same token would have enclosed itself in the same while thinking it had escaped. If Levinas's thinking of the entirely other

* "For, up to that time, it seemed to me that it is not we who sin, but some other unknown nature within us which sins. It was a joy to my pride to be set apart from culpability, and, when I had done some evil thing, not to confess that I had done it (so that Thou mightest heal my soul because it was sinning against Thee), but I loved rather to excuse myself and accuse some other unknown being which existed with me and yet was not I. In truth, of course, the whole thing was myself, and my impiety had divided me against myself [...] Thou hadst not yet placed a watch upon my mouth and a door of safekeeping about my lips, so that my heart would not slip back into wicked words in order to fashion excuses from sins" (V, x, 18).

is in some sense driven by the desire to secondarize sexual alterity, we can conclude from this that it is *this* alterity which has inspired or dictated all these maneuvers, which would thus in some sense render homage *a contrario* to what they were attempting to neutralize by calling "Il" what precedes the "il/elle" couple. In a sense which can no longer be that of an agreement or a contract, sexual difference would thus have countersigned the text of Emmanuel Levinas (of "E. L."), which would in this way have exposed itself to this countering countersignature through the very attention it paid to the question in the first place. The point, in showing this fatal possibility, is not to correct Levinas and simply to replace his "Il" with an "Elle" (Derrida must be read with extreme care here [PS, 198–201]) but, without at all denying the reserves formulated by "Violence and Metaphysics" against the very coherence of an "entirely other" in Levinas's sense (see especially WD, 126), to fold back alterity (which would thus, if one could say this, become *more other than the entirely other*) "inside" what Levinas calls the same, and which, as we have been saying from the

42 *"Rediscover the (lost) taste for holding the pen, for writing well in a sense I have mistreated, reworked, lost a long time ago (double syntax of 'lose someone') and beyond the malediction which traverses my love for the person who has lost me, rediscover an easy, offered, readable, relaxed writing"* (10–14–77), oh how fine her hands are, my survivress, she had such beautiful handwriting, that can be said in the past, quite different from mine, and very legible, stylish, elegant, more cultivated than herself, I wonder if that's possible, and how to speak of her and SA without participating in their chirography, from the lowest part of my body and to the tips of my fingers, without even feeling the resistance

start, must be inhabited or haunted by the other, which is not outside. This "other" is not a negativity which ends by exchanging and balancing in a (dialectical) economy of the same, but an absolute heterogeneity which is not external. It is in order to try to think this bizarre topology that Derrida will soon speak of invagination. We have not yet followed all the consequences of this thinking, which is going to allow us to risk paradoxes whereby the other would be no other than the same itself [*le même même*], in the doubling traced toward the double, the ghost and *Unheimlichkeit*. For the moment, let us notice how what we have just said about Levinas answers to the structure of quasi-transcendentality, which appears to let one term (writing, text, here femininity) rise only to fold it back immediately onto what it was beginning to dominate. *L'érection tombe.*

If then this analysis confirms, though complicating it, the (broadly "pro-Heideggerian") reading of Levinas in "Violence and Metaphysics," what about the interrogation of Heidegger around these problems? Before approaching the text which appears to announce

the support must have opposed to both, but no more to you, G., nor to me, and I wonder again what can have happened when my writing changed, after thirty years, then again later, when machines took it over on the sea, for I got to the sea, first when the current passed through, then here when I swim against the tide, against the waves that write on my face from the screen to tell me how lucky my mother will be, if she is, to die before me, which I infer from my fear of not dying before my uncircumcised sons, objects of my infinite compassion, not that my compassion be extended to any uncircumcised but to my own, without religion apparently having anything to do

the most direct treatment of them, we should have to return in a brief detour via *Spurs*, which appears to contain a "pro-Nietzschean" analysis of Heidegger. Derrida shows for example that Heidegger appears to miss in his reading Nietzsche's discourse on woman, or at least that he seems to subordinate it to an ontological questioning conducted with a view to the question of the truth of being (EP, 89), just as he seems to have missed the originality of Nietzsche's *writing*, according to a certain passage from *Of Grammatology* (GR, 18ff.; recalled—subscribed to—S, 115n.15). However, in showing that everything that Nietzsche says about woman comes under a problematic of *propriation* (before its determination as ap-propriation or de-propriation, as taking or giving, and therefore before any established propriety or property—be it determined as being or having—and thus also before an opposition between what one "really" or properly is and what one gives oneself out *as* in simulation or dissimulation, as we have seen for the proper name), Derrida can put forward the idea that despite a constant valorization of the proper in Heidegger, Heidegger's

with it, nor Moses the father of my mother, like for someone, me, who would be capable of inventing circumcision all alone, as I am doing here, and of founding another religion, refounding all of them, rather, playfully, doubtless according to the vague presentment that my uncircumcised sons, the only people whose judgment I fear, will have failed to fail, what culture is made of (and man, *vir,* so they say), and that for that reason they will never finish envying me or hating me, for their love hates me, and I love them with love, a dissymmetry that nobody will believe except me and G., who is always right, like God, of course, who knows how much the love of the son can come to

The throne of Elijah (Carpentras synagogue).

thought, especially around the *Ereignis*, also exceeds the metaphysical limits one might be tempted to assign it, in the defense of Nietzsche. Which leads Heidegger to the thought of the gift that we have already invoked, and tightens further the bonds we are trying to remark between gift and femininity.

It is not however in *Spurs* that Derrida follows what Heidegger says explicitly about sexual difference, even if what he says there about the gift and the *Ereignis* ought to prepare us for it. *"Geschlecht"* (G1 passim) returns to the question. Here, in a movement of a formidable complexity that we will not be able to follow in all its details, and which takes place as much with as against Heidegger, Derrida shows that Heidegger's concern to avoid *Dasein*'s being sexually marked implies the neutralization only of *binary* sexual difference, and opens the possibility, beyond Heidegger's explicit statements, of a thought of sexual *differences* irreducible to the classical binary couple (G1 passim: this problem is also a less apparent theme in "Restitutions" [TP, 261, 278, 306–9, 334–5]). The point is also to confirm that the determination of sexual difference as opposition is

be lacking, it's God weeping in me, turning around me, reappropriating my languages, dispersing their meaning in all directions, *ita cum alius dixerit: "hoc sensit, quod ego," et alius: "immo illud, quod ego," religiosius me arbitror dicere: cur non utrumque potius, si utrumque uerum est, et si quid tertium et si quid quartum et si quid omnino aliud uerum quispiam in his uerbis uidet, cur non illa omnia uidisse credatur, per quem deus unus sacras litteras uera et diuersa uisuris multorum sensibus temperauit?*,* and as I am someOne that the One God never stops de-circumcising, in other words *hounds* herself to make bleed in dispersion, *salus in sanguine,* all

profoundly in league with a homogenization, and a *certain* homosexuality, which has always taken place under the sign of the masculine (on the erasure of sexual difference in the dialectical determination of difference as opposition, cf. GL, 110aff., 124–5a, 168–9a, 173a*, 223a), whereas if we manage to think, in this reading of Heidegger, that *Dasein* can be sexually marked without yet being sexually determined according to the binary masculine/feminine opposition, one would have thought at the same stroke a plural difference which would affect the whole of metaphysical thought, in the name of the (quasi-) transcendental dispersion we have already invoked.

So we must not regret the fact that we cannot give this the proper name "woman." This is also why Derrida's relationship with "feminism" (especially outside France, no doubt) has never been, and never could be, an entirely peaceful one. For example, some have found it provocative or even shocking that Derrida should exploit terms like "hymen" or "invagination" to nickname these structures. "Hymen," in the Mallarmé text which gives its chance (as Derrida would

those who can no longer sleep for it pretend to be waiting for me somewhere I've already arrived, like the truest of false prophets, they want to deport their Elijah obsession, attraction repulsion, sucked up thrown out to the periphery of a sentence, to the periphrases of my signature.

*"So, when one man has said: '[Moses] meant the same as I,' and another: 'Not that but what I mean,' I think I can say in a more religious way: 'Why not both, instead, if both are true?' And, if there is a third, and a fourth, and any other truths that

say: cf. the cover note to TP) to "The Double Session," names "economically" the relation between inside and outside which has been bothering us since the outset: "hymen" says separation *and* the abolition of this separation, and says it in a way which can appear violent. And if, as has been claimed, the "presence" of this signifier in Mallarmé's text is not necessary to the analysis, why use it? Similarly, we could say the same for the term "invagination" as used in the analysis of Blanchot's *La folie du jour* (LG, 217; LOB, 97ff.; PAR, 243), to attempt to describe how an outside surface folds back as inside surface, and, in the case of Blanchot's *récit*, according to a still more complicated figure that we shall call a "double chiasmatic invagination of the edges" (LG, 218).

It is certain that these terms retain, and try to mark the discourse with, a sexual register (even if "invagination," for example, is a word from embryology that is much more general than might be thought) while generalizing these terms toward apparently more "abstract" structures. We have already indicated why deconstruction must necessarily run the risk of being

anyone sees in these words, why may it not be believed that he saw all these, and that, through him, the one God has tempered the sacred writings to the perceptions of many people, in which they will see things which are true and also different?" (XII, xxxi, 42).

43 I invent the word *dhavec* this day of Purim 5750, while Esther still lives on and for almost a year and a half, without ever being interested in this name Esther, in spite of my appeals, still less at this moment at which she is surviving the conscience of me, of her name as of mine, I lean over her bud-

interpreted badly (whereas philosophy would in general like to reduce such possibilities to the level of accidents), and this is perhaps the most obvious case of this risk. But unless one take refuge in a false decency with respect to nomination, one must accept that "feminine" words be grafted onto other contexts and that "feminine" predicates be extended to broader structures: this is the only way of troubling the dominant discourse, and this trouble cannot by definition be completely controlled. To be upset about this, one would have to have presupposed Derrida's mastery over textuality and the effects it produces, to have already endowed him with "masculine" privileges (or else, which comes down to the same thing, reproach him with not exercising those privileges) and to have assumed that the text obeys these phallogocentric privileges (cf. what is said about parody in Nietzsche [S, 99–101]). The only chance, as we have already said, of intervening in this classical economy involves a share of unconsciousness and nonmastery (cf. GL, 76–7a) which leaves these texts open to wild affective investments (whence adulation as well as deprecation) that

ding *escarres,* "they look good" said the reassuring nurse, they are roaring in the carnage of a protest, life has always protested in my mother, and if "bad blood" will always be for me *her* expression, if from her alone I have received it, heard it or learned it, from her impatient sighs, this is because I began with this fear, with being scared of her bad blood, with not wanting it, whence the infinite separation, the initial and instantaneously repeated i.e. indefinitely postponed divorce from [*d'avec*] the closest cruelty which was not that of my mother but the distance she enjoined on me from [*d'avec*] my own skin thus torn off, in the very place, along the crural artery where my books find their

the willed coolness of our own explication certainly does not avoid either.

The "yes, yes" of affirmation thus cannot be "essentially" feminine, even if it is not neutral. But what prevents such an essentialization-nomination is precisely what means that the determination of sexual difference as opposition cannot be separated from the most fundamental oppositions of metaphysics (cf. GL, 223), and cannot fail to be shaken up by their deconstruction. In this sense, the deconstruction of the speech/writing opposition was already a feminist gesture.

POLITICS

We are still in the tension that differentiates the same: the fact that "everything hangs together" in this way depends on the solidarity of metaphysical concepts among themselves, which in turn depends on everything we have already seen about *différance* and the trace in the constitution, or rather inscription, of any effect

inspiration, they are written first in skin, they read the death sentence held in reserve on the other side of the screen for in the end since the computer I have my memory like a sky in front of me, all the succor, all the threats of a sky, the pelliculated simulacrum of another absolute subjectivity, a transcendence which I would finally do with as she would like, she who wants my death, "*the sublime scission, the bottomless bet: to learn how to love—that cannot fail to repeat one and many closed-up rents, open again the wound of circumcision, analyze that form of secret, the 'my life' which is neither a content to be hidden nor an inside of the solitary self but hangs on the partition between two absolute subjectivities, two whole*

of identity. But this situation in no way authorizes everything to be brought back down to the same in a generalized "leveling": there is nothing less Derridean than slogans such as "everything is sexual" or "everything is political" (G1, 67), or even "everything is literature," "everything is language," etc.

It is a misunderstanding of this type that informs the discussion by Habermas in *The Philosophical Discourse of Modernity* (MIT, 1990): even supposing that one finds it acceptable to criticize Derrida on the sole basis of a secondary presentation—however excellent—of his work (the book in question is Jonathan Culler's *On Deconstruction: Theory and Criticism after Structuralism* [London, 1982]: when Jacques Bouveresse mounts a charge in *Rationalité et cynisme* [Paris: Minuit, 1985], he relies for his information on the much less rigorous explanation provided by Richard Rorty), one sees immediately that the defense of the distinction between the "genres" of philosophy and literature against their "leveling" *already* speaks on the basis of a philosophical position that Habermas can do no more than presuppose, whereas this is precisely what is in question. See

worlds in which everything can be said and put in play without reserve, with the exception not of this fact but of the bottomless stake of the other *world, I write by reconstituting the partitioned and transcendant structure of religion, of several religions, in the internal circumcision of 'my life'... I came up to write something else, for I come up now (into this loft, this 'sublime' to write*" (10–14–77), I do not have the other under my skin, that would be too simple, the other holds, pulls, stretches, separates the skin from [*d'avec*] my sex in her mouth, opposite or above me, she makes me sperm in this strange condition, it's my condition, on this suspended condition that I write to death on a skin bigger than I, that of a provisional and

too Derrida's reflections in *Parages* (PAR, 10), *Memoires* (MEM, 225–7), and *Limited Inc.* (LI, 156–8n.3). But it would have been sufficient to read attentively the last page of "Force and Signification" (WD, 29–30) to suspect the extent to which what is going on here is not answerable to a thought of intersubjectivity. This remarkable page also gives us the essentials of the relation to the other, of something feminine in this relation of alterity (signaled here as mysteriously as can be by the entirely implicit reference of a sentence in this last page to the epigraph from Freud, quoted in German more than twenty pages earlier [WD, 15]), and the relations between law and inscription.

As nothing has appeared to be less well understood than the supposed "political effects" of deconstruction, we shall say first that it is only on condition that everything not be political that politics has some chance of being thought, and that in fact deconstruction is the most radically political of discourses. Our point is not to attempt a synthesis of the most directly "political" texts of Derrida's, (for the circumstantial nature of these texts is undoubtedly more notable than elsewhere

sacrificed spokesman, who can't stand it any more, caelum *enim* plicabitur ut liber *et nunc sicut pellis extenditur super nos. sublimioris enim auctoritatis est tua diuina scriptura* [...] sicut pellem *extendisti firmamentum libri tui, concordes utique sermones tuos, quos per mortalium ministerium superposuisti nobis.* [...] *Cum hic uiuerent, non ita sublimiter extentum erat. non dum* sicut pellem caelum *extenderas, nondum mortis eorum famam usquequaque dilataueras.**

*"For 'the heavens shall be folded together as a book,' and now it is stretched over us like a skin. Indeed, Thy divine Scripture is of more sublime authority [...] Just so, Thou hast stretched out

in Derrida, and would demand a respect that limits of space do not allow us here: saying so does not imply that we accept the traditional idea whereby a philosopher's "political" texts would be "occasional," or fall into a slightly shameful empiricity, far from the essence) but to clarify essential possibilities.

Let us recapitulate briefly: if the trace inscribes in general difference in the same by marking the "presence" of the other, everything we have just put forward via "translation," "signature," "gift," "indebtedness," "promise," "affirmation," etc., helps us to think this relation in a form we might call more "ethical," without being very sure of this word (ALT, 70–1). If the originary "yes" marks the fact that there is (already) some other, that it has always already begun, we have to say that it is always already social and political (cf. GR, 109ff., and especially 130), while admitting that we do not yet know what the social and political are. Every act of foundation of a society or *polis* will be marked from the outset by the "yes" that precedes every supposedly inaugural performance. Saussure's refutation of conventionalism will be remembered again: we re-

the firmament of Thy Book like a skin, Thy wonderfully harmonious words which Thou hast imposed upon us [...] while they were living here below, it was not so sublimely extended. Thou hadst not yet spread out the heaven like a skin; Thou hadst not yet broadcast the renown of their death in all directions" (XIII, xv, 16).

ceive language like the law, which fact casts doubt on the very coherence of the question about the origin of language, and reminds us among other things that language is not essentially human (for if language is *always* received, the "first man" must have received it from some nonhuman agency, which does not mean that he received it from God or a god, although "God" is perhaps the name, or one of the names, of this very situation [HAS, 28–9]). What we said above about the refusal to think of language as in some way a separate domain over against the world, and everything we added about mechanical repetition, also implies the consequence of an essential inhumanity of language. This is also what allows Derrida to say, correcting what can still be too conventionalist in the thesis of the arbitrariness of the sign, that we must speak, rather, of a becoming-arbitrary of the "natural" symbol as of a becoming-technical of nature (GR, 47).

The *already* thus developed explains the aporias of all social contract doctrines, for example. The primitive "contract" marked by the "yes" said to the other, the contracting ring of indebtedness which closes thus

44 March 31, 1990, in two weeks, passing through March 24, *dies sanguinis* on which the adorers of the goddess ran through the streets with their severed penises in their hands before throwing them deep into the houses, I shall return close to Santa Monica, toward the first word of Laguna Beach, privatization of literature, anniversary of the initial periphrasis, end of the revolution I noted when I returned from Moscow two weeks ago, perhaps my mother will still survive the circulation of the trip around the world, in advance I love the triumph of her survival, along with billions of others forever she knows nothing of what I write, never having wanted in all her life to

in its more or less tight stricture, precedes any social contract as its condition of possibility (how do you say yes to the social contract, or sign it, if the contractors are not already bound by a code permitting a minimum of mutual comprehension?), and therefore, as we expect by now, as its condition of impossibility (for how will the social contract ever attain the originarity it is seeking if it must presuppose a priori an earlier contract?). We also know that the idea of the social contract must give to time a twist it is unable to think, insofar as at least one of the parties to the contract has its existence only through the contract it is nevertheless supposed to be able to sign, and therefore is supposed to precede. An analysis of the American Declaration of Independence (DI passim) shows, *mutatis mutandis*, how the thing is done, via an undecidability of constative and performative values (marked here in the very term "declaration," but which in fact constitutes the performative as such: there is no performative which does not also involve an at least implicit description of the state of affairs it produces) in a pseudo-present that would be the fiction of the origin-point of the State or

read a single sentence of it, which gives to the exercise with and in which G. and I are indulging its rightful dimension as a whispering, the *aparté* of a confessional where we are in for nobody, changing skin every minute to *make* truth, each his own, to confess without anyone knowing, why would one wish to know or to make that known, like a gift confession must be from the unconscious, I know no other definition of the unconscious, *ego certe, quod intrepidus de meo corde pronuntio, si ad culmen auctoritatis aliquid scriberem, sic mallem scribere, ut, quod ueri quisque de his rebus capere posset, mea uerba resonarent, quam et unam ueram sententiam*

the nation or, in this precise case, of its independence. One must already be independent in order to be able to declare oneself such, but this independence is produced only in and through the declaration of itself (see too NM, 17ff.). Just like the act of naming "properly," this identification of a collective subject is an act of reappropriative violence exercised on or against an earlier violence (what Rousseau calls the state of nature, and the fact that he thought of it as being in fact a state of peace in no way prevents it from being de jure a state of violence—because without right—as Kant saw perfectly well). This violence is that of the gift and the "yes," which always already insure a minimum of liaison to a transcendental dispersion (which without this minimum of liaison would not even be thinkable as a dispersion: this is why we said earlier that *différance* cannot be pure or absolute [see too WD, 244n.2]), but as this is not strictly speaking a state *prior* to society, for example (deconstruction never seeks such a state [cf., MEM, 58–137]), but an event repeated in each statement and act (AL, 236–7), this dispersion is always at

*ad hoc apertius ponerem, ut excluderem ceteras, quarum falsitas me non posset offendere,** I will have found or given myself nothing, save death, so long as I have not *made known* about what is not for me a fantasy of eradication or of expropriation but, close to a virtual or mimicked trance, the painful pleasure of an obsessive ideomotor drive, a scene of tearing off skin, scalping or cutting up of the growth of scale far from the sex, but not so sure, above wrists and hands, or especially on the bottom half of a peeling face, that dream in Moscow that has been haunting me for two weeks, the old epistemologist with his cheeks and chin covered

work as the element of the tension or the *band* of the social against which the contract and the laws it inaugurates exercise a contra-band.

All the "rationalist" reproaches directed against Derrida, which consist in deploring what is thought to be a promotion of discord under the sign of *différance*, whereas, they say, it would be better to work toward a consensus to be reached through rational argumentation—all such reproaches rely on a misunderstanding of the motif we are here calling dispersion (or what Lyotard calls "dissensus" at the end of *The Postmodern Condition*). The point cannot be simply to oppose a politics of dispersion to a politics of consensus, because of a fundamental disymmetry, namely that consensus can only be thought of under the aegis of the Idea in the Kantian sense (and therefore falls under the aporias described apropos of Husserl), whereas dispersion cannot be thought of in that form: an Idea of dispersion carried to the absolute is not thinkable, even as an Idea. Dispersion works with gathering and the band, to which it is not opposed (cf. TP, 340). As it is not a priori cer-

with this fascinating Thing, calling for a violent and caressing, loving and cruel manipulation who begins to detach a patched-on skin, a second skin which seems to be mine without being mine, and whose provisional half-ownership, the thick firm hairy spiny graft of a vegetable superepidermis, yellow green mossy outgrowth, pale-blooded crust of an extraterrestrial would no longer leave my desire at rest, would paralyze it too, hold it still between two contradictory movements, tear off the hedgehog to make it bleed to the point of orgasm and keep it protect it suck it along its erect fur, *"this opus must have a circum-*

tain that the right tension here is either the loosest or the tightest, we are still in the *milieu* where judgment must always be singular.

This band and contraband (although, following the logic we have expounded for signature and countersignature, we must say that every band is already contraband, has tension only in a difference of forces), more or less stable in their tension, constitute what is called the social bond as what *holds* together (more or less dispersed or gathered) the movements of dispersion and gathering (cf. PF, 18–19). One can moreover generalize this description to the formation of any ensemble at all: *socius*, subject, or even book (PC, 401ff.). Any unit owes its unity to a force that allows it to bind itself to itself, to maintain itself erect (whence the idea of replacing the word "être" with the word "bander" in *Glas* [GL, 133]), which implies a relation of itself to itself that divides the same in constituting it. The whole enigma of the law, which we have so far more or less identified with the gift, is concentrated here.

The classical political doctrines construct a *polis* constituted by a more or less sudden or gradual event

cised form [...] when, architectural or musical, a contour will be determined, we must through this turning around, in it, rediscover the indefinitely reactivable enjoyment, what makes one want to write and to come at the moment of itching the effect of circumcision to share it with others" (10–14–77).

*"And for me (and I am saying this from my heart, without any fear), were I writing something aimed at the highest authority, I should prefer to write in such a way that each man could take whatever truth about these things my words suggested, rather

of departure from nature; in this sense the doctrines of the social contract can be taken as emblematic: they condense this break into a pure event which would be the impossible performative we have just described. This departure from nature is an entry into the *nomos* (it matters little here whether *nomos* be thought of as "custom" or as law strictly speaking): now, in modern political thought at least (but no doubt since always, in fact), the desire of the *nomos* is to join up again with *physis*, which also has its "laws" (Aristotelian, Galilean, Newtonian, even Einsteinian) which provide a model of regularity and order. The laws of the city would like to be the description of essentially "natural" phenomena. (This is a particular inflexion of the general structure that we have just described, which makes it inevitable that a performative also take itself to be a constative.) The great political doctrines project the end of politics as a rediscovered state of quasi-nature, if necessary after the revolution. This type of thinking has the advantage of absorbing into its constative dimension the excess of the first performance of the law: "good" law would be absolutely constraining and not

than to put down one true opinion so plainly as to exclude other opinions, even if there were no falsity in them to offend me" (XII, xxxi, 42).

45 Already when I was taking these notes, from '77 to '84, I could not have foreseen that one day I would lift out only a few of them here or there to accompany my mother in her death, mingle my voice with the song of the four Rabbis, Azzai, Zoma, Aher, and Akiba, at the entrance to the PaRDeS,

at all coercive, like the laws of nature, which are not even prescriptive. If this desire of political thought were realized, then the *polis* would disappear into nature. This analogy between the political and the epistemological constitutes the *Aufklärung* in all its progressivity, which there is no reason to denounce or deny: but the same analogism can also authorize the worst violence in the name of rationality.

We might guess that a deconstructive politics could not be inserted into this general schema. It will attempt to think that schema and thus to exceed it: our discussion of repetition and the trace will already have sufficiently shaken the relation between nature and its others for this analogism not to be able to take place. This is why it has been possible to believe both that deconstruction was incapable of thinking the political and the social, and that it was far *too* political to be an honest philosophy (DP, 424; MEM, 142ff.). If the thought of the trace and of originary repetition disallows us from thinking any departure from nature as a unitary event (and this is also, let it be said in passing, one of the motivations for the repeated casting into doubt of the

and the unfinished incantation resounds in an amphitheater in which I do not hear everything, scarcely my own voice, only the flight, a noise of wings, the angel that last night took hold of my computer, dooming once more invention to dispossession, memory to effraction, you did not know, G., that my first novel plot, when I was 15, already told, by being it, the theft of a diary and blackmail for its return, and since then I have been teaching my Rabbis that confession, if there is such a thing, gives beyond the circle, more than appropriation or expropriation, beyond the periphery, you will think this perhaps after my death, since then I have begun to write myself things quite other than me,

usual philosophical distinction between humanity and animality, and why it was important to us to say that language was not essentially human [EC, 5; G2, 173–4; HAS, 17; LI, 136; OS, 11–12; PC, 474n.51]), we must be able to think the law before the distinction between laws of nature and positive laws (without invoking any "natural law" to insure the mediation between the two [DI, 11; cf. GR, 17]) and thus recognize and remark the excess of the law, in that it is never given. This just is the abyss of traditional political thought, called God by absolutisms, never really absorbed by the thinkers of autonomy. This is what the title of "Préjugés: devant la loi" means, for example.

In fact we should not be surprised to find ourselves thus before the law: for the concept of law is already analytically entailed by the fact of repetition, and so we have been talking of nothing else since the beginning. There is no law in general except of a repetition, and there is no repetition that is not subjected to a law (D, 123). In the same measure (the measure of the same, precisely, its rhythm) our redoubled primal affirmation cannot be *opposed* to the law (thought then as negative,

since, that is since the "great depression" of 1960, at Le Mans, which 30 years after the other began at Easter, in El-Biar, with blood in my urine, the feature of passions for another 30 years, the terror of an endless crucifixion, a thought for all my well-beloved Catherines of Siena, no one better saw through the purple of the pure cut, "this blood," she says, "was given us in abundance; thus the eighth day following His birth, the little cask of His body was pierced by circumcision… this was however so little that the creature was not yet satisfied… Stand up, then, my well-beloved daughters, you've slept enough with the sleep of negligence, let us enter the cellar opened in the flank of

forbidding), but must always compromise with the law, which, for its part, must also assume the affirmation it is often supposed to repress (LG, 224). Only if we develop these relations can we avoid the simplicity or naiveté of opposing or believing one could oppose law in general, but also the simplicity or naiveté of wanting to replace the old laws with new ones.

For in order to begin to reply to the suspicion of passive acquiescence to the law, whatever it be, we shall say that this co-implication of the law, of repetition and of affirmation, contaminates the law with a constitutive illegality which will alone allow us to understand how a given positive law could be unjust. Every law tries to ground its justice in *justesse,* transforming the violence of its performative force into a calm constatation of the state of affairs it produces, according to the play we have just seen for the contract. This schema only allows injustice to be thought on the model of falsity: the only chance of thinking a justice not thus modeled on constatation is to recognize the (necessary) possibility of an injustice already inscribed in the very structure of the

the crucified Christ (where we shall find this blood) while weeping with anguish and pain over God's wound," above all do not believe that I am quoting any more than G., no, I am tearing off my skin, like I always do, I unmask and *de-skin* myself while sagely reading others like an angel, I dig down in myself to the blood, but in them, so as not to scare you, so as to indebt you toward them, not me, "*how to circumscribe, the edge of the text, those are words to avoid so that the totality of the lexicon, bearing the marks of my other texts, a little more than 50 words, should be impossible to find in 'circumcision,' if that is the title, rummage around in all possible languages, the ML (Mohel, Milah), the word for 'word,' what*

law, not even as anticipation of its own transgression, but as its own illegality as such.

THE TITLE

The instauration of the law, in the performative act of a contract or of some legislator, presents itself as a *coup de force* opposed to a prior force of dispersion. This is not essentially different from the structure of proper name and signatures, which already imposed violence against violence, band against band. Any law (and any nomination: Babel will have made us suspect that laying down the law and imposing one's name are no strangers to each other) is a double bind or double band in this sense. Derrida shows this with respect to the function of the title (DL, 132ff., 146ff.; TB, 187–205), and by following these analyses a little we shall be able to advance toward what will perhaps be recognized as more concretely political questions.

Whatever its grammatical form, the title of a text

is the word for 'word' in each language, find again what C.L. had told me about the ML and the cut of the word, the lips or the languages in the School garden" (10–18–77), I do not know SA, less than ever, I like to read right on the skin of his language, my chosen one for a year, and like an angel but unlike angels, is this possible, I read only the time of his syllables, *et ibi legunt sine syllabis temporum, quid uelit aeterna uoluntas tua. legunt, eligunt et diligunt; semper legunt et numquam praeterit quod legunt* [...] *non clauditur codex eorum...*★

functions as its proper name. Inscribed on the outer edge of the limit or frame that circumscribes the text (and whose empirical figure is the cover), the title identifies the text, and, like any proper name, permits one to talk about it in its absence. Without a title, be it only a classification number in a library, or the recitation of the first words of a text with no title, or even the word "Untitled"—so many modalities of the title—one would be unable to make external distinctions between one text and another, and all the disciplines of reading would collapse. The title, more still than the attribution to an author's proper name, is the very operator of textual normality and legality.

But this normality and legality are instituted only by troubling a certain "legality" of language and discourse, introducing a fold into these operations of nomination and reference. "Madame Bovary" is the proper name simultaneously of a "real" text and a fictional character (in truth at least three characters). "Parages" is a common noun gathering under a title the "themes" of a book identified by its proper name "Parages." "On the Social Contract" and "Of Grammatol-

*"They read there, without temporal syllables, what Thy eternal will desires. They are reading, choosing, and loving; they read forever, and what they read never passes away [...]Their book is never closed, [nor is their scroll rolled up]" (XIII, xv, 18).

46 A circumcision is my size, it takes my body, it turns round me to envelop me in its blade strokes, they pull upward, a spiral raises and hardens me, I am erect in my circumcision for centuries like the petrified memory and an ammonite, the mineral monument of a cadaver loving grass and moss, the

ogy" seem to take more directly as their referent the content or subject of the text, but are nonetheless the proper names of these books. A complete sentence in the form of an assertion or question ("The Trojan War Will Not Take Place," "Should we Burn Sade?") becomes a proper name in turn. Here is a becoming-proper of the common and a becoming-noun of the verb and the particle that form a pendant to the becoming-common of the proper.

Nothing is unequivocal here: one can *always* nominalize non-nominal elements, make syncategoremes into quasi-categoremes (cf. D, 222n.36), and this can just as well go along with the dominant tendency which will have consisted in subordinating the syntactic to the semantic and, by degrees, the text to ontology (see for example the analyses of Aristotle in "The White Mythology" in M, 233–4, 236–7) as it can ruin this same tendency by showing, as we have done, that the name is always already infiltrated with syntactic differences. This "just as well" does not indicate a comfortable situation of choice, but as always a "differantial" tension that is the life-death of metaphysics: the point is not to

thick proliferation of the vegetable that never stops gaining on a more and more dead desire, that of my mother whose life is apparently becoming, if I am to believe them, "vegetative," we have just enough breath left to ask for pardon, for the Great Pardon, in the languages of the PaRDeS, for all the evil that my writing is drawn, withdrawn and drawn out from, an eternal skin above not you, but me dreaming of him who dreams of the place of God, burning it up in his prayer and going up toward it like ivy *scriptura uero tua usque in finem saeculi super populos extenditur* [...] sermones autem tui non transibunt, *quoniam et pellis plicabitur et faenum, super quod extendebatur, cum claritate sua prae-*

denounce the title in the name of an absolute "intertextuality," but to *suspend* it (M, 169ff., 192; PRE, 90, 93) as what gives its chance to writing.

Now the title, in this nominal function that allows the text to be recognized by the law, seems to illustrate what we have said in a still somewhat vague fashion about the position of the proper name in general, which seemed to belong without belonging to the language system: naming the "idiomatic" text it entitles, the title forms part of it without really forming part of it. It detaches itself from it, like any proper name with respect to its bearer. In naming a text, the words "Madame Bovary" on the cover of the novel do not only name something other than those same words within the diegesis of the book, but name otherwise, bridging two different worlds which work according to different laws (PRE, 107). It is by its title that the book can be named before the law, for example, whereas the character named by these same words is not susceptible to the judgment of the tribunal supposed to judge Flaubert, or at least not directly, although confusion here is almost inevitable, and the source of what is ridiculous

teriet, uerbum autem tuum manet in aeternum, [. . .] *attendit per retia carnis et blanditus est et inflammauit, et currimus* post odorem *eius,** I never like the play on words with no beyond, there remains the herb and not the verb, the furious repulsion that attracts me right up onto a skin toward the blind push of the foreign body, a more or less living, swarming and silent graft, which basically transports the intolerable envy, the enjoyment that I am, myself and nothing else, to tear off the growth and throw it far away, to introduce between it and my skin the thin blade of a writing knife *"'circumcision equipment,' p. 60 of* Family: *if I die tomorrow, people will look at this picture I am observing at*

in every trial of this type. If we decided to trouble the separation between the real world and the diegesis by taking the name "Madame Bovary" within the text as naming the text in which it is found, we would open onto all sorts of complications which depend on the bizarre status of the title. This book is called "Jacques Derrida." We should also have to follow the complication suggested here at the limit of the text and its outside by examining the subtitle, and in particular that subtitle ("novel," "récit," etc.) marking a generic belonging. There too, this mark does not simply belong to what it marks: the word "fiction" in the position of a subtitle on a book does not itself belong to the world of fiction (cf. LG passim). In fact, title and subtitle always function as *promises* (cf. MEM, 115ff.; PS, 549).

This complication of the title condenses what is concerning us here around the law. We are trying to show not only that the title of a work has an irreducibly "legal" status in that it identifies the text *for* the needs of the law (which thus dominates the text), but also that it tells us something about the law, the being-law of the law, that it dominates or exceeds in some sense

length this morning, everything will need deciphering, in particular the inscription on the blade, its place, far enough from the edge to prevent one imagining or dreaming, alas, that the letters might themselves touch, at the moment of incision, the bleeding skin, they remain above, they keep watch, they speak, what do they say? [...] *the 'shield'* [...] *in the official prayer-book: 'Blessed art thou O Lord our God, who hast not made me a woman'* [...]. *Beginning of the 20th century: circumcision is used to treat 'disorders' (loss of semen, masturbation)* [...] *the uncircumcised Jew is condemned to Gehenna"* (10–18–77), the day of the Great Pardon, presence of white, my immaculate taleth, the

the law itself. We have already caught a glimpse of this turnaround when we were saying above that the inaugural performative of the law, i.e. the event thought of in its most condensed form as social contract, depended on a radical fiction to take place, or rather, for such an event cannot take place, to produce after the fact the fiction of its having-taken-place. This structure implies that the law is made in an illegality, in a moment when it is outside the law, beside itself, and that it remains marked by this fact: it is the law of the law that it cannot ground its own legality in itself or state its own title without getting outside itself to tell a story about the event of its origin, to which however it ought to remain indifferent. The text is named on its outside surface so as to give itself a frame and thus to communicate with a broader text ("the world" in general); it thus calls for a more general and more powerful law in order to be able to impose its own idiomatic law. The law in general, itself essentially text (cf. D, 113; MEM, 143–5), must give itself a title before an external agency which is no longer of the order of the law. One can attempt to avoid infinite regress by calling this ab-

only virgin taleth in the family, like the feathers of the cocks and hens that Haïm Aimé wants to be white for the sacrifice before Kippur, the Rabbi cuts their throats in the garden after feeling under their wings, holding the knife between his teeth, then passed them over our heads while saying our names, unforgettable bloodied white animals that I wanted to save when, sometimes thrown under the bowl, they thrash around for a long time, still alive, to the point of lifting the iron lid and running again, headless and as though drunk, in the PaRDeS.

solute exteriority "nature" or "God," for example, but these names immediately fall into the abyss, naming only the very regression they were trying to block. And by naming this exteriority "on the inside" they open, according to the structure of invagination, a pocket of "exteriority" which means that the limit marked by a title or a frame no longer divides an inside from an outside but inscribes the outside inside without being able to contain it there (cf. "Parergon," TP, 11–147). This law of the law can no longer be formulated in a form acceptable to the law, it cannot present itself before a tribunal: we will call it necessity (or Necessity [EO, 116; PC, 194, 199; PRE, 130]), but as it is nothing outside singular or idiomatic, fundamentally unpredictable, undecidable (PMW, 593; PAR, 15) events in which it falls or remarks itself, we shall also call it chance (MC). Necessity—that there be this Chance.

We see in this way why Derrida will privilege in his reading those texts which inscribe this very situation, and especially "literary" texts, which oblige us to notice these structures. And we see at the same time why

*"Thy Scripture extends over the peoples until the end of the centuries [...] Thy words shall not pass away. For, the skin shall be folded up, and the 'grass,' over which it was spread, shall pass away with its beauty, but Thy word abides forever [...] He gazed through the veil of flesh, He spoke lovingly and made us ardent, and we ran after his odor" (XIII, xv, 18).

47 13, rue d'Aurelle-de-Paladines, El-Biar, it's still the orchard, the intact PaRDeS, the seamless present which continues you, the imperturbable phenomenon that you will

we would be wrong to see in texts which "reflect" on their own status no more than a narcissistic or formalist game. The apparently most "serious" and "realistic" texts are in fact those that accept the limits established by a law they are not in a position to question, and which can only function for them as a nature: by troubling tranquil reference to an outside, texts like those of Jabès, Kafka, Mallarmé, Blanchot, or Ponge (or Derrida) expose themselves to a radical exteriority which alone can produce an event (WD, 295; cf. PAR, 9–17). This is the case for certain nonliterary texts too (PC, 390–1, on *Beyond the Pleasure Principle).* What we have endeavored to formulate above in the form of theses—saying for example that the fact that there is nothing outside the text in no way enclosed us in a prison house of language but opened language to the other in general—returns here as the necessity or the chance of singularities which by remarking their singularity shake up the received limits by saying "yes, yes" to a law which never presents itself. This is what Derrida also calls the *retrait.* The law is always in retreat with respect to the domain it rules, but must nonetheless be

never see age, you no longer grow older, although everything is decided in this garden, and the law, as far as memory extends, the death of two children, Jean-Pierre Derrida, the cousin, one year older than you, knocked down by a car in front of his home in Saint-Raphaël, at school they tell you your brother has died, you believe it, a moment of annihilation from which you never recovered, and five years later, 1940, the death of Norbert Pinhas, your little brother this time, 2 years old, then expulsion from school and from Frenchness, damnation games with Claude, Claude and Claudie, boy and girl cousins, so many stolen figs, at the origin is theft and perjury, just before the 59 secrets of Ali Baba, one undecipherable secret per jar, on each date

Photograph with automobile (II)
To the right, in his mother's arms. To the left, Jean-Pierre Derrida, his cousin (cf. *Circumfession,* 47), in his own mother's arms.

remarked in it to insure the possibility of its jurisdiction. The law cannot figure among the objects subject to the law, cannot become its own case—but it is not present elsewhere, and can therefore only remark itself in the singular cases with which it is presented. In this sense titles are never established and the law is never laid down. Yet it is not sufficient to say that the texts we have cited "transgress" (cf. POS, 12) received forms according to a dialectic of newness such as that proposed by the Russian formalists, for the events of these texts do not get blunted into an achieved familiarity which would in turn need to be transgressed by new inventions. The event of a text is not masterable by a historical date (cf. SCH, 313ff.): the law imposed by historical description presupposes the relation to law in general, as it is remarked in these texts that the law thus cannot dominate. This is why literary history has little to do with literature: we read the works of the past as events neither in a personal history nor in a history of literature, but as in some sense events "in themselves."

If we reapply this situation to Derrida's texts, we will say, against a certain reception of his work, that the

a drop of blood, one date is enough to leave the geologic program behind, like the drop you saw well up on the back of the little girl allowing herself distractedly to be buggered, scarcely, with gestures that are sure but as gauche as those of a mammal at birth, she knows you've got a hard-on on your father's bed, turned as she is toward the radio, *numquid mentior aut mixtione misceo neque distinguo lucidas cognitiones harum rerum in firmamento caeli et opera corporalia,*★ that means, follow carefully, that you never write like SA, the father of Adeodat whose mother is nameless, nor like Spinoza, they are too *marranes,* too "Catholic," they would have said in the rue d'Aurelle-de-Paladines, too far from the orchard, they say discourse, like the sign of circum-

"He arrived from Portugal, I'm sure you look like him" (*Circumfession,* 47). *Cérémonies et Coutumes religieuses de tous les peuples du monde,* illustrations by B. Picard, Amsterdam, 1723.

event-character of the terms we are here calling "quasi-transcendentals," the fact that the list of them is not closed, in no way hangs on any *will* on Derrida's part to "do something new" or to "surprise" us, or to prevent us from making deconstruction into a simple reading method. The event constituted by the reading of Rousseau in the *Grammatology,* for example, did not take place in 1967 only later to become absorbed into familiarity, but comprises an essential, persisting *Unheimlichkeit.* It will be recognized that this is not anything different from what we were saying about the incompletion of signatures and survival through translation.

We should rather, then, have to say that these texts have a relation to the other which is the more remarkable and persistent in that they apparently do not cease reflecting upon themselves. As what is traditionally called literature has an essential link to these possibilities of invention of the other (PIO passim), without of course having exclusive rights to it, we see why it might have for Derrida a dignity other than that of a simple object among others of philosophical question-

cision, external *or* internal, no, no, you have more than two languages, the figural and the other, and there are at least 4 Rabbis, "... '*as for their long existence as a dispersed* nation *no longer forming a* State, *there is nothing surprising about this* [...] *and not only through the observation of* external rites *opposed to those of the other nations, but through* the sign of *circumcision to which they remain religiously attached* [...]. *I attribute such a value in this affair to the* sign of *circumcision that I believe it capable on its own of insuring this Jewish nation an eternal existence.* [...] *We find an example of the importance that can be attached to a particularity such as circumcision among the Chinese...,' S. says 'sign' and 'external rite,' why? Go back to the original, later, what follows in the text, revise: 'sign of circumcision'*

ing. If literature can appear "before the law" (of history, or philosophy, of society), it also bespeaks a relation to a law before the law. It thus exceeds the laws that attempt to tame it. This relation to a law before the law is not general but each time singular, engaging the divided idiom of the signature and the title. In calling on literature (but there is so little of it, scarcely any [D, 223]) to say something about this situation, we are not invoking an essence supposed to be known or knowable, we are not presupposing a "What is literature . . . ?" (ibid.): the point is, starting from the law and affirmation, to put to work all the unthought resources of the received concept of "literature."

Only such a relation to the law, presupposed by the text in general as more or less gathered dispersion of singularities or events, allows us to think something like freedom. The current of thought that we have linked to the doctrine of the social contract thinks freedom in terms of autonomy, of a giving-oneself-the-law. Everything we have been saying since the beginning of this book ought to make us suspect such a concept of naiveté. What we have said about writing and

and election, foreign to the understanding and to true virtue" (10–18–77), in spite of your disagreement with him on this point, and you always go beyond a disagreement, dare then compare the *schechina* of your body, that of the orchard, to its substance, and that makes you happy, for then you think of this young man, an ancestor on your mother's side, who, your cousin tells you, one day at the dawn of the last century, arrived from Portugal, I'm sure you look like him, you look more and more like your mother.

*"Do I lie? Do I bring confusion by not distinguishing the clear knowledge of these things in the firmament of heaven from the bodily works...?" (XIII, xx, 27).

the trace shows that no *autos* is possible without an inscription of alterity, no inside without a relation to an outside which cannot be simply outside but must remark itself on the inside. The unthinkable residue that the thought of the contract tries to gather up in its fabulous performance is none other than the relation to the law we have just associated with literature, and it implies fatally that autonomy is de jure impossible (cf. PS, 176). The law one gives oneself retains an irreducible relation to the law received before the law ("Come" [cf. PAR, 21–116, passim]). It alone makes possible the desire for autonomy, in making autonomy itself impossible. Pre-judged. This is what is shown, in Rousseau for example, by the indispensable resort to the figure of the legislator. The worse confusions are possible here if we think of this situation on the basis of a simple opposition between activity and passivity. To say "Yes, yes" to the law in the description we have given of it is in no way a passive obedience to a law whose justice is not even interrogated. To the contrary, it is only this pre-originary relation which makes possible the democratic discussion of the laws demanded

48 I am, I think, I gather my spirits, for there are more than one of them sharing by body, only by multiplying in me the counterexamples and the countertruths that I am, or rather, by letting them multiply without me, without narcissistic counterpart, and I stand against SA when he believes and indeed says *multipliciter significari per corpus, quod uno modo mente intellegitur, et multipliciter mente intellegi, quod uno modo per corpus significatur. ecce simplex dilectio dei et proximi, quam multiplicibus sacramentis et innumerabilibus linguis et in unaquaque lingua innumerabilibus locutionum modis corporaliter enuntiatur! ita crescunt et multiplicantur fe-*

in principle by a thought of the contract. If the contract really founded the laws in as absolute a way as it would wish (i.e., as we said, in such a way that they would be as constraining as the laws of nature), it is hard to see how one could have any idea of justice against which to measure the current laws. Without such an idea, which is thought of traditionally under the name of natural law (but which we can no longer in all rigor allow ourselves to think under the aegis of nature, unless we take infinite precautions to separate nature from its metaphysical oppositions to the law, precisely, to technology, etc.), there would not even be any possibility of talking about justice, nor of encouraging the famous rational discussion with a view to a consensus, that people rather bizarrely try to *oppose* to Derrida.

And yet it is inadequate to say simply that the thoughts of a social contract presupposes the more "archaic" relations—in an obviously nontemporal sense—explored by Derrida. The deconstruction of the speech/writing opposition kept the old name "writing," at the risk of certain confusion, as the only

tus aquarum. adtende iterum quisquis haec legis★... here I am, peripheral and transiently, only the series of the 59 widows or counterexemplarities of myself, the first to have received from very high up the order to put an end to the secular endogamy so as to go in search of Saint Foreskin, the gram of the "*lost part of self, which has moreover the form of the Ring, return upon oneself in the alliance, so that if in place of my mother, symbolic and inaccessible holder of my ring, had been substituted my wife, another virgin and holder in whom I confide the secret unknown to me and of whom I am the more jealous, at the very moment that this latter, she's always been*

possibility of marking the philosophical field as it is constituted. The deconstructions begun here of the couples active/passive, nature/*polis*, etc., are not content simply to seek out, before political thought, metaphysical antiquities for a specialized collection. Unlike Wittgenstein, for example, deconstruction does not think that philosophy leaves everything as before, but has indeed the pretension of intervening in practice. This is also what distinguishes it from a critique in the Kantian sense (TP, 19–20). But just as, in the retention of the name "writing," we also marked a definite indebtedness with respect to the old concept of writing and to the proper names of the texts that had elaborated that old concept, even under the sign of evil, the point is not, in this thought of the affirmative law, to reject or ruin what the doctrine of the social contract tried to make possible as liberty, democracy, or rational discussion (cf. PS, 340–1). Getting this point wrong—and deconstruction allows us to think through, as always possible, this mistake which does not befall it like an external accident, but arrives in a programmed way, without surprise for us (cf. MEM, 138–9)—has led to

the last, symbolically entrusts the symbol, the alliance is lost, the third introduced, the gaping opened, and I must set off again after the Grail, wandering again, wandering laid bare, whatever the simulacra of station, reconciliation, the alliance for a new departure being marked, at a given precise date, by the real loss, this time, of that symbol, in my wallet thus swollen, my father's ring entrusted to me by my mother when he died, and the day of that loss a de-cision *was taken in me without me* [...]. *Jealousy and virginity, my two nipples"* (9–3–81), and it is always toward a West, mine in the end, that the decision pushes me to fly, to the extent that being "exported" now from

descriptions in terms of "critique of modernity" or "hatred of democracy" which rest on a deep misunderstanding, which must be called unjust, as much of the relations of indebtedness with respect to received thinking (here, Heidegger) as of deconstructive strategy in general.

We have already invoked, with reference to Levinas, the thought of a lesser violence in an economy of violence. That the law is always laid down in illegality shows again this primordial violence we are also calling Necessity. Traditional political thinking recognizes the fact of this violence but projects its end de jure in its various projects. We know that the attempt to realize the state of absolute nonviolence, which would be the end of politics in both senses of the word "end," can produce the worst violence. A politics thought of as an economy of violence does not allow itself the dream of realizing peace (which does not exclude the possibility of dreaming of peace as a dream made possible by what disallows its realization). This implies that politics is *now*, not projected into a utopian future, but in the event of the tension which is not to be *resolved*. Decon-

Moscow to Los Angeles, with a brief landing in Paris, just time enough to remind my loved ones of my existence, I am sighing to know until when I will be going round myself in this way, phantom or prophet charged with a mission, heavily charged with a secret unknown to him, the sealed text of which would be in his pocket, commenting on it until he has no breath left for the 59 nations in love with him who want thus compulsively to reject-deport him, *Vos autem,* genus electum,** you are waiting for an order from God who, calling your mother back to him to give you the starting signal, the race and history begin-

struction is not a thought of the absolute also in that one cannot absolve oneself from this tension, nor therefore acquit oneself of the indebtedness it implies.

THE INSTITUTION

If deconstruction has an effect on philosophical discourse, one ought to expect it to have one too on the philosophical institution in the broader sense, if it is true that "text" is not to be confused with "discourse." Touching on institutions is moreover one of the features that is supposed to distinguish deconstruction from a simple critique (TP, 19–20). Derrida has participated in several movements tending to change the existing philosophical institution or to create new institutions: "cofounder" of the Group for Research on Philosophical Teaching (GREPH), and more recently of the Collège International de Philosophie. One should not see in this simply a secondary or marginal activity concerning the socio-professional status of

ning at this point, finally allows you to speak, one evening you'll open the envelope, you'll break the seals like skins, the staples of the scar, unreadable for you and for the others, and which is still bleeding, so that finally ceasing from eyeing your pocket they may enter at dawn the terrible and sweet truth you bear.

*"... that what is understood in but one way by the mind may be expressed in many ways through the body, and what is expressed in but one way through the body may be understood in many ways by the mind. Notice the simple love of God and

philosophy teachers, for example, but an effort to rethink philosophy in its relations with its institutions. This is an integral part of what "deconstruction" means.

These relations are not simple. Modern philosophy has an obvious institutional link with the university, not only in that it has found a place (an increasingly cramped space) within it, but in that it is responsible for the modern concept of the university. It is not only that philosophy is carried out in general within the university: the university is a philosophical institution, its concept is due to philosophical reflection. This situation gives philosophy a double place, which corresponds curiously to what we have said, and are going to say, about quasi-transcendentality. It is to philosophy that is due the division of intellectual labor that decides the organization of the university into faculties or departments, including the one it is to be found in. Philosophy is a discipline among many others, an element of a series, but at the same time it departs from this immanence to describe and even construct the se-

neighbor—by how great a multiplicity of symbols and what innumerable tongues, and in each language by countless ways of speaking, it is proclaimed corporeally. It is this sense that the offspring of the waters increase and multiply. Pay attention again, whoever is reading this" (XIII, xxiv, 36).

**"But, you, 'a chosen race,' [the weak things of the world]" (XIII, xix, 25).

ries of which it is nonetheless *a-part* (DP, 428ff.). Bigger than the university of which it is but a part: part bigger than the whole.

In spite of its medieval or even ancient roots, this organization of the university is really modern. It takes its inspiration from the philosophical projects that preceded the foundation of the University of Berlin in 1810. The university is ruled by an Idea in the Kantian sense, the idea of a totality of the teachable (PR, 6). What is more, it gives philosophy the privilege of saying the truth about the whole of the university, according to a traditional schema: positive knowledge lacks secure foundations so long as philosophy has not given them to it. At the same time, this privilege of philosophy can and even must go along with a lack of real power in and outside the institution whose truth it nonetheless speaks. In *The Conflict of the Faculties*, the object of a commentary by Derrida, Kant gives philosophy all power to speak the truth to the other faculties (even the "higher" faculties, i.e. law, medicine, and theology), as well as to the government powers to which it is subject, but no real power to take actual de-

49 April 10, 1990, back in Laguna, not far from Santa Monica, one year after the first periphrasis, when for several days now I have been haunted by the word and image of mummification, as though I were proceeding with the interminable embalming of Mother alive, surviving or dying, surrounding her tightly with my 59 prayer bands, and now last night a dream throws me back toward her again, and toward her words, these words for her, who will never read them, up to this last word for "word," she had just died, everything was laid out in her room around her, in El-Biar rather than in Nice, the shroud prepared, this does not stop me from walking out in the

cisions (DP, 425). Philosophy should speak the truth but not lay down the law. We should, then, have to assume the possibility of making a theoretically rigorous distinction between a constative-theoretical language, that of philosophy, and a performative-prescriptive language, that of power. We have already experienced the fragility of these distinctions.

Philosophy has not kept these privileges in the university: the Idea that in principle ought to open onto the possibility of an infinite progress just seems finished. And insofar as deconstruction puts into question the distribution of finite and infinite, of fact and right, then it ought to encourage this decline. We would, then, be tempted to say that any reform aiming to reinforce the position of philosophy in its institutions could only be a reactive attempt to reclaim rights that had been justly lost, and that deconstruction should not participate in such reforms. Yet Derrida has never simply recommended that philosophy disappear, and this is, *mutatis mutandis*, the reason for the reproach that has been directed against deconstruction in the United States (where its influence has been above all felt in lit-

street, arm in arm with a young lady, under an umbrella, nor from seeing and avoiding, with a feeling of vague guilt, my Uncle Georges, my mother's younger brother who thus bears the same name as his sister, whom he often nicknamed Geo, who is limping, for he really does limp and his step is part of my life, he beats the time of family morals, he marks the family like the stamp on a coin or a flag flown, and I hear him limping toward the dead woman's house, to which I go too after a detour to discover that my mother was not inert and even, after a few hypotheses on my part about the movements of fermentation that continue after death, awake enough for a tear to run down

erature departments), where it is supposed to have restored a factitious dignity to an old canon of literary texts whose ideological foundations would supposedly be threatened elsewhere by truly radical critiques. But deconstruction only ever takes place, for reasons of principle, through a more or less relaxed attachment to what has traditionally been called philosophy, which it never simply repudiates, and it suspects any gesture that proclaims a simple "exit" from philosophy of remaining in it all the more certainly. Derrida recognizes a definite privilege, when it comes to the possibility of shaking up logocentrism, of new "disciplines" such as linguistics or psychoanalysis, but we have also seen the vigilance he puts into the study of the most traditionally metaphysical elements of these same disciplines. It is certain that, in fact, a large part of what was until recently the domain of philosophy has been taken over by the "human sciences": the point for deconstruction is not to deplore a nibbling away of privileges lost to philosophy as a region of the university, or even as the queen of all regions of the university, but to show how this change remains a prisoner of classical schemas. So

her cheek and for her to reply to my question in the form of a consolation "Why are you crying, Mother?", with her hand held out, "I don't agree with this, these magic spells, I should have had the injection straight away," "Of course not, mother," and later in the night, the words "counterfeit coin," in English, come to be associated with the word "slip" in the same sentence, to denounce when I wake what I am doing here, letting my mother go or letting her down, already burying her under the word and weeping her in literature *subito destitutus sum, et libuit flere in* conspectu tuo *de illa et pro illa, de me et pro me, et dimisi lacrimas, quas continebam, ut effluerunt quantum uellent, substernens*

we see that the reserves formulated with respect to the human sciences (to simplify: they think they get us out of metaphysics and make philosophy out of date; in fact they are more tangled up in metaphysics than the philosophy they are fighting) cannot in principle remain at the level of discursive analyses, but owe it to themselves to think of new institutional possibilities. It does not follow that we simply and reactively defend philosophy against a generalized and threatening positivism—that of the human sciences—but, exactly following the movement of reinscription characterizing discursive deconstruction, that "philosophy" must undergo a twist: the philosophy we defend is no longer exactly the philosophy that is being attacked (this is a fundamental principle of the GREPH, for example); and this is almost a rule of deconstructive politics, which accepts the possibility of a negotiation without for all that accepting what is still too frank, oppositional, and direct about "negotiation" in general. Double gesture again: we recognize a primordial indebtedness toward a tradition that the point is not however to preserve or celebrate as such.

eas cordi meo [...] *et nunc, domine, confiteor tibi in litteris. legat qui volet et interpretetur, ut uolet, et si peccatum inuenerit, fleuisse me matrem exigua parte horae, matrem oculis meis interim mortuam,*★ and for 59 years I have not known who is weeping my mother or me—i.e. you *"when he says 'you' in the singular and they all wonder, who is he invoking thus, who is he talking to, he replies, but you, who are not known by this or that name, it's you this god hidden in more than one, capable each time of receiving my prayer, you are my prayer's destiny, you know everything before me, you are the god (of my) unconscious, we all but never miss each other, you are the measure they don't know how to take and that's why they wonder whom, from the*

However, if we insist on strategy without finality, on a ruse which does not aim at a determinate goal and which is not a ruse of reason, then it is hard to see what an institutional politics of deconstruction could be. What is the use of the generalized questioning of the institution if one does not have another institution in mind to replace the old one? This classical question (you criticize the existing order of things: what do you propose to put in its place?), which tends to reinforce the political order as order of an order, precisely, and which regulates many "political" reactions to deconstruction in the Anglo-American countries, is itself exceeded by deconstruction. If deconstruction had a goal or a regulating idea, it would be: that something come about, that something happen, that there be some event (cf. SS): an "institution" ruled according to this Idea (which is not really one, not depending at all on a projection to infinity) ought in some sense to make a void to welcome this event. Such an institution would have to be, on the one hand, autonomous enough to recognize the fundamental alterity that, as we have seen, makes possible and impossible the foundation of

depth of my solitude, I still address, you are a mortal god, that's why I write, I write you my god" (9–4–81), to save you from your own immortality.

*"I was suddenly bereft. It was a relief to weep in Thy sight about her and for her, about myself and for myself. I gave free course to the tears which I was still restraining, permitting them to flow as fully as they wished, spreading them out as a pillow for my heart [...] And now, O Lord, I am confessing to Thee in writing. Let him who wishes read and interpret it as he wishes. If he finds it a sin that I wept for my mother during a little part

an institution in general (autonomous enough to recognize the impossibility of autonomy, then), but, on the other hand, sensitive enough to the event of this alterity to undo itself and reconstitute itself at a very rapid rhythm. And yet, it is inadequate here to think of a space closed in on itself "in" which things—events in the cultural or spectacular sense—would happen (this is where deconstruction also communicates with questions of architecture [cf. PF passim]). We have insisted enough on the impossibility in principle of constituting any such "inside" for this to be clear. It was precisely the old model of the university that posited a separation between inside and outside, which left it open to all sorts of critiques, and impotent faced with a fragmentation of knowledge that it no longer contains, even in the form of an Idea. A new philosophical institution ought to welcome all sorts of "external" parasitings: it could no longer be thought solely under the sign of truth, and is from the outset bound up in power. The distinction between performative and constative that rules the Kantian model of the university is not rigorous, philosophy is *also* performative in its efforts to

of an hour, the mother who was dead for the time being to my eyes, [who had wept over me for many years that I might live before Thy eyes—let him not be scornful]" (IX, xii, 33).

50 *"What has entered my life this year, from May '80 to August '81, irreversibly I fear, is the* sinister, *not the disaster which still had something of the sublime about it and, up to and including the whiteness of its name, some candor, not the disaster that put a spell on my life, but the sinister, the bad-mouthed disaster, eight letters again which come out badly in ISTER, disaster losing even its height, gri-*

speak the truth, there is no pure theory before or outside of the questions of right or duty (LI, 135), and this is why we insist to such an extent on the event.

In this perspective, responsibility is neither on the side of pure truth nor subject to the governmental or technocratic powers that demand that thought submit to the demands of efficiency and utility, but is stretched by, and toward, the coming of the event. In this sense the institution would not be an ivory tower or a tower of Babel, but would allow for dissemination, including the "confusion" of tongues: this is the effort of the Collège International de Philosophie.

Which is not, it is important to recall, a "deconstructive" institution and could not be one. The point is not that deconstruction is pure anarchy and that therefore it could give rise to an institution only by betraying itself: the possibility of the institution is given with the trace in its iterability, which simultaneously gives its impossibility. Institutions in general are in deconstruction "before" deconstruction is in institutions. So we must not deplore a definite institutionalization of deconstruction (especially in the United States, but

macing disaster obliging one to crawl, which no longer even allows one to walk, the word 'sinister' imposed itself alongside the word disaster, in its proximity of resemblance and difference, like its black brother of evil portent, while I was walking in the sun ruminating about all the bad things that have happened this year, and may nobody be allowed to be told the whole series of them, the addresses of such a narrative being party enough to it for the panorama to be forbidden to them, and to me, so that I am alone with everything, and after all, is that not what I wanted?" (9–4–81), now this morning it seems to me I am seeing a word, "cascade," for the first time, as happens to me so often, and each time it's the birth of a love affair, the origin of

even there in an unequal, *différante* way [cf. MEM 12ff.]) or express the wish that it should give rise to institutions replacing universities. If it is remarked in the institution it allows us to think, then that is already an event, to be remarked again.

THE SERIES: (QUASI-) TRANSCENDENTAL QUESTIONS

We have taken a series of terms from Derrida, who took them from texts read not according to a program or a method (cf. DR, 273) but, at least in (irreducible) part, according to the flair and the chance of encounters with what is bequeathed or repressed by the tradition. We have said several times that these terms are singular in the sense that they remain more or less attached to the text from which they were taken, and never achieve the status of metalinguistic or metaconceptual operators. And yet, as we have recognized from the argument around context and citation, these terms cannot for all that remain enclosed in a supposed immanence

the earth, without counting the fact that the 52 + 7 and a few times that I have thought I was, like a cascade, falling in love, I began to love each word again, so many words like clean proper names, but the word cascade, you see, itself, I do not see, it falls under my eyes, have you ever seen a word, what's called seen, however long you turn around it, and how to bring off a confession, how to look at yourself right in the eyes and show your face if a word is never seen face on, not even the word *milah,* for "word," and if I have said all my perjuries made of words, only said them, when what I would have liked to announce to G., my mother who since always has no longer been able to hear

of the text, from which they have departed at least sufficiently to be noticed by Jacques Derrida. They thus have what we might call a disappointed transcendental ambition, they depart from their element (like the fish in the Adami drawing commented on in "+R" [TP, 157ff.]) only to plunge back into it, they raise their heads long enough to breathe (GL, 115b) before taking their place again in the text. *L'érection tombe.* By naming this situation "quasi-transcendental" (a term we borrow from Rodolphe Gasché, but which is regularly used by Derrida himself, at least since *Glas* [AL, 291, 307; GL, 151–62a; PC, 403; TB, 186]), we committed ourselves to returning to this more directly.

> We should have to put the quasi-transcendental into a relation with other uses of the prefix "quasi-" or the adverb "quasiment," associated with metaphor or catachresis (RM, 21–2), with ontology (RLW, 292), "contemporaneity" (PS, 382, omitted from translation NA), tautology (HAS, 5); property (HAS, 60); negativity (DES, 11), the contract (F, 57, omitted from translation at xxxviii), the concept (LI, 122) and the date (SCH, French edition only, 84). But as the point

me, and make G. understand, G. who speaks well of me so well, what you have to know before dying, i.e. that no only I do not know anyone, I have not met anyone, I have had in the history of humanity no idea of anyone, wait, wait, anyone who has been happier than I, and luckier, euphoric, this is a priori true, isn't it?, drunk with uninterrupted enjoyment, *haec omnia uidemus et* bona sunt ualde, *quoniam tu ea uides in nobis,** but that if, beyond any comparison, I have remained, me the counterexample of myself, as constantly sad, deprived, destitute, disappointed, impatient, jealous, desperate, negative and neurotic, and that if in the end the two certainties do not exclude one another for I am

1984: return to his kindergarten in El-Biar (with Martine, his niece).

here is never simply to make a list of signifiers, we that wantedshould of course have to associate to this the "simili-transcendental" of *Glas* (GL, 244), everything that comes under the simulacrum, and therefore fiction, literature, and, little by little, *all* the terms and turns that have detained us up until now. In this respect, it would perhaps be justifiable to privilege one local reference to a "*quasi-natural* production" (F, xxviii): the "quasi-" always tells us something about a nature's dissimulatory exit from itself (cf. EC, 9).

The term "transcendental" first of all calls up a Kantian conception of philosophy: the point would be to elucidate the conditions of possibility of experience. Since Kant, it has been possible to contest the universality of the structures discovered in this way, especially to set against Kant the historicity of the transcendental domain. Thus Foucault can elaborate a notion of historical a priori, and Habermas his own notion of the quasi-transcendental. One can also change the support of these structures, moving from the rational subject to language, for example: this is what justifies Ricoeur's description of structuralism as a Kantianism without a

sure they are as true as each other, simultaneously and from every angle, then I do not know how still to risk the slightest sentence without letting it fall to the ground in silence, to the ground its lexicon, to the ground its grammar and its geologics, how to say anything other than an interest as passionate as it is disillusioned for these things, language, literature, philosophy, something other than the impossibility of saying still, as I am here, me, I sign.

* "All these things we see, and they are very good; for, Thou seest them in us" (XIII, xxxiv, 49).

subject. This gives rise to an exchange between philosophy and "human sciences," and even to the latter's pretension to absorb philosophy. This is not how Derrida proceeds: we have seen him put the human sciences, be it linguistics, rhetoric, anthropology, or psychoanalysis, through severe examinations that it would be difficult not to call philosophical, at least in part. If Derrida undeniably contests the transcendental privilege, and this is the very object of deconstruction (cf. GL, 156), this is not in the name of the "positivities" recognized by the human sciences, which fall constitutively short of transcendental questioning—in a moment we shall see according to what law—but in the name (without a name, as we have constantly verified) if not of an ultra-transcendental, then at least of a passage through the transcendental (cf. GR, 60–2).

There is no doubt that if we were trying to find predecessors for Derrida in his relationship with philosophy, the name of Heidegger would immediately impose itself. Derrida says very early on that nothing of what he does would have been possible without Hei-

51 I am no longer far from touching land at last, she is watching, she is waiting for me to have finished, she is waiting for me to go out, we will leave together, she was holding my hand, we were going up by the route known as the little wood and I began to invent the simulacrum of an illness, as I have all my life long, to avoid going back to nursery school, a lie that one day I forgot to recall, whence the tears when later in the afternoon, from the playground, I caught sight of her through the fence, she must have been as beautiful as a photograph, and I reproached her with leaving me in the world, in the hands of others, basically with having forgotten that I was sup-

degger (M, 22ff.; POS, 9–10). We know that the name "deconstruction," which quickly took off both in the United States and in France—but without Derrida's ever assuming it as the name of a method or even of a theory (cf. EO, 85–6)—to name "what Derrida does," is in part a translation of Heidegger's *Destruktion.* For the question of time, for example, every reader of *Kant and the Problem of Metaphysics* sees very quickly the relations between Heidegger's "repetition" of Kant's temporal syntheses as a function of the transcendental imagination and what Derrida puts forward about *différance.*

See especially M, 48ff. Derrida invokes the transcendental or productive imagination more often than one might think on a first reading: from "Force and Signification" (WD, 3ff.) to *Psyché* (EN, 122; PIO, 57–8) and *Memoires* (MEM, 64), it appears as an important focus of his thought. As the transcendental imagination is also, in Kant, the place of production of the schemata, which alone insure the communication between intuition and concept, and therefore between the empirical and the transcendental, then we sense its im-

posed to be ill so as to stay with her, just, according to our very alliance, one of our 59 conjurations without which I am nothing, accusing her in this way of letting me be caught up again by school, all those cruel mistresses, and since then I've always been caught up by school, while she was smiling at me in silence for her capacities for silence and amnesia are what I share best, no arguing with that, that's what they can't stand, that I say nothing, never anything tenable or valid, no thesis that could be refuted, neither true nor false, not even, not seen not caught, it is not a strategy but the violence of the void through which God goes to earth to death in me, the geologic program, me, I've never been able to contradict myself, that's saying, so I write,

portance for our concerns here. We can also note the remark from *Margins* which identifies the transcendental imagination as a place where Hegel's critique of Kant looks most like a confirmation of Kant (M, 78–81), and especially the remark in "Plato's Pharmacy" which makes the *pharmakon* into the *milieu* of differentiation in general (what we have here tended to call "the same"), and affirms that in this respect it would be "analogous" to what philosophy will later call the transcendental imagination (D, 126). This is not without its links to *chora*, and implies still that from a certain point of view the whole of Derrida is already "in" Plato (for those who read ... like Derrida, and therefore do not believe that we really know what "in Plato" means), as his ghost or his double (MEM, 64 links the transcendental imagination and the ghost; cf. EC, 17–18): we should need a quite different history of philosophy to account for these relations.

More generally, the quasi-concept of the trace elaborated by Derrida occupies a position that it has been possible to think is identical with that of Being in Heidegger, which would come down to making *différance*

that's the word, convenient for forgetting, one can always come and go, go off ahead light of foot, I am still so young, all I'm saying is nursery school, *la maternelle,* the unforgettable power of my discourses hangs on the fact that they grind up everything including the mute ash whose name alone one then retains, scarcely mine, all that turning around nothing, a Nothing in which God reminds me of him, that's my only memory, the condition of all my fidelities, the name of God in the ash of Elijah, an evening of rest that never arrives, seven days after the 52-week year, Domine deus, pacem da nobis—omnia enim praestitisti nobis—*pacem quietis, pacem sabbati, pacem sine uespera* [...]. *Dies autem septimus sine uespera est nec habet occasum,*★ and as

into a repetition of the ontico-ontological difference, in spite of what Derrida himself says about it (GR, 22–3). In spite of the reservations or at least the questions with respect to Heidegger expressed throughout his work, from what is said in the *Grammatology* (GR, 20–24) and in the same pages of *Positions* that recall the debt to Heidegger (POS, 9–10, cf. 54–6), through "Ousia and Grammè" and "The Ends of Man" (M, 31–67, 111–36), to *"Geschlecht"* (G1 passim), arriving (provisionally) at *Of Spirit* (OS, especially 7–13), it is true that any reading that wanted at all costs to establish Derrida's originality—which is not our primary concern, because we doubt the relevance and coherence of any such project—would sometimes have difficulty in separating them, or would have to resign itself to seeing Derrida as a sort of perfected Heidegger: whence for example a reading of *Of Spirit* that sees in it simply a still Heideggerian deconstruction of a term (*Geist*) inadequately deconstructed by Heidegger himself. It is undeniable that there is a Derrida who is a defender and illustrator of Heidegger, but this is especially true, we think, when the point is to enforce re-

I say nothing, well-known program, I write to alienate, drive mad all those that I will have alienated by not saying anything, I am just to confide in them the memory of me who am in for nobody, since a date immemorial, since I've been scared, me, in the evening, of the fear I inspire, fear of the deathly silence that resounds at my every word, *"even if—Elie were to be written as a novel in 4 columns, at 4 discursive levels (cf. above... although I gave up the 4 notebooks at least a month ago), no doubt I should not make the distinction apparent in typographical of topographical form, from one sentence to the next of the apparently continuous tissue but according to strict internal criteria, the 4 breaths relaying each other"* (9–4–81).

spect for the complexity of Heidegger's thought against hasty and inadequate appropriations or critiques, which has led certain just as hasty readers to make Derrida into a "Heideggerian," albeit a "dissident" rather than an "orthodox" one (cf. MEM, 221), and thus to suspect him of guilty or embarrassing complicity as to Heidegger's political commitments. This structure, which one might be tempted to believe was freshly set up by the very recent "Heidegger affair," has in fact informed a certain reception of Derrida from the start (cf. POS, 55–6).

We do not believe that that is the right way to approach these problems. Everything we have said about reading, tradition, translation, and the signature ought to prevent us from envisaging these questions in this naively historicist form. Quite apart from the fact that Derrida's readings are never simply confirmations or simply critiques, if we wanted to establish Derrida's originality with respect to Heidegger we should have *already* to be in possession of the truth about Heidegger, or think we were, which would be difficult to do without passing through the readings carried out by

*"O Lord God, grant us peace—for Thou hast provided all things for us—the peace of rest, the peace of the Sabbath, the peace without an 'evening' [...] Now the seventh day is without an 'evening' and has no setting" (XIII, xxxv, xxxvi, 50, 51).

Derrida himself. Heidegger's originality would thus be in part produced by Derrida, who would be in turn one of Heidegger's originalities. But the paradoxes of self and other would let us suspect that Derrida's proximity to Heidegger implies an alterity that is more important than in the case of any other thinker. Derrida is right up against Heidegger. Little by little, and of course with variations of accent, one ought to be able to extent the form of this argument to all the authors of the tradition, which immediately disqualifies the form of the question, and helps us to understand how Derrida could write that we are perhaps on the eve of Platonism, without that implying any return to the sophists (D, 109–10).

So in spite of these possible reference points, then, it is not through historical inquiry that we shall try here to understand the "quasi-transcendental," which, on the other hand, following a reversal we have already seen at work, might make us understand something about the historicity of any historical inquiry. We have seen that in Derrida what makes possible immediately

52 *"Supposing that—*Glas *or* The Postcard *have a 'selector,' a principle or choice or discrimination (thematic or formal), for example the two columns,* Gl., *or the figure* 7, *etc., in* The Book of Elie, *on the other hand, would the principle of selection, without which no book, nor any form, would appear, not be the principle of selection itself, circumcision as retrenchment, mark, determination, exclusion, whence the impossibility of writing, whence the interminable reflection, whence the infinite delay, whereas, haven't I said this enough, what interests me is not the principle of selection in general but this idiom that makes or lets me write... if even—"* (9–4–81), and I am interested by, interested in the selection or election of me, let us say Jacob,

makes impossible the purity of the phenomenon made possible. What allows a letter to be sent and received, a postal network, simultaneously makes the nonarrival of this letter possible too. What makes a performative possible (iterability) means that a performative can always be "unhappy." What allows language to be transmitted in a tradition opens meaning to a dissemination which always threatens any transmission of a thought. What makes the statement of the *cogito* possible also makes possible its repetition after my death or in my madness. This last example will help us here. Only the ideality of the sign "I" allows the movement of transcendence with respect to the "I" stating it: this ideality depends on the repetition which implies the possibility of my death as a figure of my necessary finitude. Having thus "produced" the transcendental, philosophy puts death in with the empirical and the accidental, whereas it was necessary to the production of what now secondarizes it. This is what we were earlier calling a *necessary* or *essential* possibility. This analysis does not ruin the transcendental by bringing it back down

only by curiosity, not of me, for me or by me, but, as ought to go without saying, by the very thing, the other, then, which would have chosen, blessed or cursed me, chosen at birth, at the moment when the youngest son that I am did not come after the eldest, René Abraham, but the second, Paul Moïse, dead I know not how or from what a few months before I was conceived, I who was thus like the twin brother of a dead one who must have died rue Saint-Augustin in Algiers where I must have been brought myself a few weeks after my birth, July 15 in a villa in El-Biar, during the holidays, during a burning hot summer, for don't go thinking that Saint Augustine whom elsewhere I ven-

to a harsh reality of death, but contaminates it with the contact of what it attempted to keep at bay, whereas it lived only on the basis of that keeping at bay.

We thus have a double movement which, when elucidated, will help us to understand what struck us at the outset, namely an apparent tension in Derrida between apparently immodest assertions embracing the whole of metaphysics and a minute attention paid to the finest grain of the texts read. We are now in a position to explain the coherence of these two movements. If one says that finitude is in some sense the condition of transcendence, one makes it into the condition of possibility of transcendence, and one thus puts it into a transcendental position with respect to transcendence. But the ultra-transcendental thus produced puts into question the very structure of transcendence, which it pulls back down onto a feature that transcendence would like to consider as empirical. If we formalize this situation to the extreme, we produce a proposition ("the empirical is the transcendental of the transcendental [of the empirical]") which is readable only if its terms undergo a displacement from one occurrence to

erate and envy, would invade me in this way right up to the Pacific between Laguna Beach and Santa Monica if I were not obsessed, in the night of my learned ignorance, by the non-knowledge of what happened in the rue Saint-Augustin between 1929 and 1934, the date at which we came back to El-Biar, this time to set up home there permanently until 1962, on the edge of an Arab quarter and a Catholic cemetery, at the end of the Chemin du Repos, just before the birth of my sister Janine Félicité, and when the jealousy of the surviving twin began to be unleashed in me, fixing itself onto the elder, basically the double of the unknown false twin, so *that* one was not dead,

another, which entails the deconstruction of the primary opposition, and the "anasemic translation" of its terms. This deconstruction moves toward a comprehension of any discourse ruled by the empirical/transcendental opposition and everything that goes along with it: but this movement, which would traditionally be represented as a movement upward, even beyond what has up until now been recognized as transcendental, is in fact, or at the same time, a movement "downward," for it is the empirical and the contingent, themselves necessarily displaced, in this movement, toward the singular event and the case of chance, which are found higher than the high, higher than height, in height's falling. *L'érection tombe.* "Quasi-transcendental" names what results from this displacement, by maintaining as legible the trace of a passage through the traditional opposition, and by giving this opposition a radical uncertainty which we shall call "undecidability" on condition that we take a few supplementary precautions.

We must not fall into the trap of believing that undecidability would at last be the right word for what we

*intendi considerationem in eos qui gemini nascuntur, quorum plerique ita post inuicem funduntur ex utero, ut paruum ipsum temporis interuallum, quantamlibet uim in rerum natura habere contendant, colligi tamen humana obseruatione non possit litterisque signari omnino non ualeat, quas mathematicus inspecturus est, ut uera pronuntiet. et non erunt uera, quia easdem litteras inspiciens eadem debuit dicere de Esau et de Iacob: sed non eadem utrique acciderunt,** from this I always got the feeling of being an excluded favorite, of both father and mother, not excluded and therefore distinguished like all favorites, not cloven or ambiguous but excluded *and* favorite, at two juxtaposed moments, and precisely like the elder, invulnerable

are trying to say here, and that it would moreover have the advantage of communicating with a mathematical modernity and thus legitimate deconstruction in everybody's eyes. As early as his first book, Derrida shows with Husserl how Gödel's undecidability remains in a relation that must be described as dialectical with the decidability it respects and maintains as a horizon (OG, 53n.48, 56): in *Positions*, Derrida emphasizes the analogical value of this name (POS, 42–3); later he distinguishes between two forms of undecidability, themselves in an undecidable relation to each other (MEM, 137; PAR, 15; cf. NA, 29, PIO, 55–6, and, more generally, GL 2b, 51a, 127b, 210–11a, 225aff.).

We have already justified, with respect to conceptual history, the fact that we must maintain this legibility of the old conceptuality, to the greater annoyance of conventionalists and revolutionaries. We can draw another version of this justification from the analyses in *Glas*, which will help us to understand why the quasi-transcendental, unlike what happens in Foucault or Habermas, is not to be taken as a historicizing or cul-

and wounded to death before even getting past the first cape, the very same evening, I mean seven days old, and it's still going on, read the papers.

*"I directed my consideration to those who are born as twins. In many cases they proceed so close upon one another from the womb that the small time interval (however much importance in the nature of things people may attribute to this) can hardly be grasped by human observation and cannot be registered in those symbols which the astrologers would study in order to foretell true events. Yet, they will not be true, for a man looking

turalizing relativization of the transcendental. Let us imagine that one attempt to criticize, as is often the case, transcendental discourse in the name of the concrete realities of life, by saying for example that this discourse is an attempt at legitimation on the part of one class (or its representatives) trying to maintain its concrete domination over another class. And so one would say that the transcendental discourse is in reality the ideological product of an historical situation whose truth would be found, for example, in the economy. In doing so, one has quite simply put the economic in a transcendental position without being able to think that fact, given that this very position is supposed, in this transcendental explanation, to be no more than an ideological effect that the analysis ought to denounce. This is the structure which produces all the—insoluble—problems of the traditional "left intellectual" and his infinite bad conscience, which, when exhibited, turns into the self-righteousness of immediate legitimacy. One can state as a law that any attempt to explain transcendental effects by invoking history must presuppose the historicity of that same history as the very

at the same symbols would have had to say the same things for Esau and Jacob. But, the same events did not befall both men" (VII, vi, 10).

53 *"Although I haven't written any of it yet, I already know what's missing from this book of Elie, and that's the dedication, but when the dedicatee, man or woman, appears, the book will already have been written, no point anymore"* (8–16–81), so I have never found the time to write, when there are only seven more circumferences to go round, one week before the day with no

transcendental which this system of explanation will never be able to comprehend. This is what we earlier called transcendental contraband, and it cannot resolve the paradox (*plus de . . .*) according to which it is the very concept to which appeal is made to explain everything that will never be understood in the explanation. This is basically the stumbling block of any empiricism whatsoever. No doubt the worse naivetés in this respect affect sociological "explanations" of philosophy. From this point of view, discourses like those of Foucault and Habermas—which recognize that one cannot do without transcendental analysis but which still want to limit that analysis by invoking a certain historical periodization of the transcendental itself—no doubt avoid the worst contradictions, but deprive themselves at the same stroke of the means to understand the historicity of those periods, and appeal rather feebly to diverse motors of history as a way out. There is nothing surprising about this apparently paradoxical situation after what we have said about the law which can only establish the legality of its own case by exposing its titles to a more general law. Every law "finally"

evening, and today, April 15, 1990, rainy Easter Sunday, like at the end of *Glas,* when I have just telephoned Nice and learned that there's "nothing new," she can only survive, she is "calm," she "is eating," although the state of one of her bedsores has again got worse, I wonder, having thought I was dying last night and already set it all up, the discovery and return or not of the body, the papers and the rumors, when in truth I began this voyage, this year, this year's turn which comes back on itself without any revolution being certain in me as far as I know, at what moment, were it only for a moment, I wait for the moment which is looking for me, the decision deciding my life without me, I began to "initialize," as Macintosh says, not only

communicates with an absolute out-law which would be in a "transcendental" position with respect to any given legality, and which we have called the gift of the law, or the promise. The point is not at all to endorse the structure whereby "regional" disciplines necessarily appeal for their legitimacy to a last instance—i.e. philosophy—even thought of as "fundamental ontology," but to show how any attempt to unseat philosophy from a classically defined region can only replace in the final instance something which will play the part of philosophy without having the means to do so. Thinking one can do without philosophy, one will in fact be doing bad philosophy: this entirely classical philosophical argument (WD, 152, 287–8) cannot be refuted without the deconstruction of the general structure, and such a deconstruction is therefore no longer philosophy, without for all that falling into the empiricism that philosophy can always see in it (GR, 161–2).

We shall say still more strictly, following *Glas,* that every system excludes or expels something which does not let itself be thought within the terms of the system,

these disks, with names as diverse and as unarbitrary as Santa Monica, Angels, Lag 90, Word, etc., but the trellis of the periphrases for them to have begun to float onto the screen, calling me to fish out the aleatory in a rigorous order even if you don't understand it at all yet, caught up as you are in these pacific algae around the invisible knot, unbeknownst to me, as though the screen gave me to see my own blindness and suddenly I look at this gray and slightly domed surface as the opaque eye of a blind man who will never leave me in peace, because his light continuous snoring tells me that I will never put into a "table" of "letters," impossible letters, the jealousy both of Esau and Jacob, of Moses and Abraham, double of doubles, the one dedicated to

and lets itself be fascinated, magnetized, and controlled by this excluded term, its transcendental's transcendental.

> This excluded term could, for example, be madness; this would be the other side of Foucault's work, and one can say that the mad project of exceeding the totality so as to think it is what Derrida attempts to sign with the word *déjà*. One might be tempted to think that what is driving our own work here is the still madder project of exceeding this *déjà* itself.

The reading work carried out by Derrida consists in the location of these excluded terms or these remains that command the excluding discourse: the supplement (masturbation or writing) in Rousseau (OG, 203–34); the index in Husserl (SP, 27ff.); the *parergon* or vomit in Kant (EC, 21–5; TP, 44–94), etc.

THE CLOSURE

This situation has given rise to two types of more or less inevitable misunderstandings that explain in part

the other, *inueni haec ibi et non manducaui. placuit enim tibi, domine, auferre* opprobrium *diminutionis ab Iacob, ut* maior *seruiret* minori, et uocasti gentes in hereditatem tuam,* it remains to be understood of time, and of the time of writing, i.e. the inheritance of the last will of which nothing has yet been said, I'm sure of that, that touches the nerve of that for which one writes when one does not believe in one's own survival nor in the survival of anything at all, when one writes for the present but a present that is *made,* you hear, in the sense in which SA wants to *make* truth, only out of the return upon itself of that refused, *denied,* survival, refusals and denials attested by the writing itself, the last will of the word of each word, where my writing enjoys this

the strong positive and negative reactions that Derrida has always provoked among his readers. These reactions are produced by the impossibility of not seeing that deconstruction is no longer exactly philosophy, without for all that being another discourse philosophically locatable as "regional." For on the one hand, one can see in this work a "postphilosophical" operation which, condemning itself to note the "closure" of metaphysics, has no possible occupation left other than that of rifling through the dustbins of philosophy to get out of them the meager nourishment that the tradition had not managed to swallow. Which is why Derrida does not "do" philosophy, but "reads" philosophy, philosophy on this view having nothing better to do. On the other hand, one can consider that, philosophy having never done other than appropriate what previously was outside it, all deconstruction does is accomplish philosophy in its most traditional aspects. Does not Derrida himself open *Margins* on a description of philosophy proceeding in this way (M, x; cf. 177)? We can tighten up this alternative by saying that the first option would make Derrida into the anti-Hegel par ex-

self-privation, exulting in giving itself as a present, before witnesses, the mortality that inheritance primarily means, for *je me donne ici la mort* can be said only in a language made a present to me by its colonization of Algeria in 1830, a century before me, *I don't take my life, mais je me donne la mort.*

*"I found these things there, but I did not partake of them. For, it pleased Thee, O Lord, to remove from Jacob the reproach of his minority, in order that the older might serve the younger, and Thou didst call heathens unto thy Inheritance" (VII, ix, 15).

cellence, and the second the direct legatee of Hegel. Having chosen one's side of this divide, one can of course praise or criticize Derrida for what one thinks he is doing, which gives a matrix of four possibilities of reception which would accommodate most of the reactions Derrida has provoked up until now. The facility with which one can produce arguments on both sides recalls Kant's antinomies (and the presentation of some of Derrida's texts in two columns is not foreign to this reference), and suggests at the same stroke that we cannot remain content with this. It goes without saying after what we have just been arguing about quasi-transcendentality that we will not get out of this situation by sharpening the distinction between phenomena and things in themselves, for this distinction is a form of what quasi-transcendentality casts into doubt. Our problem has been constantly to stand *between* or short of, in the milieu of differentiation, and this is what we must try to formalize further: so we will not say that Derrida answers to one rather than to the other of these descriptions, *nor* that he answers to one *and* the other, *nor* that he answers to *neither* one nor the

54 Her triumph of life—perhaps I shall see her still alive, on my return from California, we exchanged a few words on the telephone, between Laguna Beach and Nice, Sunday, April 8th, I know less than ever what she is saying, hearing, thinking or feeling, what she recognizes without recognizing of me speaking to you basically asking myself the same question about you, no?, nobody will ever know what is happening between us, nor how I can be sure that you will not understand much of what you will nonetheless have dictated to me, inspired me with, asked of me, ordered from me, I am as deprived of understanding what is going on on the other side, her side, as I am of understanding Hebrew, for I'm reaching the end without

other. The fact that we have to double up the neither/nor here (the form of our proposition is "neither (either a or b) nor (a and b) nor (neither a nor b)," which we can formalize further as $\sim ((a \wedge b) \text{ v } (\sim a \sim b))$, or, to bring out in what way it would be a "contradiction," $\sim((\sim(\sim a \sim b)) \text{ v } (\sim a \sim b))$ (read as "it is false that of the propositions 'at least one of a and b' and 'neither a nor b,' one is true"), would be, precisely, the mark, in a propositional logic, of the questioning of opposition and negation in their philosophical versions, and one index among others that one cannot formulate everything in a logic, but at most in a *graphic*.

The *first version*, which would tend to assimilate Derrida to the "postmodern," rests on a hasty assimilation of "closure" (in the expression "closure of metaphysics") and "end." We should say first quite simply that this is a reading error to be corrected, and refer to the passages in which the necessity of a distinction between closure and end is clearly asserted: as Derrida has done on several occasions (GR, 4, 14; POS, 13; SP, 102; WD, 250, 300). And we shall also insist on the complexity of the idea of "closure," which should not be

ever having read Hebrew, see someone who multiplies dancing and learned circumvolutions in a foreign language for the simple reason that he must turn around his own unknown grammar, Hebrew, the unreadability he knows he comes from, like his home, but *"will anyone ever know which of the two of us is the more vulnerable, the French grammar of this sentence marking no gender, and that's how it gets into the shy retrenchment of the frightened animal, he pronounces an atrociously tragic sentence, then makes its quotation marks appear, abandons it to anonymity and puts forward an analysis of it, for example a grammatical analysis, in the most neutral of tones, but the analysis does not close the* Trauerspiel, *it dramatizes all the more, here, for who in the end is more vulnerable than the other to*

imagined as a circular limit surrounding a homogeneous field: that would be a metaphysical thinking of the closure, which would on this view separate an inside from an outside, and would facilitate the analogical transfer of this inside/outside onto before/after, which is none other than the confusion we are trying to avoid here: the closure is rather to be thought as an invaginated form that brings the outside back inside and on the contrary facilitates the understanding of the Derridean always-already (cf. M, 24, and especially RM, 14). It is certain that Derrida does not intend to assimilate closure and end of metaphysics.

But now the *second* possible reading thinks it can see its way. For how does this closure without exteriority differ from a, say, Hegelian version of philosophy, which is not content to do critique in the Kantian sense by establishing the limits which define a rational use of thought or language, but also wants to incorporate the beyond implied in any position of a limit in general, to avoid remaining subject to the infinite declared to be unknowable (this is the principle of Hegel's critique of Kant)? According to this reading, the accomplice of de-

analysis?" (9–3–81), before speech, among the Jews alone, there is circumcision, the sacred tongue will have slipped over me as though over a polished stone, perhaps, but I bury the deep things, I must have pretended to learn Hebrew, I lied to them about language and school, I pretended to learn Hebrew so as to read it without understanding it, like the words of my mother today, at one moment, in 1943, with a Rabbi from the rue d'Isly, just before the *bar-mitzvah,* which they also called the "communion," at the moment when French Algeria in its Governor-General, without the intervention of any Nazi, had expelled me from school and withdrawn my French citizenship, the undertaking of Décremieux thus being annuled, a decree less old than

construction is not the postmodern announcement of the end, but Hegelian philosophy that the postmodern would thus only confirm by what it thought was its opposition. By trying to reconnoiter the margins of philosophy and to bring the new human sciences into its domain of influence, one would on this view be simply repeating or accomplishing Hegelianism. If one tries to find what is the excluded term of the postmodern debate, for example, as the very condition of that debate according to quasi-transcendental logic, then one reintegrates that excluded term into the inside of the closure, and one is still and forever doing metaphysics. One would thus suspect deconstruction, under its radical appearances, of being no more than a complicated strategy to be able to do philosophy (idealist philosophy, what's more) in a fundamentally conservative fashion. Under the appearance of a contestation of Hegelian philosophy, deconstruction would have found the means to play an interminable game with it, a game that one must above all not win, on pain of having to take note of the end of any "foundationalist" philosophy and the uselessness of continu-

my grandfathers, it is true, Abraham and Moses, so that thus expelled, I became the outside, try as they might to come close to me they'll never touch me again, they masculine or feminine, and I did my "communion" by fleeing the prison of all languages, the sacred one they tried to lock me up in without opening me to it, the secular they made clear would never be mine, but this ignorance remained the chance of my faith as of my hope, of my taste even for the "word," the taste for letters, *nam si primo sanctis tuis litteris informatus essem et in earum familiaritate obdulcuisses mihi et post in illa uolumina incidissem, fortasse aut abripuissent me a solidamento pietatis, aut si...*★

ing indefinitely to call it into question. In spite of its apparent actuality, deconstruction would be merely a ruse with a view to legitimate an antiquarian interest for the history of philosophy. Not that one should simply turn the page of philosophy, but one can do some philosophy, outside this stifling library in which you'd like to lock us up. Analytic philosophy, for example, asks and resolves serious problems in short, clear, and clean articles, without getting lost in these quotations and commentaries, and it can pride itself on real progress in understanding without making a fuss about it.

We have already invoked as a "definition" of deconstruction the effort to interrupt the Hegelian *Aufhebung* (see again POS, 40–1). This is not done by "forgetting" Hegel, for he does not forget us (WD, 251). We also know that direct opposition to Hegel only fuels his dialectical machinery, and that we must therefore proceed according to a nonoppositional difference. Whence the impression of an interminable game, and whence too the vulnerability to Hegelianization of any attempt at a rapid description of deconstruction, in-

* "For, if I had been first informed by Thy holy writings and if Thou hadst grown dear to me through my familiarity with them, and if I had later fallen upon those other books, perhaps they would have torn me away from a firm foundation of piety; or, if..." (VII, xx, 26).

cluding by Derrida himself. But to see in that a complicity, whereas analytic philosophy, for example, would have escaped that complicity, is not a valid consequence. The point, in deconstruction, is not to reintegrate remains into philosophy, but, by rendering explicit the quasi-transcendental conditions even of speculative philosophy, to introduce a radical nondialectizable alterity into the heart of the same. What can the Hegelian dialectic not think while finding in it its condition of possibility? We have already dryly indicated that we should not indicate as a response the proper name of any entity, but that "the gift" might be the nickname we need here.

The direct analysis of Hegel is found essentially in three texts: "From Restricted to General Economy" (WD, 251–77), "The Pit and the Pyramid" (M, 71–108), and the left-hand column of *Glas*. As is only to be expected, the quasi-transcendental we are looking for is differently named in these texts, according to the singularity of the crossing: in the first case, it would be, at Bataille's side, the laughter of a sovereignty without mastery; in the second, Egypt and a machine function-

55 He prayed to the sun with his hands behind his back, at the approach of the sacrifice as much as of its interruption, his hand raised over me, there are several of them around the *mohel,* they are looking between my legs, they are calling me and I can't hear anything, the women are in the other room, it's my birthday, of myself I can see only a birthmark, that stain on the right eye, *"but in Elie, everything would be said in the first person, I, I, I and from one sentence to the next, even within the same sentence, it would never be the same I, whence the unreadability, unless there is a code, for example the tense of the verb, or another feature, grammatical or not, to guide the writing and allow the attentive or hardworking reader to reconstitute the scenography of narrators, as if one*

ing without assignable goal. Let us also pass over all the moments located in *Glas* when the *Aufhebung* runs the risk of bogging down, in the position of African fetishism (especially GL, 207a), in the figure of Antigone within the dialectic of the family and the ethical community (G1, 142aff.), and, massively, in the position of the Jew in the dialectic with the Greek, supposedly sublated in Christianity.

THE JEW

Let us pause here before trying to formulate these relations more precisely. Our decision to privilege the term "quasi-transcendental" has called up a Kantian filiation that we have wanted to complicate but not simply deny. Now Hegel's philosophy is not only a sustained critique of Kant's thought, but a thought which, when it comes to the moral law at least, puts Kant in the position of the Jew. Not only is Derrida Jewish, but he follows these moments very closely in Hegel's text, and this situation cannot fail to engage with something too

could get across lines of different colors for example from 1 to 5, from 2 to 3, from 4 to 7, from 6 to 8, etc." (8–16–81), and I tell myself this morning in the mirror who are you talking to, I've missed you, you've missed me, there are still a few days to be spent here before passing from life to death, hers or mine, I have begun to enter old age and see my eyebrows turn white without having known the writing of conversion, that convent that the Ruzyne prison made me dream of for a few hours, in Prague, between Christmas and New Year 1982, when in a terrified jubilation, before seeing the infernal cell, before that Czech officer had screamed and threatened me, hand raised, before putting on the striped pyjamas, I thought that at last, at last, I was going to be

with respect to Heidegger and Levinas. Nothing is symmetrical here, but we must note the fact that Hegel places Kant in the position of the Jew, the better to criticize his thought, and Levinas (with respect to whom Derrida says he never has any objection [ALT, 74]) puts himself in the position of the Jew to criticize Heidegger's thought. Certain readers have noted a certain stylistic family resemblance between Derrida's writings and the interminable commentaries of the Talmudists. We too may have facilitated a "Jewish" reading of his thought by insisting above on the law which is not given to understanding, but that there is, to be negotiated, without any possibility of absolution. It is easy to imagine a scenario which would appropriate Derrida for a Jewish thought in some way opposed to a tyranny of the Greek *logos,* for a thinking of the law opposed to (or at least unassimilable by) a thought of Being, for a thought of justice which would not be (subordinated to) a thought of truth, a passability which would not be a mastery, etc. Such a schema, with everything that might be satisfying about it, would stumble somewhere on the relation of Derrida to Heidegger, which

able to rehearse, and then write, write for years in pencil on a clean whitewood political prisoners' table, I see the film of my whole life, henceforth, ten years after my birth, and for ten years now, framed by two sets of bars, too heavy, metal interdictions, the expulsion and the incarceration, out of school and into prison, that's what I return to every day, that's what I'm becoming, that's what I was, that's where I write, each time caught up again by one and freed from the other, more locked up in one than in the other, but which, each time from the feeling of an illegible accident, of a wound as virtual, as unmemorable as it is undecipherable to the fortuitous victim of the modern sacrifice which would give me space, to me, irreplaceably,

one might be tempted to describe as aberrant, or even pathological. It is certain that this type of scenario informs certain recent reactions to the Heidegger and de Man affairs, and what some people have seen as a quite perverse refusal on Derrida's part to decide, condemn, pass a judgment without appeal.

We think that these are simplifications. Let us look briefly at *Glas,* on Hegel, Kant, and the Jews. The Jew for Hegel remains under the sign of the cut: cut from maternal nature after the flood (GL, 37aff.), cut off from and in opposition to the community and love with Abraham, condemning himself to wandering in the desert outside any fixed domicile, marking this cut with the sign of circumcision (41aff.) to remain attached to the cut itself, subject as a finite being to the infinite power of a jealous God from whom he cuts himself. In order to insure his own mastery, the Jew is mastered by the infinite he cannot understand. The cut, which finds it simulacrum in circumcision, leaves the Jew subordinated to an infinite he does not understand, and therefore he remains entirely plunged in the finite, in matter. The Jew is alienated, in a relation not with a

where they got me, where they will never get me, they masculine or feminine, the irreplaceable mission no longer leaving you, any more than here, the choice between the aleatory and the calculable, myself finding myself where I am, on this day, only by no longer trying to rediscover myself according to some regular and geological relation between chance and necessity, up to the other to invent me, I'm crying for having lost the irreplaceable with hands behind back, not yet sacrificed but already tied up, and I weep the very tears of the unique, et euacuatum est chirografum, *quod erat contrarium nobis? hoc illae litterae non habent. non habent illae paginae uultum pietatis huius, lacrimas confessionis,* sacrificium *tuum...*★

transcendent truth but with a transcendence which takes the (formless) form of the command and the incomprehensible law—which cannot therefore be rational—but which one undergoes without mediation in its letter and not its spirit (51aff.). Now Kant, structurally, occupies the position of the Jew in Hegel's system (34a). Autonomy according to Kant, for example, obedience to the "thou must" of the moral law, would merely interiorize the absolute heteronomy of the Jewish God, would not then be true autonomy, but, on its own terms, pathological (58a): like the Jews, Kant remains caught in the oppositional thought of the understanding, spread out between a formalism of the law and an empiricism of events. By claiming to fix the limits of what a finite subjectivity can know, Kant disallows himself the ability to think the infinite, whose slave he would thus remain.

One sees how one might be tempted to take Kant's part against Hegel here, and assimilate what we have said of the law to this Jewish setup. One would thus have gone beyond the two readings that have just tempted us: Derrida would be neither the Kant of the

*"... and the handwriting was canceled, which was against us. Those writings do not contain this. Those pages do not show the countenance of this piety, the tears of confession, Thy sacrifice" (VII, xxi, 27).

56 The bedsores are opening again, my sister tells me on the telephone, especially the one on the *sacrum,* I feel everyone's ambiguous impatience, raw guilt around this sign of life in which the inside still appears and the blood protesting and the skin which does not want finally to close on its silence, like a clean shroud, like an eyelid of sleep, like in that dream last

Aufklärung, nor the Hegel who absorbs everything into philosophy, but in some sense Hegel's Kant, the Jew, condemned to the interminable elaboration of a law always in retreat, mysterious, jealous of its truth that one will never know, but whose traces one will follow, traces that will never give rise to a present perception or to an experience (215a). And by interminably following the traces of an *other* Hegel (of another reading of metaphysics), which says something other than what it says, Derrida, Hegel's shadow or double, would have made him into his doubly mysterious God, who, pretending to show himself in full daylight, would simply hide all the better. In spite of all Hegel's efforts to overcome the cut, Derrida would have insisted on cutting him from himself, cut himself from him, and he therefore remains fascinated, while claiming to show that the fascinated one is Hegel, attached to the very thing he would like to cut himself from. So he tries to show that basically Hegel was never able to get himself out of Judaism. Wishing to make sure of the finite mastery of the letter of philosophy, Derrida would make himself the slave of an infinite that he ad-

night in which I was explaining to Jean-Pierre Vernant, during a private conversation in an underground place, that if he was accusing himself of not being without responsibility for the death of the child, because at its birth he had nipped its neck very gently, this was a way of giving some sense to something that had none, then, half-awake, I understood more clearly the extent to which avowal, even for a crime not committed, simply secretes meaning and order, an intelligibility that arrests, by finally agreeing to confine the asubjective and endless culpability of chaos, the subject agape but its lips finally cut out by the word, M/L., remaining, as subject, the fearful avowal of this

mits he cannot understand. Whence the wandering in the desert (cf. WD, 64–78) of deconstruction which will never announce the truth. Or else, at best (or at worst), Derrida would be in the position of Moses, proposing an unintelligible liberation in so abstract and forced a rhetoric, a writing so artificial and full of ruses that one would say it was a foreign language (GL, 48a). This writing would be like the Jewish tabernacle, a construction of bands, empty inside, signifier without signified, containing nothing at the center (49a).

STRICTION

For Hegel, interior Africa and its fetishism will sublate in the process of religion, the Jew will be sublated in and through the Christian, Antigone in the becoming of ethics. Everything that can appear to be an obstacle to dialectics can be interpreted by the latter according to opposition, and therefore contradiction, and therefore sublation. Whence both the improbability of Hegelian science, and the difficulty of not being already

corruptibility, the subject in truth constituted by the category of this accepted accusation, the hiatus finally circumscribed, edged, the subject configured by the knife of this economy, and the better for it, desirable too, but I think, to confide this to my friends the birds of Laguna Beach on the rock white with their excrement, that having murdered none of my dead brothers, nor my little cousin Jean-Pierre killed by a car, what is called killed, I must have kept myself from these crimes by ruminating my life in them, turned around them to protect my sons from them, like gods, forewarn them even against circumcision, and warned-of suicide, that perfect crime they could still impute to

inscribed within it. And yet, one can still try to link up these remains in a series which will make us understand something more about dialectics without quite entering into it, without being ruled by the *Aufhebung*. This is predicted again by the passage on fetishism, in which interior Africa, in its predialectical status, figures an undecidability: dialectics will interpret the relation between this undecidability and itself in dialectical terms; but one might perhaps interpret this relation as an effect of undecidability—and *this* undecidability would still be in an undecidable relation with sublating dialectics (GL, 210).

One could say the same thing about the Jew (Kant) and Antigone, but also about any moment at all of the dialectic, which thus turns round into the other of itself: it is thus in principle at any moment at all of his analysis that Derrida could have written that the logic of the *Aufhebung* opens to a reading (a rewriting) which says expense and loss rather than exchange and recuperation (GL, 167a). But *this* perpetual possibility is no longer of the order of the dialectic (and would also be,

me, all my prayers, all my tears of love, what I prefer to my life bleeding like the overflow of these murders I carry within myself, the question of me, with respect to which all other questions appear derived, as for example the question remains derisorily secondary of knowing whether I committed them or not, these infanticides, really or not, as the philosophers, jurists and psychoanalysts would say, against the other or against me, in the absence of a girl or in order to spare the sister, for that very purpose, she, the word, the password, our lifelong secret, the inside of the ring, *"you know and that's why I'm running after you, I keep you and look for you, I would like to hide nothing from you,*

for example, the unpredictable laughter of Bataille [WD, 252, 255ff.]).

But it is the sun which furnishes the moment in *Glas* at which these questions are condensed the most intensely. We are in Hegel's philosophy of religion, and we will have in mind what we have just been saying about the Jewish God. At the very beginning of religion, God is the sun: at the end, the fire of absolute light—short of and beyond representation. The first moment would be that of a light without figure, pure element that could be thought to be without negativity, without a shadow. Here, apparently, we have pure expense and gift, play without work, without trace or time. Once more, it is difficult to see why things would not remain like this. How does the dialectic get going or, if one must suppose that it is already going, how is it to understand this moment "before" it that is not even a moment? The dialectic has already shown its resources in our previous "examples," and here it says: for this pure light to be itself in its burning, it must already be other than itself. To *be* loss or expense, it

you are my first letter as Proust says, 'I have sent postcards and you are the first letter I have written,' you my pardoner who knows there's nothing to pardon, and I am your absolved one, you need me as absolved, innocent absolved, you would not love me if I were innocent or guilty, only innocent absolved of a fault which it seemed to me I had committed, before me, when it fell upon me like life itself, like death" (9–6–81), *Et manifestatum est mihi, quoniam bona sunt, quae corrumpuntur.*★

★"It was made manifest to me that it is because things are good that they can be corrupted" (VII, xii, 18).

must be *kept*, must keep itself as what it is, keep its loss, be its own keeping, therefore be other than itself, become its opposite. If the loss must keep itself in order to be loss, it is no longer pure loss, it loses itself as loss. This is negativity, the shadow that allows history to begin. The pure gift of pure light *binds* itself to be the gift that it is, and that therefore it is no longer, from the moment that it is bound. The original fire that burns without being must also burn *itself* as fire in order to become what it is in this auto-destruction. The fire burns but must burn itself as pure fire in order to burn still. Even if one is determined to think in this way what precedes in some sense what is, what allows what is to be, one cannot *hold* to it without allowing into being what one claims escapes it as its origin (see too WD, 246, on Artaud). Philosophy, as ontology, science of being, is indebted to this gift that it cannot think without losing it, but this loss (of loss) was always inscribed in the gift or the loss itself. The gift gives rise to philosophy, and cannot not do so: but losing itself immediately in philosophy, it does not give itself as gift, but as beginning of exchange. The gift gives itself out

57 Whether they expelled me from school or threw me into prison, I always thought the other must have good reason to accuse me, I did not see, I did not even see my eyes, any more than in the past I saw the hand raising the knife above me, but basically they were telling me, that's their very discourse, in the beginning the *logos,* that it was enough to seek, to track down the event by writing backward, never seeing the next step, it was enough to write to prepare the moment when things turn round, the moment at which you will be able to convert and finally see your sacrificer face on, not to accuse him in turn at last, but to make the truth, *"It would be enough to begin with any*

as philosophy, and this is already the simulacrum and the beginning of being. It returns to philosophy by subjecting itself to the return of indebtedness. The binding-itself of the gift which attaches its "there is" to being is stricture (*il y bande, il lia* [GL, 236]), which folds back pure donation into exchange and reappropriation. This striction is not yet an ontological category; it exceeds the ontological in speaking its possibility. It is the matrix (GL, 244a; this would still be *chora* if we were reading Plato) which "produces" the transcendental on the basis of an absolute outside which is immediately folding back into the inside: transcendental (of the transcendental). Quasi-transcendental of all the quasi-transcendentals we have developed. Everything we have tried to say about Derrida's thought is concentrated in the tightening of this striction. It binds, here, the discourse that is trying, in a strangulated way, to have it out with that thought. This is what means that we do not escape philosophy, but also what means that there is no end to philosophy, whose closure just is this more or less loose striction. Striction gives rise to the dialectical negativity it is not yet, but this not-yet is not

old shock, in apparently the most aleatory fashion, and all the rest, yes, would come RUNNING, lovely word, without delay, like some mad thing, and it would not be aleatory, but why, to begin with scenes of guilt in some sense faultless, without any deliberate fault, situations in which the accusation surprises you, and afterward the having-been at fault, even before any reflection, has to be, not taken on board, for that is just impossible, but you have to let yourself be 'charged,' as they say in English, and struggle with that charge, doubtless significant enough to serve later as a paradigm a whole life long, for there is nothing fortuitous in the fact that these scenes play in their Confessions an organizing and abyssal role" (9–6–81), know that I am dying of

yet that of the dialectic. This striction remains heterogeneous to dialectics, as the "examples" we have picked out testify. They all carry the trace of a predialectical striction, the ash of this fire (cf. FC).

BEING AND THE OTHER

We see, then, that Derrida is neither more nor less Hegelian than Kantian. *Glas* and the reading of Hegel no more give us the truth about Derrida than do the other texts, even if it is undeniable that the Hegelian weight bearing on all our thought can give *Glas* a contingent privilege in the formation of Derridean texts. But we went through it only in order the better to return to what was announced above around the figures of the Jew and the Greek, represented here by Levinas and Heidegger. We have already invoked several times the last page of "Force and Signification," which already thinks of writing as a certain feminine alterity in Being. It is indeed very tempting to place this thought of the other on the side of Levinas (having carried out the

shame, but of a shame in which I persevere all the more in that I have nothing to do with it, I'm not admitting anything and yet I am ready to justify or even repeat the very thing I'm being accused of, even tirelessly to provide you with arguments of my own vintage to establish this fault which nonetheless is all Hebrew to me, for I am perhaps not what remains of Judaism, and I would have no trouble agreeing with that, if at least people really wanted to prove it, and we'll have to get up early, at dawn on this day with no evening, for after all but after all what else am I in truth, who am I if I am not what I inhabit and where I take place, *Ich bleibe also Jude,* i.e. today in what remains of Ju-

"correction" about sexual difference we have pointed out), and therefore on the side of a certain "Jewish" thought, whereas Heidegger, in everything that attaches him to the Greek tradition and a certain privilege of Being, would be foreign to this thinking. How is this a simplification?

Let us first pick out, in the last sentence of "Violence and Metaphysics," and the last note called up by the last word of this last sentence, the quotation from Joyce's *Ulysses*: "Woman's reason. Jewgreek is greekjew. Extremes meet" (WD, 153; cf. the oblique reminder of this in GL, 38a). This is the end, all in questions, of a text which already opened on a doubling of the question of the question, and which undertakes, among other things, a defense of the rigor and necessity of Heidegger's thought of Being against Levinas's hasty reading. This whole text attempts to show the incoherence of Levinas's formulation of an absolute alterity, and affirms the unavoidable necessity of speaking alterity in the philosophical language of the Greek *logos*: if Jewish thought is other than Greek thought, it cannot be absolutely external to it, but folded, along

daism to this world, Europe and the other, and in this remainder I am only someone to whom there remains so little that at bottom, already dead as son with the widow, I expect the resurrection of Elijah, and to sort out the interminably preliminary question of knowing how they, the Jews and the others, can interpret circumfession, i.e. that I here am inhabiting what remains of Judaism, there are so few of us and we are so divided, you see, I'm still waiting before taking another step and adding a word, the name from which I expect resurrection—and of my mother, *cum iam secura fieret ex ea parte miseriae meae, in qua me tamquam mortuum sed resuscitandum tibi flebat et feretro cogitationis*

the nonenveloping figure of invagination, into this nonidentical same which has been one of our most constant themes (cf. here WD, 152). Our detour via Hegel and his way of thinking the Jew under the sign of the cut (only to overcome this cut in dialectics, which is the destiny of a thought of difference as cut rather than as stricture [TP, 340]) allows us now to understand that the refusal of absolute separation, the impossibility of thinking, following Levinas, peace in the form of the diaspora of absolutes (WD, 116n.42), does not oblige us to accept the Hegelian logic which would think of the difference between Jew and Greek in the perspective of a (Christian) reconciliation. And already, *Glas* insists on this too, Jew and Greek in Hegel are not different entirely according to the laws of the dialectic (read in series and parallel GL, 45a, 52–3a, 70a, 75aff., 91–2a, 213a), but already rolled up together in forbidden and inevitable analogies.

But to say this is in no way to absorb Levinas into the *logos* with which he must nonetheless compromise, and make of him a Greek in spite of himself. The second text by Derrida on Levinas, already invoked

offerebat, ut diceres filio uiduae: iuuenis, tibi dico, surge, *et reuiuesceret et inciperet loqui et traderes illum matri suae.*★

★"... since she already felt safe in regard to this aspect of my wretchedness, in which she wept for me as for one dead but destined to be restored to life by Thee. She was offering me on the bier of her thoughts, so that thou wouldst say to the son of the widows: 'Young man, I say to thee, arise!' and he would come back to life and begin to speak again and Thou wouldst return him to his mother" (VI, i, 1).

around sexual difference, tries again to formulate this relation in a more precise fashion, under the name of *seriature*. This text will help us to tighten up the thought of stricture, which is still too loose; we are going to follow it very closely, folding certain descriptions of Levinas's writing back onto Derrida himself. For there is in this language of tension, bands, laces (cf. TP, 255–382 passim) the danger of making it difficult to think the event which, in order to be an event, ought to interrupt the continuity which images of force or torsion run the risk of implying. Seriature attempts to name a bond still, but a bond made of interruptions which would be so many events. Derrida indeed proposes to name "interruptions" the moments, thought and enacted by Levinas, in which discourse, deploying its contents or its themes in the continuity of its Said, is cut or torn by the dimension of the Saying, the address, which opens to the other, makes itself responsible for the other in making the other responsible for it. This dimension, heterogeneous to thematization, and that any thematization must presuppose, has clear links with the gift, for example. We provisionally cede the

58 It only happens to me, so it is enough to pivot 5 words, 5 times one word of my language, it only happens to me, and you have the whole of this circumfession, the sieving of the singular events that can dismantle G.'s theologic program, but to offer it to him, for this is a present for him alone, the sigh faced with the repetition compulsion and the destiny neurosis, the *hubris* of the prophet sent off for having had himself assigned a mission whose undecipherable letter arrives only at himself who understands it no better than anyone else, save for that very fact, the despair of the innocent child who is by accident charged with a guilt he knows nothing about, the little

Said to dialectics, which takes up and integrates the rents, the better to show how it must nonetheless presuppose an alterity, its Saying, that it cannot speak as such. Only this alterity makes possible reconciliatory activities, which must thus retain the trace of what does not belong to them, conceal a remainder, ash. But in order to mark or remark these interruptions, they must be said in a Said which cannot simultaneously say its Saying. Whence what we have called complicity, and the necessity of a certain contamination. How can those texts which attempt all the same to think the tearing of the Saying in the Said (Levinas's text, but also Derrida's) differ from those that do not think of this? The tearing of the Saying (but also of *différance*) leaves traces even in those discourses which care nothing about this—just as deconstruction is in some sense already at work "in" Plato or Hegel's writing. So why would it not be sufficient to write like Plato or Hegel, if the trace is there in any case, and we can do nothing about it? And what if this is Necessity? In short, is there a difference between transcendental contraband and the quasi-transcendental?

Jew expelled from the Ben Aknoun school, for example, or the drug-factor incarcerated in Prague, and everything in between, and here he is bending beneath the burden, he takes it on without taking it on, nervous, worried, hunted, cadaverized like the beast playing dead and melding with the foliage, literature in short, to escape the murderers or their pack, cadaver carrying himself, heavy like a thing but light so light, he runs he flies so young and light futile subtle agile delivering to the world the very discourse of this impregnable inedible simulacrum, the theory of the parasite virus, of the inside/outside, of the impeccable *pharmakos,* terrorizing the others through the instability he

The watchtower of Ruzyne prison, near Prague.

To the extent that the interruption depends in some sense on the other to whom we say "Come" (AT, 33–5; cf. PAR, 20–116), its trace is left to the chance of what we have called the countersignature of the other. It is thus not really "in" the discourse in question, and this is why the signature of this discourse is structurally incomplete. This trace must necessarily be able to pass unperceived, or rather, for the trace is not a phenomenon, efface its effacement, not get itself remarked. It is not implausible, for example, to believe that Derrida says nothing other than his "objects," for example Levinas and/or Heidegger. Showing that this is nonetheless inadequate or unjust will depend on a writing obliging one to read the trace "as such" in its very retrac(t)ing: what is called writing's *restance* (LI, 51ff.; PS, 180). This is also what we have called giving (the other's) chance its chance. That there always be this chance is what we have called Necessity—ethics would begin in *this* chance given to necessary chance (which is not "in itself" ethical). The effort to give *a* (proper) name to this trace of the trace immediately absorbs it into the (transcendental) Said. We therefore need a multiplicity

carries everywhere, one book open in the other, one scar deep within the other, as though he were digging the pit of an *escarre* in the flesh, *"2nd dream last night, impatience faced with telling it, broadly speaking a gift from Marie-Claire Pasquier in a sort of library, a book bound in leather that I open elsewhere to explore its complicated structure, several books in one, 1 white-paged diary, then three books, three titles that I could comment on to infinity to the point of lodging the whole of my story in it, 1. My mother myself (gift from B. John/son), 2. The village people, 3. THE MOURNING WELL!!"* (10–22–81), in a dream-body in which his mother would only survive in order to wait for him and save him again, that one, Moses's

of names forming a series: what has here been the non-finite series of the quasi-transcendentals. The series gives us to read not so much "full" terms subsequently mounted together like pearls on a string, as the spacing which is the *différance* of each of these terms, and that we have explicated here on the basis of Saussure. Each term of this series names an event of interruption: the serialization marks the interruption between these interruptions, and in doing so, prevents them from being clean or absolute cuts (cf. "The without of the pure cut," in TP, 83–119). There is therefore relation and contamination between the interruptions, as there is between the interruptions and what they interrupt (this is the quasi-), in the very fact of the series in its more or less strict bond. Tension of liaison and deliaison, of stricturation and destricturation (cf. TP, 340), of gathering and dispersion (PF, 17–19).

This situation disallows discourse any purity and propriety. We have insisted regularly on the impossibility in principle of cutting oneself cleanly from the metaphysical *logos*, and we have now complicated this proposition by remarking a supplementary complicity

vicar, *Lacrimae ergo amantur* [...] *uidebat enim illa mortem meam* [...] *exaudisti eam nec despexisti lacrimas eius* [...] *nam unde illud somnium, quo eam consolatus es* [...] *"non" inquit; "non enim mihi dictum est: ubi ille, ibi et tu, sed: ubi tu, ibi et ille...,"** where the cut ought to attach for he who is not circumcised remains "cut" from his community, which leaves them to explain that circumcision is older than Abraham who repeated it one Great Pardon Day and then the time without circumcision, this very time, no?, the interruption in the practice after the departure from Egypt when Yahweh commands Joshua to take up again the stone knives, and tomorrow very close to Santa Monica, at

between the interruption that affects metaphysical discourse in spite of itself and the interruption remarked as interruption in the deconstructing discourse—this is also why this discourse is not in an external and critical position with respect to its "objects." It is not a simply "active" discourse operating on a "passive" discourse. Without the perpetual risk that the remarking discourse fall back into the remarked discourse (that there be this risk is necessity again), there would be no ethical possibility for a responsibility. This responsibility is therefore situated at the limit where the same and the other touch in their very interruption. We have already seen with respect to the pre-originary gift in the reading of Hegel that if one were determined to keep this gift pure, one would efface it all the better: to save the loss is to lose it as loss. To affirm a *pure* play is to oppose it to the work which works on the basis of this opposition to understand the game and therefore to work on it. What deconstruction affirms, what it says "yes, yes" to, is not pure game or expenditure, but the necessity of contamination.

UCLA, to the crowd and in its language I shall speak of the Final Solution, and I shall start in on the ultimate periphrasis, may as well say the ultimate flight, after having heard them hear me tremble.

★"Tears, then, and sorrows are loved [...] she saw my death [...] Thou didst hear her and didst not despise her tears [...] For, whence came the dream by which Thou didst console her [...] She answered, 'No, what was said to me was not, "Where he is, you are," but, "Where you are, he is" ' " (III, ii, 3; xi, 19–20).

This necessary contamination, this parasiting of the other by Being and of Being by the other would be precisely why Derrida is not Levinas, who for his part wants none of any such contamination. Levinas would like, for example, to retain the possibility of "hearing a God uncontaminated by Being" (quoted in PS, 182), and therefore radically cut from Being, and would like to have us recognize in this possibility something as important as the Heideggerian demand to retrieve Being from forgetting. But everything we have seen since the beginning makes the purity of such a possibility unthinkable.

Which could lead one to believe that we are coming closer to Heidegger again, following a pendulum movement that would be none other than the invisible hyphen in "Jewgreek," or else that we are presenting Derrida as producing a synthesis of Heidegger and Levinas. But if synthesis there be, we must be careful not to think of it as a measured mixture of being and

59 To speak of the child's hell you prefer "minimalist" decency, question of taste, *et solidasti auctoritatem libri tui,** at the moment when here you are trembling, Tuesday, May 1, 1990, 7 o'clock in the morning in Laguna Beach, she's still alive for you, over there in Nice, 20, rue Parmentier, 4th floor, it is 4 in the afternoon there, your brother and sister have not yet arrived, you will see her, perhaps you will still hear her when you get back, it's enough to recount the "present" to throw G.'s theologic program off course, by the very present you are making him, *Everybody's Autobiography,* yours which tells *you* so well

the other, or as the final *Aufhebung* of this opposition or this difference, which would be history itself (WD, 153). Following what we have put forward about the double and the ghost, one can say that to the extent that Derrida doubles Levinas or Heidegger so closely, he is precisely "more other" than any other. We can moreover extend this logic: it is only by passing very close to metaphysics that Derrida will have succeeded in writing the least metaphysical discourse imaginable. Derrida is right up against Levinas and Heidegger, neither Jew nor Greek, neither a thinker of the law nor a thinker of Being (MEM passim). For example, this motif of contamination, which seemed to refer us back, from the absolute other who would be God, to Being, also marks a decisive difference with Heidegger. For if, for the latter, Being is nothing outside the entities in which its retrac(t)ing is marked, this thought nonetheless wants to retain a certain purity, as thought, with respect to technology. Everything we have said about possibly mechanical repetition as an essential possibility of archi-writing marks the necessity of a contamination of any essence by a generalized "tech-

that *there is no thinking that one was never born until you hear accidentally that there were to be five children and if two little ones had not died there would be no G.S.,* you archive the system, MacWrite Macintosh SE Apple of PaRDeS, you are unrecognizable, as you were to that young imbecile who asks you, after your talk on the Final Solution, what you had done to save Jews during the war, but though he may well not have known, until your reply, that you will have been Jewish, it recalls the fact that people might not know it still, you remain guilty of that, whence this announcement of circumcision, perhaps you didn't do enough to save Jews, he might be right, you always think the other is

nology" (MEM, 109–10, 139; OS, 10). It is moreover at this price that we can manage to complicate the anthropologizing reading that can always haunt Heidegger. This is to be put alongside a refusal to subscribe to Heidegger's idea that "science does not think" (MEM, 109), but above all, here, alongside what Heidegger says about writing, defending manuscripture against the typewriter, which supposedly destroys the unity of the word (G2, 178ff.): now Derrida's thinking calls any such unity into question: his texts work on sublexical graphic and phonic units, like the "gl" of *Glas* or the "tr" of " + R," but other less obvious ones too (cf. FC, 11, 59); and he is interested in nonlinguistic inscription, in drawing and painting. If writing had for Derrida a privileged empirical version, this would be less manuscripture, or even typescript (although he takes a certain pleasure in recalling that Nietzsche was one of the first writers to possess if not to use such a machine [G2, 168–9; PS, 496], and in reminding the reader that he too uses one [LI, 95]), but the computer, which he has been using for a short while (PS, 496 again). Not just because of the "memory" traces of an electronic ar-

right, at the beginning or the end of the book, perhaps you didn't do enough, not enough to save yourself first of all, from the others or again from the Jews, you have not yet "seen" like those circumcised ones among the Wonghi, who receive the order to open one eye then the other after the operation, immediate simulacrum of a resurrection, but you see yourself beginning to overrun this discourse on castration and its supposed substitute, that old concept of narcissism, that worn edge topology, resurrection will be for you *"more than ever the address, the stabilized relation of a destination, a game of a-destination finally sorted out, for beyond what happens in the P.C., it is now the work to dispatch it*

chive, which can only with difficulty be thought according to the opposition between the sensible and the intelligible, and more easily as differences of force or capacity (although this is already important [cf. WD, 228], helping us to think writing in a more complicated relation with space and time): but also because of the possibilities of folding a text back on itself, of discontinuous jumps establishing quasi-instantaneous links between sentences, words, or marks separated by hundreds of pages.

It is not at all by chance that Derrida talks of Joyce's books in terms of supercomputers (AL, 147–8), nor that his thought should communicate in an essential way with certain discourses on so-called artificial intelligence. Nor that we should have conceived this book a little on the model of a "hypertext" program which would allow, at least in principle, an almost instantaneous access to any page or word or mark from any other, and which would be plugged into a memory containing all of Derrida's texts, themselves simultaneously accessible by "themes," key words, references, turns of "style," etc. (which our list of references sim-

that must win out, toward the secret that demanded, like a breath, the 'perversity' of the P.C., not to be finished with a destinerrancy which was never my doing, nor to my taste, but with a still complacent and therefore defensive account of the Moira" (7–6–81), too late, you are less, you, less than yourself, you have spent your life inviting calling promising, hoping sighing dreaming, convoking invoking provoking, constituting engendering producing, naming assigning demanding, prescribing commanding sacrificing, what, the witness, you my counterpart, only so that he will attest this secret truth i.e. severed from truth, i.e. that you will never have had any witness, *ergo es,* in this very place, you alone

ulates for better and worse), and then to a larger memory making accessible, according to the same multiple entries, the texts quoted or invoked by Derrida, with everything that forms their "context," therefore just about the (open) totality of the universal library, to say nothing of musical or visual or other (olfactive, tactile, gustative) archives to be invented. Such a textual machine would not in the last instance be a pedagogical, technical tool, nor an efficient and technologist way of "learning Derrida," although it is undeniable, and not at all regrettable, that it would also lend itself to such uses—for the program would also include instructions displaceable according to a chance that would exceed any programming mastery by opening that mastery to it. Such a machine would suspend reading in an open system, neither finite nor infinite, labyrinth-abyss (cf. WD, 123, 160, 298–9), and would thus also retain the memory of the traversals tried out, following their nose, their flair, by all its readers, these being so many texts to plug back into the general network. Joyceware (AL, 148), Derridaware, Derridabase. But this machine is already in place, it is the "already" itself. We are

whose life will have been so short, the voyage short, scarcely organized, by you with no lighthouse and no book, you the floating toy at high tide and under the moon, you the crossing between these two phantoms of witnesses who will never come down to the same.

*"Thou didst establish the firmament of the authority of Thy Book" (XIII, xxxiv, 49).

inscribed in it in advance, promise of hazardous memory in the monstrous to-come, like the monumental, pyramidal, but so humble signature, so low, effaced, of Jacques Derrida, here below, now, here.

ENVOI

We have, obviously enough, been clumsy. Trying to repeat faithfully the essential features of Derrida's thought, we have betrayed him. By saying that deconstruction is, finally, none other than necessity, and that it is always already at work in the most "metaphysical" texts, we have absorbed Derrida, his singularity and his signature, the event we were so keen to tell you about, into a textuality in which he may well have quite simply disappeared. Every one of Derrida's texts is an event, we said thematically, missing them all. Each of these texts has an address or several addresses we have pretended to ignore the better to be able to digest them ourselves. In the best case, we have said everything about deconstruction *except* the supplementary remark whereby it is *named* in texts signed by Jacques Derrida.

This is what forbade us from attempting a "Derridean" reading of Derrida, the only way of respecting this thought by betraying it again: we have said the limits of commentary and interpretation in limiting ourselves to commentary and a little (very little) interpretation. Double bind in which our absolute fidelity has been infidelity itself. This is why this book will be of no use to you others, or to you, other, and will have been only a hidden pretext for writing in my own signature behind his back.

ACTS (THE LAW OF GENRE)

After the simulacrum of a duel, the *second round* of this work begins precisely as another round, in the sense of games or cards. Be it biography, bibliography, or iconography, I shall play, no doubt out of provocation with respect to my partner, J.D., or any other reader, a game which consists in following "the law of genre" (one of the titles of *Parages*) or received norms, the very norms that J.D. has never stopped calling into question, in a theoretical mode but also in his work as a writer. These constraints appear particularly artificial in the establishment of the *Curriculum vitae,* an expression I prefer to that of biography: it gestures toward rhythm and speed, race or cursiveness ("Life will have been so short," J.D. writes often, more or less, and here again, *in fine*). In *Curriculum vitae,* I also hear the ironic allusion to the passage of a *mobile,* to the "academic" character of a professional "career" (J.D.'s having been that of a *homo academicus,* certainly, and through and through, but so unacademic too). To take only one example, the distinction between the *public* and the *private* was manhandled, along with a few other distinctions, in *The Post Card.* There, it is the target of jokey or serious questions. Its paradoxical mise en scène exhibits the laws of *différance,* of "destinerrance," of "clandestination," of iterability, of undecidability, etc., which come along to disturb so many assurances or insurances taken out against the signature, the relation between fiction and reality, fiction and truth, literature and philosophy, art and technology, private life and political stage: *night and day.* Faced with *The Post Card,* as with *Glas, Circumfession,* or *Mémoires d'aveugle: l'autoportrait et autres ruines,* the establishment of a "biography," however thin, becomes a challenge. Betting and deciding arbitrarily, I have therefore decided to impose some contractual clauses on myself and thus to put to the test of such an exercise some conventions which can be challenged. Within the limits of the pages still available in this book, I have therefore chosen *the day,* the poverty of the day, what in any case allows itself to be violently attracted by visibility. I have selected only the public "deeds," i.e. *overexposed* ones, or, as they say, "objectively verifiable" on the basis of accessible documents. Everyone knows that these are not always the most significant, the most interesting, or the most determining. At least they are "true" in the sense that some people still give to that word, i.e. unquestionable because questionable: exposed to counterevidence, they belong to the order of the *contestable* or the *refutable.* The documents that count most in my eyes, including for "private life," are still in the bibliography: decipherable in the published writings if only they are read in a certain way.

The selection is less schematic for the years preceding 1962, the date of the first publications, years which were therefore, if one can say so, less "public."

For among these facts, a choice still had to be made. Sometimes I have given a privilege to those which seemed likely to cast some light on some passages of *Circumfession.* This questionable *curriculum* (questionable in the first instance by J.D. himself) is thus not only cursive, selective and limited, *it only fits this book.* For another book, J.D.'s "life" would, in the end, have been quite different. It would give rise to a quite different presentation, and therefore to another discussion. This reserve doesn't just depend on the fact that the "living person" who says it here (pp. 170, 273, 306) is still quite young. So this is *one life* of Jacques Derrida. Among others.

I first of all thought of marking with an asterisk, in the bibliography, the works by J.D. in which the autobiographical dimension is most marked, those I have just quoted or some others, such as the *Borderlines* in *Living On* (in *Parages*), or *Punctuations* (in *Du droit à la philosophie*). But I gave up on the idea, because all of J.D.'s texts are in some way "autobiographical," and I felt confirmed in this decision by *Mémoires d'aveugle:* "Like Mémoires, the Self-Portrait always appears in the reverberation of several voices. And the voice of the other commands, makes the portrait resound, calls it without symmetry or consonance. If what is called self-portrait depends on the fact that it is called 'self-portrait,' an act of nomination ought to allow me, quite legitimately, to call anything at all a self-portrait, not only any drawing ('portrait' or not) but everything that happens to me and that I can cathect myself with or let myself be cathected by. Like Nobody, as Ulysses says when he blinds Polyphemus. [...] The incompletion of the visible monument depends on the ecliptic structure of the *trait,* which is merely remarked, but is impotent to reflect itself in the shadow of a self-portrait. These are so many reversible propositions. One can also read pictures of ruins as the figures of a portrait, or even a self-portrait."

As for the pictures, "figures of a portrait, or even a self-portrait," my choices obey the same convention: this is *one life* among others, real ones, possible ones, fictive or secret ones. A nonfinite number of other narrative links are plausible, with or without right of inspection. Let us remember at least the opening of J.D.'s polylogue introduction to *Droit de regards,* then read on; for this would perhaps be the best means of access to the clichés of this "Curriculum": "*—You will never know, and nor will the rest of you, all the stories I managed to tell myself while looking at these pictures. —These pictures? In that case they would have to give something to be* *seen or recognized, finally, at the moment a plot unravels. Now I got this feeling, at least, that someone is trying their best to hide something from us. We are being fascinated and seduced by a ciphering of all the diagonals: the story of a secret which perhaps does not exist and which is being struggled over in silence during a game of draughts. No one wants to show us anything. It's an assemblage or a disassemblage: it is not constructed with pictures; I would almost see in it the contrary of a construction and it operates with photographs and photographs of photographs. Wrong way round constructions, a bit as one talks about constructions in analysis or police constructions. —[...] These stories are not infinite in number, of course, but remain almost innumerable. And the arrangement of the 'pictures' above all makes the story of it all interminable."*

Some of the biographical reference points I am now going to select, in their "objective" and "conventional" form, have already been mentioned and commented upon in two works to which I refer the reader: Michel Lisse, *Jacques Derrida* (Brussels: Hatier, 1986), and Maurizio Ferraris, *Postille a Derrida* (Turin: Rosenberg and Sellier, 1990). Most of the others were communicated to me by J.D. in a rather discontinuous or aleatory way (conversations or documents), with an enthusiasm that was, let's say, uneven. But I thank him all the same.

G.B.

The maternal branch of the family at the beginning of the century: great-grandfather in the center; grandfather and grandmother to his left; mother in front of her, sitting in the front row.

CURRICULUM VITAE

1923 Marriage of Aimé Derrida and Georgette Safar. They set up house in the rue Saint-Augustin in Algiers. A town hall document (October 21, 1871) certifies that Georgette Safar's grandfather, "born in Algiers during the year eighteen hundred and thirty-two," "fulfills the conditions for naturalization prescribed" by a decree dating from 1871, and "has declared that he takes the name of Safar as surname and as forename that of Mimoun." Seven witnesses had certified that the parents of "the above named," who had "just signed in Hebrew," "had been established in Algeria before eighteen hundred and thirty." Until the Crémieux decree of 1875, the "indigenous Jews" of Algeria are not French citizens. They lose their citizenship and become "indigenous Jews" again under the Vichy regime.

1925 Birth of René Derrida.

1929 Birth of Paul Derrida, who dies less than three months later, on September 4, 1929.

1930 Birth of Jackie Derrida, July 15, in El-Biar (near Algiers, in a holiday house).

1934 The family leaves the rue Saint-Augustin for El-Biar. Purchase of a villa (the "garden," the "orchard," or the "Pardes" of "13 rue d'Aurelle-de-Paladines") with the help of a loan that will only be paid off just before the departure for France, in July 1962, when Algeria becomes independent. Birth of Janine Derrida.

1935–41 Nursery and primary schools at El-Biar. In 1940–1, intense "Pétainization" of the school in an Algeria which was never occupied and never saw a German soldier: "Maréchal here we are," sending of letters and drawings to the Marshall, raising of the flag every morning by the top pupil in the class, except if he is Jewish (J.D., who has not yet been expelled from school, whereas his brother and sister already have been, has to give up his place before the flag to the second in his class). Article 2 of the Jewish Statute of October 3, 1940, excluded the

Jews from teaching and the law ("The Maréchal is the most severe, he insists in particular that there should be no Jew in the legal and teaching professions," quoted by Y. C. Aouate; "Les mesures d'exclusion antijuives dans l'enseignement public en Algérie (1940–43)," in *Pardès,* 8 (1988).

1938 Birth of Norbert Derrida, January 11. He dies of tubercular meningitis on March 26, 1940.

1941 J.D. joins the first year at the Lycée de Ben Aknoun, near El-Biar.

1942 On the first day of the school year, J.D. is expelled from school and sent home (episode evoked in *The Postcard,* p. 87–8). In his zeal, the terrible Rector Hardy had just lowered the cutoff point of the *Numerus Clausus* from 14% to 7%: "The highest percentage cannot exceed 7%; any fraction above the last unit must then fall; example: class of 41 pupils; 7% = 2.87: number of Jewish pupils that can be admitted = 2" (quoted in *Pardès,* op. cit., p. 118, and the author of the article recalls that "there was no equivalent of this measure in France, not even during the worst years of the German occupation that were to follow." Marrus and Paxton see in this "a much more important step toward segregation than anything that was done in metropolitan France"). Unleashing of antisemitism, henceforth officially authorized, physical and verbal violence, also among children. Declaration of a headteacher in the classroom when Jewish names are called: "French culture is not made for little Jews" (op. cit., p. 126). After the Allied landing, November 8, 1942, and during the "two-headed" government (De Gaulle–Giraud), the return to "normality" took eleven months, until October 1943. J.D. is then enrolled, until the spring of 1943, at the Lycée Emile-Maupas (the name of a street behind Algiers Cathedral where Jewish teachers expelled from the public system had set up some teaching). J.D., who finds the atmosphere hard to take, secretly absents himself for almost a year. No doubt these are the years during which the singular character of J.D.'s "belonging" to Judaism is imprinted on him: wound, certainly, painful and practiced sensitivity to antisemitism and any racism, "raw" response to xenophobia, but also impatience with gregarious identification, with the militancy of belonging in general, even if it is Jewish. In short, a double rejection—of which there are many signs, well before *Circumfession*. (In passing, let me say that J.D. surprises me less than he thinks or pretends to think when he exhibits his circumcision here: for a long time now he has been talking of nothing else, as I could show with supporting quotations, and, to limit myself to the places in which he names it, in *Glas, The Postcard, Schibboleth* (especially), *Ulysses Gramophone*. As for what might link the "this is my body and I give it to you" of the Eucharist to the exhibition of the circumcised body, we can add to these same texts the seminar that they tell me J.D. is currently devoting to the "rhetoric of cannibalism," to what he calls the "aimance" of "loving-eating-the other" and, of course, to the great question of transubstantiation.) I believe that this difficulty with belonging, one would almost say of identification, affects the whole of J.D.'s oeuvre, and it seems to me that "the deconstruction of the proper" is the very thought of this, its thinking affection.

1943–47 Return to the Lycée de Ben Aknoun (first of all, in '44–5, in huts near to the lycée which had been turned by the English into a military hospital and a camp for Italian prisoners). Disordered, unruly, and sporty schooling—a "bad lad" he says; more sports field than classroom: football—matches with Italian prisoners—, running, all sorts of competitions occupy a preponderant place in his life. J.D. dreams of becoming a professional footballer. Uneven studies. Failed *baccalauréat* in June 1947. At the same time, unease, maladjustment, withdrawal, "private diary," intense reading (Rousseau, Gide, Nietzsche, Valéry, Camus). Publication of poems he has told me he "hates" in little North African reviews (since 42–3, "liberated" Algiers had become a sort of little cultural and publishing capital).

1947–48 Philosophy class at the Lycée Gauthier in Algiers (marked by reading Bergson and Sartre). Thinks he has known for a long time that he must write ("literature," rather), and thinks of a job as a teacher (literature, rather) as the only possible, if not desirable, job. After passing the *baccalauréat,* in June 1948, he hears by chance a broadcast about career orientation in which a literature teacher in *hypokhâgne*[1] praises this class and the diversity of the literary disciplines that allows one to put off the choice of specialism—and mentions that he had had Camus as a pupil. Without knowing any more about it, without even ever having heard of the Ecole Normale Supérieure, J.D. goes to see this teacher the next morning and enrolls in the Upper Literature class of this third lycée, the large Lycée Bugeaud in Algiers.

1948–49 The movement toward philosophy takes shape. "Awed" reading of Kierkegaard and Heidegger.

1949–50 First trip to "metropolitan" France, first trip at all, on the boat the *Ville d'Alger* to Marseille. Boarding student at the Lycée Louis-le-Grand in Paris. Painful experience. Uneven and difficult start to studies, except perhaps in philosophy. J.D. remembers intense reading of Simone Weil (in a pathos of vague Christian mysticism), of the "existentialists" (Christian or other), wrote essays described as "Plotinian" by Etienne Borne in spite of the obligatory schooling of the time (Sartre, Marcel, Merleau-Ponty, etc.). Fails entrance examination to the Ecole Normale Supérieure.

1950–51 Still in *khâgne* at Louis-le-Grand. More and more difficult living conditions. Fragile health. Returns to El-Biar for three months. On his return leaves the school dormitory: *chambre de bonne* in the rue Lagrange. Nervous collapse, sleeplessness, sleeping tablets and amphetamines, has to give up the entrance exam at the first paper.

1951–52 Third year of *khâgne* at Louis-le-Grand, where he meets some of those who for the most part remained his friends, whether or not he was subsequently with them again at

1. The first of two years (the second known as *khâgne*) that some students continue with at high school after the *baccalauréat,* in preparation for entry into one of the Grandes Ecoles. The level of work in these *classes préparatoires* is generally recognized to be more demanding than that of the first two years at University.

the Ecole Normale Supérieure, into which he is admitted at the end of the year (for example, R. Abirached, M. Aucouturier, J. Bellemin-Noël, L. Bianco, P. Bourdieu, M. Deguy, G. Granel, H. Joly, J. Launay, L. Marin, M. Monory, P. Nora, J. C. Pariente—already in *hypokhâgne* in Algiers—, J. M. Pontévia, M. Serres).

1952–53 Ecole Normale Supérieure (ENS). Gets to know Althusser on his first day (also born in Algiers), who is already a *caïman,*[2] with whom he becomes friends and will later be a colleague for almost twenty years. Beginning of a normal "career," after some more failures (in psychology, in ethnology). First meeting with Marguerite Aucouturier. Intermittent militant in noncommunist far-left groups. Stalinist communism is dominant at the rue d'Ulm.

1953–54 Trip to Louvain (Husserl Archives). Writes "The Problem of Genesis in the Philosophy of Husserl" (higher studies dissertation), published in 1990 by the Presses Universitaires de France. Makes friends with Foucault, whose lectures he attends.

1955 Fails the philosophy *agrégation*[3] oral examination, having abandoned the third written paper in the same conditions as in 1951.

1956–57 Passes the *agrégation,* receives a grant as a *special auditor* at Harvard University—on the somewhat fictitious pretext of consulting microfilms of unpublished work by Husserl, whose *Origin of Geometry* he begins to translate and introduce. Reads Joyce. In June 1957, in Boston, marriage with Marguerite Aucouturier (they will have two sons, Pierre, born in 1963, and Jean, in 1967).

2. School slang meaning a director of studies.

3. The *agrégation* is a competitive examination which qualifies successful candidates for higher teaching posts. Success in this examination guarantees the candidate a state job for life, and it is consequently highly prized. A first stage of the examination consists in written papers: those achieving a high enough mark in these move on to the oral examination at which the final results are decided.

1957–59 Military service in the middle of the Algerian war. Asks to be sent to a teaching post in a school for soldier's children (Koléa, near Algiers). For more than two years, second-class soldier in civilian clothing, he teaches French and English to young Algerians or French Algerians. Lives with Marguerite and his friends the Biancos in a villa in Koléa, teaches in a private school and translates press articles. Often sees Bourdieu in Algiers. J.D. has always (at least since 1947) condemned the colonial policy of France in Algeria but hoped, until the last moment, in 1962, that a form of independence would be invented that would make cohabitation possible with the French Algerians. He even put pressure on his parents not to leave Algeria in 1962. Soon afterward recognized his illusions on this matter. J.D. often speaks of his "nostalgeria."

1959–60 First paper (Conference at Cerisy), return to France, first teaching post at the lycée in Le Mans, in *hypokhâgne,* with his friend Genette (met at the rue d'Ulm). Serious "depressive" episode at the end of the school year. First trip to Prague to Marguerite's family.

1960–64 Teaches at the Sorbonne ("general philosophy and logic": assistant of S. Bachelard, G. Canguilhem, P. Ricoeur, J. Wahl). Second trip to Prague. Independence of Algeria: his whole family moves to Nice. First lecture to the Collège de Philosophie (on Foucault and in his presence; on the latter's advice he reads Roger Laporte, one of his most faithful friends). First publications in *Critique* and *Tel Quel*. Meets Philippe Sollers (to whom he is bound by a "great friendship" until 1972). Jean Cavaillès prize (modern epistemology) for the *Introduction* to *The Origin of Geometry.* Admitted to the CNRS but immediately resigns to take up a teaching post at the ENS, invited there by Hyppolite and Althusser. He is to remain there, with the post of maître-assistant, until 1984. In 1968, Bernard Pautrat becomes his other colleague there.

1966 On the invitation of René Girard, participates in Baltimore (Johns Hopkins University) in a big colloquium since become famous—and one which marked the beginning of a spectacular intensification in the reception given to certain French philosophers or theorists in the United States. J.D. meets Paul de Man and Jacques Lacan there, and sees Barthes, Hyppolite, Vernant, Goldman again.

1967 Lecture to the Société française de philosophie ("Différance"). Joins the editorial committee of *Critique,* from which he resigns discreetly in 1973 (since when has been part of its honorary committee). Publishes his first three books. After 1967–8, most of the "public facts and deeds" can be reconstituted on the basis of "publications." I shall therefore limit the points of reference to a minimum. Although things are more complex, and demand analyses that would be too long, in the nonacademic "cultural" space, many signs on the other hand could testify to the more and more manifest contrast between the foreign and French academic scenes. On the one hand, outside France, the greatest hospitality (more or less regular teaching posts in dozens of universities, hundreds of lectures in Europe and outside Europe, election to several academies (Academy for the Humanities and Sciences of New York, American Academy of Arts and Sciences, etc.), prizes (Nietzsche prize in 1988), honorary doctorates (Columbia, Essex, Louvain, New School, Williams College [Cambridge, 1992, became an "affair," after the *non-placet* expressed in the first place by three dons made a ballot [336 to 204 in favor of J.D.] necessary for the first time in 30 years]); on the other, in France, a resolute blocking (suffered equally by all those with whom he is associated in his work, be they colleagues or students), the doors of the university definitively closed (for example, after 1980, and although he had been urged to defend his thesis to be a candidate for a chair, succeeding Paul Ricoeur, this post is immediately suppressed by A. Saulnier-Seité, then minister of education, and when another post is given in replacement and on certain conditions, the university colleagues who had "invited" J.D. to apply, and those of the national body, vote against him). Spectacular and revealing situation whose analysis would have to appeal to too many texts and too many indices for me to do anything other here than mention the interest or necessity, in principle, of carrying it out. The analysis of these institutional phenomena has always been for J.D. a theoretical task and a locus of commitment (cf. *Du droit à la philosophie*).

1968 J.D. appears somewhat withdrawn or even reserved about some aspects of the May '68 movement, although he joins in the marches and organizes the first general assembly at the ENS. Frequent meetings, during these weeks, with Maurice Blanchot (one of the friendships and admirations that clearly count the most for J.D.). In July 1968, first of a series of seminars at the University of Berlin (on the invitation of Peter Szondi, with whom he becomes friends and whom he sees again several times in Paris with Celan, who was also his colleague at the ENS). Other friendships among those that matter most to him also date from Berlin (where he will present *Glas* as a seminar for six months in 73–4): Samuel Weber, Werner Hamacher, Rodolphe Gasché—and of these it must be said that, like many others it is difficult to enumerate here, they cross frontiers in the airported style of a cultural and linguistic nomadism. From '68 onward, J.D., "travels" more and more, in and outside Europe.

1970 Aimé Derrida dies of cancer at the age of 74.

1971 First return to Algeria since 1962. Sees the "garden" again. Lectures and teaching at the University of Algiers. Lecture to the Congrès des sociétés de philosophie de langue française in Montreal ("Signature, Event, Context").

1972 "Nietzsche" conference at Cerisy (with Deleuze, Klossowski, Kofman, Lacoue-Labarthe, Lyotard, Nancy, Pautrat, etc.). Three more books, special issues of *Lettres françaises* and *Le Monde*. Definitive break with Sollers and *Tel Quel* (in spite of proximity and a certain solidarity, especially between '65 and '69, J.D. had never been part of the review's committee and had never stopped marking his independence—which his partners did not like, especially in terms of the theoretico-political orientations of the group, its Marxist dogmatism and its pro-PCF[4]

4. The French Communist Party.

zeal until at least 1969, its Maoist dogmatism subsequently. As for the meaning and conditions of this break, I have often heard J.D. invite people on the one hand to "read the texts," including his own and especially those of the collection[5] and the review in the years '65–'72, at least up to and including *Tel quel—mouvement de Juin '71—Informations* of 30 April 1972; and on the other hand not to trust "at all" the public ["grossly falsifying"] interpretations-reconstructions of this final sequence by certain members of the *Tel Quel* group). First trip to Hungary.

1974 Inaugurates the collection "La philosophie en effet" with S. Kofman, Ph. Lacoue-Labarthe, and J.-L. Nancy with the Editions Galilée, which had just been founded by Michel Delorme, who will take it on again after a period with Aubier-Flammarion. Drafts the *Avant-projet* for the foundation of the Groupe de recherche sur l'enseignement philosophique (Greph) and founds this group with friends, colleagues, and students, the following year (on the activity that followed, see *Du droit à la philosophie*).

1975 Meets Adami and Titus-Carmel. Makes friends with them and writes texts for some of their exhibitions. Participates in the Cerisy conference on the work of Ponge, whom he had met (like many others, since 1965: J. Genet, P. Klossowski, P. Boulez, A. Cuny, N. Sarraute, L. R. des Forêts, R. Antelme) at the home of his friends Yves and Paule Thévenin. After having been linked above all to the Johns Hopkins University, begins to teach a few weeks a year at Yale, with Paul de Man and J. Hillis Miller (the great American critic he had met at Johns Hopkins in 1968 and whom he will follow again to Irvine in California when he leaves Yale in 1986). Beginning of what has been called a little misleadingly the Yale School (H. Bloom, P. de Man, J. Derrida, G. Hartman, J. H. Miller), of the debates and wars around the "invasion" of "deconstruction in America."

5. Apart from being a review, *Tel Quel* was also the name of a collection of books published by the Editions du Seuil, including Derrida's *L'Ecriture et la différence* and *La dissémination*.

1979 Along with others, takes the initiative of organizing the Estates General of Philosophy held at the Sorbonne (see *Du droit à la philosophie*). This is when the first press photographs of J.D. appear, taken on this big public occasion. J.D. has often explained why he had done everything he could to avoid public photography up to that point. First trip to black Africa for the colloquium at Cotonou (see *Du droit à la philosophie*).

1980 Defense of a *Thèse d'Etat* at the Sorbonne (see "Punctuations," in *Du droit à la philosophie*). Opens the Congress of French Language Philosophy in Strasbourg ("Envoi" in *Psyché*). Cerisy conference "On the basis of J.D.'s work" organized by Lacoue-Labarthe and Nancy, no doubt the French philosophers closest to J.D. in thought and friendship over more than twenty years (see *Les fins de l'homme*).

1981 With Jean-Pierre Vernant and some friends, founds the Jan Hus Association (help for dissident or persecuted Czech intellectuals) of which he is subsequently vice-president. The same year, goes to Prague to run a clandestine seminar. Followed for several days, stopped at the end of the week, finally arrested at the airport, and, after a police operation on his suitcase in which they pretend to discover a brown powder, he is imprisoned on the charge of "production and trafficking of drugs." Signature campaign for his release. Released ("expelled") from Czechoslovakia after the energetic intervention of François Mitterrand and the French government.

1982 Appears with Pascale Ogier in *Ghost Dance,* a film by Ken McMullen. Entrusted by J-P. Chevènement[6] to coordinate a mission (composed of F. Châtelet, J. P. Faye, and D. Lecourt) to found the Collège international de philosophie. First trips to Japan and Mexico. First of a series of trips to Morocco, on the invitation of his friend Abdelkebir Khatibi. Regular seminar at San Sebastian. Named A. D. White Professor at Large at Cornell University.

6. The then minister of Research and Technology.

1983 Foundation of the Collège international de philosophie, of which J.D. is the first elected director. Participates in the organization of the exhibition "Art against Apartheid," and in the initiatives to create the cultural Foundation against Apartheid (J.D. being part of the guiding council) and the writers' committee for Nelson Mandela (see the texts about this in *Psyché*). Elected to the Ecole des hautes études en sciences sociales (director of studies: *Philosophical Institutions*). Death of Paul de Man (on the "de Man affair," which breaks out in 1987, at the same time as the "Heidegger affair," see *Memoires for Paul de Man,* and *Of Spirit*).

1984 Second trip to Japan. Frankfurt: lecture to Habermas's seminar and opening lecture to the Joyce conference (*Ulysses Gramophone*).

1985 First trip to Latin America (Montevideo, Buenos Aires; second meeting with Borges—the first had taken place in an aeroplane between Ithaca and New York.)

1986 On the invitation of Bernard Tschumi, begins to work with the American architect Peter Eisenman on a project for the Parc de la Villette (*Choral Work,* see *Psyche*). This collaboration is to give rise to numerous meetings and publications in the milieu of architectural research. Collaborates on a film about Caryl Chessman (with J-Ch. Rosé).

1987 "Plays" in the work by video-artist Gary Hill, *Disturbance* (see "Videor"). Reads *Feu la cendre* with Carole Bouquet for the "Bibliothèque des voix" (Editions des femmes).

1988 Third trip to Jerusalem. Meeting with Palestinian intellectuals in the occupied territories (see "Interpretations at war," 1990). Georgette Derrida's third fall, since when she has been under medical supervision at home (see *Circumfession*).

1989 Opening address to the large colloquium organized by the Cardozo School of Law in New York (where J.D. teaches at the City University) on *Deconstruction and the Possibility of Justice.* This colloquium marks an important scansion in the rapid development of "deconstructive" research in philosophy or legal theory in the United States. Co-president, with J. Bouveresse, of the Commission on Epistemology and Philosophy (within the Bourdieu-Gros commission set up by the Ministry of Education—see *Du droit à la philosophie*).

1990 Seminars at the Academy of Sciences of the USSR and the University of Moscow. Opening lecture to the international colloquium organized by S. Friedlander at the University of California (Los Angeles) on *The Final Solution and the Limits of Representation*. Organization of an exhibition of drawings at the Louvre (J.D. inaugurates the series "Parti pris," see *Mémoires d'aveugle: l'autoportrait et autres ruines*). First return to Prague since his imprisonment in 1981.

[**1991**, December 5: Death of Georgette Derrida.]

Photography with automobile (III)
With his father, mother, and brother in the Bois de Boulogne, near El-Biar, before his sister was born.
"There is also the word *'voiture'*—to think that we have spent our life *en voiture,* and several *voitures* that meet, are immobilized in front of each other at the first rendez-vous, ... and I pass you and you pass me [*je te double et tu me doubles*] and the routes that are lost in the night, ... and *je t'envoiture* again ...,"
The Post Card, p. 200.

Return in 1984 to 13, rue d'Aurelle-de-Paladines, in El-Biar. The garden, or *pardes,* and J. D.'s room on the right, hidden by a tree.

Same date in the same garden, with his sister and the Algerian owner of the house.

Primary school in El-Biar, in 1939–40 (J. D. sitting, fifth from the left).

Lycée Ben Aknoun, in tenth or eleventh grade (1946) (J. D. standing in the second row from the back, third from the left).

Same period, on the Ben Rouilah playing fields, near Ben Aknoun: "We used to play until it was pitch dark: I dreamt of becoming a professional footballer."

1949–50, In the "khâgne": boarder at the lycée Louis-le-Grand.

Photograph with Automobile (IV)
1956, in Normandy, with Robert Abirached ("first car": as old as its owner: a 1930 Citroën C4).

With Gilles Deleuze, Jean-François Lyotard, Maurice de Gandillac, Pierre Klossowski, and Bernard Pautrat at the 1972 Cerisy-la-Salle conference on Nietzsche: "Women, what title would have been more precise and resounding? ... Woman will be my subject ... Woman will thus not have been my subject," *Spurs: Nietzsche's Styles.*

At Cerisy-la-Salle with Francis Ponge at the conference devoted to his work in 1975 (on the board, in capitals, the legend that figures at the center of *Signsponge:* "Let us inscribe without speaking a word the legend, in monumental capitals...").

Estates General of Philosophy, at the Great Amphitheater of the Sorbonne, in 1979. "This reserve perhaps comes to him from what remains essentially *undecided* today in the destination of philosophy. … An affirmation does not demonstrate in the same mode. It engages, decides, pronounces—here for philosophy. … Affirmation, *if there is affirmation,* is unconditional" ("Philosophie des états généraux").

At Cotonou (Benin) in 1978, on the occasion of a colloquium of African philosophers on *Philosophy and the Development of the Sciences in Africa:* "It is by *treating differently* every language, by *grafting* languages onto each other, by *playing* on the multiplicity of languages ... that one can fight ... against the colonizing principle" ("La crise de l'enseignement philosophique," in *Du droit à la philosophie*).

At the Gare de l'Est, Paris, January 2, 1982, on his return from Prague after his arrest.

A scene from *Ghost Dance,* during filming at the Select, with Pascale Ogier. "I believe on the contrary that the future belongs to ghosts, and that modern image technology, cinema, telecommunications, etc., are only increasing the power of ghosts."

Press conference at UNESCO on the publication of *Pour Nelson Mandela* (Paris: Gallimard, 1986), with E. Jabès, M. Tlili, O. Bhêly-Quênum, and H. Cixous. "The postscript is for the future—in what is most undecided about it today. For I wanted to talk about the future of Nelson Mandela, of what cannot be anticipated, caught, or captured by any mirror" ("Admiration de Nelson Mandela ou les lois de la réflexion," in *Psyché*).

Second meeting with Borges, at his home in Buenos Aires, in 1985. "This wound is also a sign of election … of an assigned mission: in the night, by night itself. In order to evoke the great tradition of blind writers, Borges then turns around an invisible mirror. At the same time as a celebration of memory, he sketches a self-portrait" (*Mémoires d'aveugle*).

At the Mutualité in 1989, alongside Harlem Désir and the collective "89 for equality," demanding voting rights for immigrants in local elections. "The combat against xenophobia and racism *also* goes via this right to vote. So long as it is not gained, injustice will reign, democracy will be limited to that extent, and the riposte to racism will remain abstract and impotent."

During preparation of the exhibition *Mémoires d'aveugle* at the Louvre. "—Notice that at the date at which I have this dream about a blind man, about sons and old men and eyes, the theme of this exhibition has not yet been chosen ...—That's just like an exhibition by you. It comes down to you inscribing the chronicle of an exhibition in your own memories.—No, I'd be tempted, rather, by the self-portrait of a blind man. Legend: 'This is a drawing of me' " (*Mémoires d'aveugle*).

BIBLIOGRAPHY

Abbreviations Used in Text

AL	*Acts of Literature*
ALT	*Altérités*
AT	"Of an Apocalyptic Tone . . ." (see *Psyché*)
ATM	"At This Very Moment . . ." (see *Psyché*)
CH	"'Chora'"
D	*Dissemination*
DES	"Desistance" (see *Psyché*)
DI	"Declarations of Independence" (see *Otobiographies*)
DIA	"Dialangues"
DL	"Devant la loi"
DP	*Du droit à la philosophie*
DR	*A Derrida Reader*
DRB	"The Deaths of Roland Barthes" (see *Psyché*)
EC	"Economimesis"
EN	"Envoi/Sending: on Representation" (see *Psyché*)
EO	*The Ear of the Other*
F	"Fors"
FC	*Feu la cendre*
G1	"Geschlecht" (see *Psyché*)
G2	"Geschlecht II" (see *Psyché*)
GL	*Glas*
GR	*Of Grammatology*
HAS	"How to Avoid Speaking" (see *Psyché*)
IF	"An Idea of Flaubert" (see *Psyché*)
LG	"The Law of Genre" (see *Parages*)
LI	*Limited Inc.*
LIP	"Languages and Institutions of Philosophy" (see *Du Droit à la philosophie*)
LOB	"Living On: Borderlines" (see *Parages*)
M	*Margins of Philosophy*
MEM	*Memoires for Paul de Man*
MP	"Me—Psychoanalysis" (see *Psyché*)

NA	"No Apocalypse, Not Now" (see *Psyché*)
NM	"Nelson Mandela . . ." (see *Psyché*)
NY	"Numbers of Yes" (see *Psyché*)
OG	Introduction to Husserl's *Origin of Geometry*
OS	*Of Spirit*
PAR	*Parages*
PC	*The Post Card*
PF	"Point de Folie" (see *Psyché*)
PIO	"Psyché: Invention of the Other" (see *Psyché*)
PMW	"Like the Sound of the Sea Deep within a Shell: Paul de Man's War"
POS	*Positions*
PR	"The Principle of Reason" (see *Du Droit à la philosophie*)
PRE	*Préjugés—devant la loi*
PS	*Psyché: Inventions de l'autre*
PUN	"Punctuations"
RLW	"Racism's Last Word" (see *Psyché*)
RM	"The *Retrait* of Metaphor" (see *Psyché*)
S	*Spurs*
SCH	*Schibboleth*
SCR	"Scribble"
SI	*Signsponge*
SP	*Speech and Phenomena*
SS	"Some Statements and Truisms . . ."
T	"Title: To Be Specified" (see *Parages*)
TB	"Des Tours de Babel" (see *Psyché*)
TEL	"Telepathy" (see *Psyché*)
TP	*The Truth in Painting*
TW	"Two Words for Joyce" (see *Ulysse Gramophone*)
UG	"Ulysses Gramophone" (see *Ulysse Gramophone*)
WD	*Writing and Difference*

1. Books

Apart from the books strictly speaking by Jacques Derrida, I have collected under this rubric the texts (prefaces or essays)

Saint Augustine, Frontispiece for *The City of God* (16th century). With copyist's instruments in his hand, like the Socrates in *The Post Card,* Saint Augustine seems to be writing to the dictation of the angel behind him: "sagely reading others like an angel" (*Circumfession,* 45).

which have appeared in *books* and have not been collected elsewhere. I have cited them in the language of their original publication, which was not always French. Through lack of space, I have referred only to English translations. Most of these works have been translated into a dozen languages. With the exception of *Glas,* which is translated only into English, and *The Post Card* (being translated into Italian, and not translated into Japanese), all these books have been translated into English, German, Spanish, Italian, and Japanese, or, for those that appeared after 1982, are being translated into these languages. As with everything in this bibliography, I have drawn very deeply on the rich and rigorous work of documentation carried out by Elisabeth Weber, whom I should like to thank here. In *A Derrida Reader—Between the Blinds,* preceded by an essay "Reading Between the Blinds," Peggy Kamuf provides a bibliography (New York: Columbia University Press, 1991). See too Albert Leventure, "A Jacques Derrida Bibliography 1962–90," *Textual Practice,* vol 5, no. 1 (Spring 1991). [My thanks to Suhail Malik for his invaluable work in finding and collating references to available English translations throughout Derridabase.] G.B.

1962

L'Origine de la géométrie, by Edmund Husserl. Translated with an introduction—(Paris: Presses Universitaires de France, 1962); tr. John P. Leavey, Jr. (Brighton: Harvester, 1978).

1967

De la grammatologie (Paris: Minuit, 1967); tr. Gayatri Spivak, *Of Grammatology* (Baltimore: Johns Hopkins University Press, 1976).

La Voix et le phénomène (Paris: Presses Universitaires de France, 1967); tr. David Allison, *Speech and Phenomena* (Evanston: Northwestern University Press, 1973).

L'Ecriture et la différence (Paris: Seuil, 1967); tr. Alan Bass, *Writing and Difference* (University of Chicago Press, 1978).

1972

La Dissémination (Paris: Seuil, 1972); tr. Barbara Johnson, *Dissemination* (University of Chicago Press, 1982).

Marges de la philosophie (Paris: Minuit, 1972); tr. Alan Bass, *Margins of Philosophy* (University of Chicago Press, 1984).

Positions (Paris: Minuit, 1972); tr. Alan Bass, *Positions* (University of Chicago Press, 1981).

1973

"L'Archéologie du frivole"; introduction to Condillac, *Essai sur l'origine des connaissances humaines* (Paris: Galilée, 1973).

1974

Glas (Paris: Galilée, 1974; [reprint, Denoël/Gonthier, 1981, 2 vols.]); tr. John P. Leavey, Jr., and Richard Rand, *Glas* (University of Nebraska Press, 1986).

1975

"Economimesis," in S. Agacinski et al., *Mimesis des articulations* (Paris: Flammarion, 1975), pp. 55–93; tr. Richard Klein, "Economimesis," *Diacritics* 11:2 (1981), 3–25.

1976

L'Archéologie du frivole: Lire Condillac (Paris: Gonthier-Denoël, 1976); tr. John P. Leavey, Jr., *The Archeology of the Frivolous: Reading Condillac* (Pittsburgh: Duquesne University Press, 1980).

Eperons. Sporen. Spurs. Sproni (Quadrilingual) (Venice: Corbo e Fiore).

"Fors: les mots anglés de N. Abraham et M. Torok," preface to Abraham and Torok, *Cryptonymie: Le verbier de l'homme aux loups* (Paris: Aubier-Flammarion, 1976), pp. 7–73; tr. Barbara Johnson, "Fors," *The Georgia Review* 31 (1977), 64–116.

"Où commence et comment finit un corps enseignant," in *Politiques de la philosophie,* ed. Dominique Grisoni (Paris: Grasset, 1976), pp. 55–97.

1977

"L'Age de Hegel," in *GREPH, Qui a peur de la philosophie?* (Paris: Flammarion, 1977), 73–107; "La philosophie et ses classes" (full version of shortened text first printed in *Le monde de l'éducation* 4, March 1975), ibid., 445–50; "Réponses à La Nouvelle Critique" (first printed in *La Nouvelle Critique* 84 and 85, May and June, 1975), ibid., 451–58.

1978

Eperons: Les styles de Nietzsche (Paris: Flammarion, 1978); tr. B. Harlow, *Spurs* (University of Chicago Press, 1979).

La Vérité en peinture (Paris: Flammarion, 1978); tr. Geoff Bennington and Ian McLeod, *The Truth in Painting* (University of Chicago Press, 1987).

"Scribble (pouvoir/écrire)," introduction to W. Warburton, *Essai sur les hiéroglyphes* (Paris: Aubier, 1978); tr. Cary Plotkin, "Scribble (writing-power)," *Yale French Studies* 58 (1979), 116–47.

Il fattore della verità (Rome: Adelphi, 1978).

1980

La Carte postale de Socrate à Freud et au-delà (Paris: Aubier-Flammarion, 1980); tr. Alan Bass, *The Post Card* (University of Chicago Press, 1987).

"Ocelle comme pas un," preface to Jos Joliet, *L'Enfant au chien-assis* (Paris: Galilée, 1980).

1982

L'Oreille de l'autre: Otobiographies, transferts, traductions; Textes et débats avec Jacques Derrida (Sous la direction de Claude Lévesque et Christie Vance McDonald) (Montréal: VLB, 1982); tr. Peggy Kamuf et al., *The Ear of the Other* (New York: Schocken, 1985); second edition, University of Nebraska Press, 1988.

Sopra-vivere (Milan: Feltrinelli, 1982).

1983

D'un ton apocalyptique adopté naguère en philosophie (Paris: Galilée, 1983); tr. John P. Leavey, Jr., "Of an Apocalyptic Tone Recently Adopted in Philosophy," *The Oxford Literary Review* 6:2 (1984).

Signéponge, with parallel translation by Richard Rand (University of Chicago Press, 1983); also (French text only), Paris: Seuil, 1988.

1984

La Filosofía como institución (Barcelona: Juan Grancia, 1984).

Otobiographies: L'enseignement de Nietzsche et la politique du nom propre (Paris: Galilée, 1984); translations: "Declarations of Independence," tr. Thomas Keenan and Thomas Pepper, in *New Political Science* 15 (1986), 7–15; "Otobiographies," tr. Avital Ronell, in *The Ear of the Other* (see *L'Orielle de l'autre,* 1982, above).

Feu la cendre/Cio'che resta del fuoco (Firenze: Sansoni, 1984).

1985

Lecture de droit de regards, by M.-F. Plissart (Paris: Minuit, 1985); tr. David Wills, "Right of Inspection," *Art and Text* 32 (1989), 19–97.

"Préjugés: devant la loi," in Lyotard et al., *La faculté de juger* (Paris: Minuit, 1985).

1986

"Forcener le subjectile," preface to *Dessins et portraits d'Antonin Artaud* (Paris: Gallimard, 1986).

Mémoires: for Paul de Man, translated by Cecile Lindsay, Jonathan Culler, and Eduardo Cadava (Columbia University Press, 1986 [second enlarged edition 1989]).

Parages (Paris: Galilée, 1986); partial translations: "Living On: Border Lines," tr. James Hulbert, in Bloom et al., *Deconstruction and Criticism* (New York: Seabury, 1979), pp. 75–175; "The Law of Genre," tr. Avital Ronell, *Glyph* 7 (1980), 202–29; "Title (to be specified)," tr. Tom Conley, *Sub-stance* 31 (1981), 5–22.

Schibboleth: pour Paul Celan (Paris: Galilée, 1986); earlier version in English in G. Hartman and S. Budick, eds., *Midrash and Literature* (New Haven: Yale University Press, 1986), pp. 307–47.

"Proverb: 'He that would Pun'," preface to *Glassary* (companion volume to *Glas*) by John P. Leavey, Jr., and

Gregory Ulmer (Lincoln and London: Nebraska University Press, 1986).

Caryl Chessman: L'écriture contre la mort (with J. C. Rosé), film, TFI-INA-Ministry of Culture.

1987

"'Chora,'" in *Poikilia: Etudes offertes à Jean-Pierre Vernant* (Paris: EHESS, 1987).

De l'esprit: Heidegger et la question (Paris: Galilée, 1987); tr. Geoffrey Bennington and Rachel Bowlby, *Of Spirit: Heidegger and the Question* (University of Chicago Press, 1989).

Feu la cendre, with a reading of the text by the author and Carole Bouquet (Paris: Editions des femmes, 1987).

Psyché: Inventions de l'autre (Paris: Galilée, 1987); the following translations of individual essays are referred to in *Derridabase: ATM,* "At This Very Moment in This Work Here I Am," tr. Ruben Berezdivin, in Robert Bernasconi and Simon Critchley, eds., *Re-Reading Levinas* (London: Routledge, 1990), 11–48; *DES,* "Desistance," tr. Christopher Fynsk, in Philippe Lacoue-Labarthe, *Typography* (Cambridge, Mass.: Harvard University Press, 1989), 1–42; *DRB,* "The Deaths of Roland Barthes," tr. Pascale-Anne Brault and Michael Nass, in Hugh J. Silverman, ed., *Continental Philosophy I: Philosophy and Non-Philosophy since Merleau-Ponty* (New York and London: Routledge, 1988), 259–97; *EN,* "Sending: On Representation," tr. Peter and Mary Ann Caws, *Social Research* 49, no. 2 (1982), 294–326; *G1,* "*Geschlecht:* Sexual Difference, Ontological Difference," tr. Ruben Berezdivin, *Research in Phenomenology* 13 (1983), 65–83; *G2,* "*Geschlecht* II: Heidegger's Hand," tr. John P. Leavey, Jr., in John Sallis, ed., *Deconstruction and Philosophy: The Texts of Jacques Derrida,* (Chicago: University of Chicago Press, 1987), 161–96; *HAS,* "How to Avoid Speaking: Denials," tr. Ken Frieden, in Sanford Budick and Wolfgang Iser, eds., *Languages of the Unsayable: The Play of Negativity in Literature and Literary Theory* (New York: Columbia University Press, 1989), 3–70; *IF,* "An Idea of Flaubert: 'Plato's Letter,'" *MLN* 99 (1984), 748–68; *NA,* "No Apocalypse, Not Now (full speed ahead, seven missives, seven missiles)," tr. Catherine Porter and Philip Lewis, *Diacritics* 14, no. 2 (1984), 20–31; *NM,*

"The Laws of Reflection: Nelson Mandela, In Admiration," tr. Mary Ann Caws and Isabelle Lorenz, in *For Nelson Mandela* (New York: Seaver Books, 1987), 13–42; *NY,* "A Number of Yes," tr. Brian Holmes, in *Qui Parle* 2, no. 2 (1988), pp. 120–33; *PF,* "Point de Folie—maintenant l'architecture," tr. Kate Linker, in Bernard Tschumi, *La Case Vide* (London: Architectural Association, 1986), 4–20; *PIO,* "Psyché: Inventions of the Other," tr. Catherine Porter, in Lindsay Waters and Wlad Godzich, eds., *Reading De Man Reading* (Minneapolis: University of Minnesota Press, 1989), 25–66; *RLW,* "Racism's Last Word," tr. Peggy Kamuf, *Critical Inquiry* 12 (1985), 290–9; *RM,* "The *Retrait* of Metaphor," tr. Frieda Gasdner, Biodun Iginla, Richard Madden and William West, *Enclitic* 2, no. 2 (1978), 5–33; *TB,* "Des Tours de Babel," tr. Joseph F. Graham, in Joseph F. Graham, ed., *Difference in Translation* (Ithaca: Cornell University Press, 1985), 165–248; *TEL,* "Telepathy," tr. Nicholas Royle, in *The Oxford Literary Review* 10 (1988), 3–41.

Ulysse gramophone: Deux mots pour Joyce (Paris: Galilée, 1987); translations: "Two Words for Joyce," tr. Geoff Bennington, in Derek Attridge and Daniel Ferrer, eds., *Post-Structuralist Joyce: Essays from the French* (Cambridge: CUP, 1984), pp. 145–59; "Ulysses Gramophone: Hear Say Yes in Joyce," tr. Tina Kendall, in D. Attridge, ed., *Acts of Literature* (London: Routledge, 1992), 256–309.

1988

Limited Inc., ed. Gerald Graff, tr. Samuel Weber and Jeffrey Mehlman (Evanston: Northwestern University Press, 1988).

Mémoires: pour Paul de Man (Paris: Galilée, 1988); tr. Jonathan Culler et al., 2d ed. (Columbia University Press, 1989).

1989

"Some Statements and Truisms about Neo-logisms, Newisms, Postisms, Parasitisms, and other small Seismisms," in D. Carroll, ed., *The States of Theory* (Columbia University Press, 1989).

". . . Una de las virtudes más recentes . . . ," preface to Christina de Peretti della Rocca, *Jacques Derrida: Texto y Deconstrucción* (Barcelona: Antropos, 1989).

1990

Du droit à la philosophie (Paris: Galilée, 1990); the following translations of individual essays are referred to in *Derridabase: LIP,* "Languages and Institutions of Philosophy," tr. Sylvia Söderlind, Rebecca Comay, Barbara Havercroft, and Joseph Adamson, *Recherches Sémiotiques/Semiotic Inquiry* 4, no. 2 (June 1984), 91–154; *PR,* "The Principle of Reason: The University in the Eyes of its Pupils," tr. Catherine Porter and Edward P. Morris, *Diacritics* 13, no. 3 (1983), 3–20.

Che cos'è la poesia? (quadrilingual) (Berlin: Brinckmann und Bose, 1990).

"Donner le temps (de la traduction)"/"Die Zeit (der Übersetzung) geben," in G. C. Tholen and M. O. Scholl, eds., *Zeit-Zeichen* (Weinheim: VCH Acta Humaniora, 1990).

"Interpretations at War: Kant, le Juif, l'Allemand," in *Phénoménologie et Politique: Mélanges offerts à Jacques Taminiaux* (Brussels: Ousia, 1990), pp. 209–92.

Mémoires d'aveugle: L'autoportrait et autres ruines (Paris: Musée du Louvre, 1990).

Le problème de la genèse dans la philosophie de Husserl (Paris: PUF, 1990).

Heidegger et la question: De l'esprit et autres essais (Paris: Flammarion, 1990).

1991

Jacques Derrida (in collaboration with Geoffrey Bennington) (Paris: Seuil, 1991); tr. Geoffrey Bennington, *Jacques Derrida* (Chicago: University of Chicago Press, 1992).

L'autre cap, suivi de la démocratie ajournée (Paris: Minuit, 1991).

Donner le temps: 1. *La Fausse Monnaie* (Paris: Galilée, 1991).

1992

Acts of Literature, ed. Derek Attridge (London and New York: Routledge, 1992).

Cover of *The Post Card* (Socrates and Plato, frontispiece of *Prognostica Socratis Basilei,* 13th century, Oxford, Bodleian Library, ms. Ashmole 304, fol. 31 v°). "Socrates writing, writing before Plato ... like the negative of a photograph waiting twenty-five centuries to be developed—in me, of course ... Socrates, he who writes—sitting, bent, docile scribe or copyist, Plato's secretary, I guess. He is in front of Plato, no, Plato is *behind* him ... but standing..."

2. Articles

I have collected here, in their original language, those articles which are not collected in Derrida's books. G.B.

"Sur *Lebenswelt und Geschichte* de H. Hohl," *Les Études philosophiques* no. 1, 1963.

"Sur *Phänomenologische Psychologie* de E. Husserl," *Les Etudes philosophiques,* no. 2, April–June 1963.

"Sur *E. Husserl's Theory of Meaning* de J. N. Mohanty," *Les Etudes philosophiques* no. 4, 1964.

"D'un texte à l'écart," *Les Temps modernes* 284, March 1970.

"A-coup" (J.D. et al., Trente-huit réponses sur l'avant-garde), *Digraphe* 6, 1975, Paris.

"Où sont les chasseurs de sorcières?," *Le Monde,* July 1, 1976.

Round Table with *Greph,* "Qui a peur de la philosophie?," *Noroît,* nos. 224, 225, 226, 227, January–April 1978.

"Economies de la crise," *La Quinzaine littéraire,* August 1–31, 1983.

"La langue et le discours de la méthode," *Recherches sur la philosophie et le langage,* no. 3, Grenoble, Groupe de recherche sur la philosophie et le langage, 1983.

"Mes chances. Au rendez-vous de quelques stéréophonies épicuriennes," *Tijdschrift voor filosofie,* no. 1, March 1983, Leuven (repr. dans *Confrontation* 19, "Derrida," 1988).

"Bonnes volontés de puissance: Une réponse à Hans-Georg Gadamer," *Revue internationale de philosophie,* no. 151, 1984, fasc. 4, *Herméneutique et Néostructuralisme: Derrida-Gadamer-Searle,* Univ. of Brussels/PUF.

"Ce que j'aurais dit . . . ," *Le Complexe de Léonard ou la Société de création* (Actes de la Rencontre internationale de la Sorbonne, February 1983), Paris, Les Ed. du *Nouvel Observateur*/J.-C. Lattès.

"Les événements? Quels événements?" *Le Nouvel Observateur, 1964–1984,* no. 1045.

"Les philosophes et la parole: Passage du témoin de François Georges à Jacques Derrida," *Le Monde,* October 21–22, 1984.

"Women in the Beehive: A Seminar with J.D.," *Subject/Object,* spring, 1984, Brown Univ.

"Epreuves d'écriture," Participation ("Les Immatériaux," by J.-F. Lyotard and Th. Chaput), Paris, Centre Georges-Pompidou, 1985.

"Le langage," *Douze Leçons de philosophie,* presentation by Christian Delacampagne, Paris, *La Découverte/Le Monde.*

"But, beyond . . . ," tr. P. Kamuf, *Critical Inquiry,* autumn 1986.

"Pardonnez-moi de vous prendre au mot," *La Quinzaine littéraire,* no. 459, March 16–31, 1986.

"Petite fuite alexandrine (vers toi)," in *Notes: Monostiches, One-Line Poems,* published by Raquel, no. 1, May 1986; repr. in E. Hocquard, Raquel, *Orange Export Ltd. 1969–1986,* Paris, Flammarion.

"Antwort an Apel," tr. by Michael Wetzel, *Zeitmitschrift: Journal für Asthetik,* no. 3, 1987.

"L'Oeuvre chorale" with Peter Eisenman, *Vaisseau de Pierres 2. Parc-Ville Villette,* Champ Vallon, 1987.

"On Reading Heidegger," *Research in Phenomenology,* vol. 27, 1987, *Topic: Reading Heidegger,* Humanities Press.

"Reply," Jardine, A. and Smith, P., *Men in Feminism,* Methuen, 1987.

"La réponse de J.D." (to V. Farias), *Le Nouvel Observateur* 27, November–December 3, 1987.

"Les chances de la pensée," *Légende du siècle,* no. 5, April 19, 1988.

"Derrida-Bourdieu: Débat" (Letter to *Libération,* March 19–20, 1988).

"Heideggers Schweigen," in *Antwort: Martin Heidegger im Gespräch.* Pfullingen, Neske, 1988.

"Machtmissbrauch," (Letter to *Die Frankfurter Allgemeine Zeitung* March 16, 1988).

"The Politics of Friendship," *The Journal of Philosophy,* no. 11, November 11, 1988.

"Une nouvelle affaire," (Letter to *La Quinzaine littéraire,* February 16–29, 1988).

"Une lettre de Jacques Derrida," *Libération,* March 3, 1988.

"Like the Sound of the Sea Deep within a Shell: Paul de Man's War," tr. Peggy Kamuf, *Critical Inquiry* 14, spring 1988.

"Biodegradables: Seven Diary Fragments," tr. P. Kamuf, *Critical Inquiry* 15, no. 4, summer 1989.

"Comment donner raison? How to concede, with reasons?" (bilingual, tr. J. Leavey), *Diacritics* 19, no. 3–4, fall-winter 1989, *Heidegger, Art and Politics.*

"La démocratie ajournée," *Le Monde de la Révolution française: Gazette du bicentenaire* (monthly), no. 1, January 1989.

"Point de vue" (answer to the question "Le seuil de tolérance, c'est quoi pour vous?"), *Libération,* January 22, 1990.

"Force de loi. Le 'fondement mystique de l'autorite,'" in *Deconstruction and the Possibility of Justice, Cardozo Law Review,* New York (bilingual), October 1990.

"Videor," in *Passages de l'image,* Centre Georges-Pompidou, 1990.

"A letter to Peter Eisenman," in *Assemblage: A Critical Journal of Architecture and Design,* no. 12, August 1990.

"L'autre cap," in *Liber* no. 5, Ocober 1990 (*Le Monde,* September 29, 1990).

"Let us not forget—Psychoanalysis," *Oxford Literary Review* 12, nos. 1 and 2, 1990.

"La voix de l'ami," in homage to Henri Joly, *Cahier du Groupe de recherches sur la philosophie et le langage,* Grenoble, no. 12, 1990.

"Louis Althusser," eulogy given on the death of Louis Althusser, *Les Lettres françaises,* no. 4, December 1990.

3. Translations

L'Origine de la géométrie, by Husserl, PUF, 1962.

"Les frontières de la théorie logique," by W. V. Quine (with R. Martin), *Les Etudes philosophiques,* no. 2, 1964.

"Le monde-de-la-vie et la tradition de la philosophie américaine," by M. Farber (*ibid.*).

4. Interviews

I only give references in this selection to the interviews not collected in *Positions* or *Du Droit à la philosophie.* G.B.

Cartoon by Tim for a double page in
Le Monde, 1973.

"Culture et écriture: La prolifération et la fin du livre," *Noroît,* no. 132, November 1968.

"Avoir l'oreille de la philosophie," with Lucette Finas, *La Quinzaine littéraire,* no. 152, November 1972.

"Jacques Derrida" (interview), *Almanach de Shakespeare and Company,* no. 2, 1975.

"Entre crochets" (I), with D. Kambouchner, J. Ristat, D. Sallenave, *Digraphe,* no. 8, 1976.

"Littérature, philosophie et politique sont inséparables," with Agacinski, Kofman, Lacoue-Labarthe, Nancy, Pautrat, *Le Monde,* November 30, 1976.

"Ja, ou le faux-bond" (II), *Digraphe,* no. 11, 1977.

"An Interview with Jacques Derrida," with J. Kearns and K. Newton, *The Literary Review,* no. 14, April 18–May 1, 1980.

"Jacques Derrida, Europas 'svazarte' filosof," interview with Horace Engdahl, *Expressen,* April 23, 1981, (Sweden).

"Jacques Derrida sur les traces de la philosophie," with Ch. Descamps, *Le Monde,* January 31, 1982, et *Entretiens avec Le Monde,* I, *Philosophies,* Paris, *La Découverte/Le Monde.*

"Je n'écris pas sans lumière artificielle," with A. Rollin, *Le fou parle,* no. 21–22, November/December 1982, Balland.

"Choreographies," with Ch. V. McDonald, *Diacritics,* summer 1982.

"Dialangues: Une conversation avec Jacques Derrida," with Anne Berger, *Fruits,* no. 1, December 1983.

"Derrida l'insoumis," with Catherine David, *Le Nouvel Observateur,* no. 983, September 9–15, 1983.

"Derrida, philosophie au Collège," with J.-L. Thébaut, *Libération,* no. 692, August 11, 1983.

"Voice II," with V. Conley, *Boundary* 2, no. 2, winter 1984.

"La visite de Jacques Derrida," *VU!,* no. 38–39, Tokyo, January 1984.

"Jacques Derrida: Deconstruction and the Other," in R. Kearney, *Dialogues with Contemporary Continental Thinkers,* Manchester Univ. Press, 1984.

"Plaidoyer pour la métaphysique," with J. F. Lyotard, *Le Monde,* October 28, 1984.

"Artists, Philosophers and Institutions," *Rampike* special double edition, 3, no. 3, and 4, no. 1, *Institutions, Anti-Institutions,* Toronto.

"Deconstruction in America: An Interview with Jacques Derrida," J. Creech, P. Kamuf, J. Todd, *Critical Exchange,* no. 17, winter 1985.

"On Colleges and Philosophy," with G. Bennington, *Documents* 5, Institute of Contemporary Arts, 1986.

"The crisis in Knowledge. Poststructuralism, Postmodernism, Postmodernity," *Art Papers,* January/February 1986, Atlanta Press.

"Jacques Derrida. Leer lo ilegible: Deporte y modernidad," *Revista de Occidente,* no. 62–63, 1986, Madrid.

"Deconstruction, a Trialogue in Jerusalem," with G. Hartman and W. Iser, *Mishkenot Sha'ananim Newsletter,* no. 7, December 1986, Jerusalem.

"Entrevista: Del materialismo no dialectico," with K Jihad, *Diario* 16, no. 69, August 3, 1986.

"Architecture et philosophie," with Eva Meyer (1984), (tr. *Beseda, Revue de philosophie et de religion,* no. 4, 1986, Leningrad-Paris).

"Gespräch," *Französische Philosophen im Gespräch,* Munich, Klaus Boer Verlag, 1986.

"Jacques Derrida on the University," with I. Salusinszky, *Southern Review* 19, no. 1, March 1986, Adelaide, Australia.

"Une carte postale de l'Amérique," with V. Vasterling, *Krisis. Tijdschrift voor filosofie,* no. 22, March 1986, Amsterdam.

"Ma l'ideologia non è azione," *Panorama,* November 8, 1987, Milan.

"Entretien" (D. Cahen, "Le bon plaisir de Jacques Derrida," France-Culture), *Digraphe,* no. 42, December 1987.

"Heidegger, l'enfer des philosophes," with D. Eribon, *Le Nouvel Observateur,* November 6–12, 1987.

"Labyrinth und Archi-Textur, 1984," with E. Meyer, *Das Abenteuer der Ideen,* Internationale Bauausstellung, Berlin, 1987.

"Autobiographical Words: Why Not Sartre?" (in Japanese), *Revue de la pensée d'aujourd'hui* 15–18, 1987.

"Artaud et ses doubles," with M. Olivier, *Scènes Magazines,* no. 5, February 1987, Genève.

"Interview with Jacques Derrida," in I. Salusinszky, *Criticism in Society,* Methuen, 1987.

"Some Questions and Responses," *The Linguistics of Writing,* with D. Attridge et al., Manchester Univ. Press, 1987.

"A Conversation with Jacques Derrida," *Precis* 6, 1987, Columbia Univ. Graduate School of Architecture, New York.

"Controverse sur la possibilité d'une science de la philosophie," with F. Laruelle, *La Décision philosophique,* no. 5, Osiris, 1988.

"The Derridean View," *BM* 4, September 1988, City Univ. of New York.

"Le philosophe et les architectes," *Diagonal,* no. 73, August 1988.

"Y a-t-il une langue philosophique?" *Autrement,* no. 102, November 1988, *A quoi pensent les philosophes?*

"Il faut bien manger ou le calcul du sujet," with J.-L. Nancy, *Confrontation,* no. 20, winter 1989.

"Conversation with Christopher Norris," *Architectural Design, "Deconstruction II"* (video-interview, March 1988), Academy Ed., repr. in *Deconstruction Omnibus Volume,* London, 1989.

"Jacques Derrida, autor de la teoria de la 'deconstrucción' . . . ," with Cr. de Peretti, *El Independeiente,* no. 12, December 24, 1989, Madrid (dossier on J.D.).

"Entrevista con Jacques Derrida," *Politíca y Sociedad,* with Cr. de Peretti, no. 3, 1989, Madrid.

"Rhétorique de la drogue," *Autrement,* no. 106, April 1989.

"Istrice. 2. Ick bünn all hier," with M. Ferraris, *Aut aut,* no. 235, January/February 1990.

"A Discussion with J. Derrida," with P. Kamuf et al., *The Writing Instructor* 9, no. 1–2, 1990, Univ. of Southern California.

"Jacques Derrida on Rhetoric and Composition: A Conversation," with G. Olson, *Journal of Advanced Composition* 10, no. 1, 1990, Univ. of South Florida.

"Un penseur dans la cité: 'Le philosophe n'a pas à parler

comme tout le monde . . . ,'" *L'evénement du jeudi,* April 12–18, 1990.

"Le dessein du philosophe," with J. Coignard, *Beaux-Arts,* no. 85, December 1990.

"Jacques Derrida ici et ailleurs," with R. P. Droit, *Le Monde,* November 16, 1990.

"Le programme philosophique de Jacques Derrida," with R. Maggiori, *Libération,* November 15, 1990.

5. Works on Jacques Derrida

Some books and special issues including bibliographical detail are marked by "B."

Books

Finas, L., Kofman, S., Laporte, R. Rey, J.-M., *Ecarts: Quatre essais à propos de Jacques Derrida,* Paris, Fayard, 1973.

Parret, Herman, *Het Denken van de grens: Vier opstellen over Derrida's grammatologie,* Leuven, Acco, 1975.

Toyosaki, Koitchi, *In the Margin's Margin or Graft without Subject: Re(-)marks on Derrida* (in Japanese), Tokyo, Epaves, 1975.

Laruelle, François, *Machines textuelles: Déconstruction et libido d'écriture,* Paris, Seuil, 1976 (partly on J.D.).

Levesque, Claude, *L'Etrangeté du texte: Essais sur Nietzsche, Freud, Blanchot et Derrida,* Montréal, VLB, 1976.

Santiago, Silviano, *Glossario de Derrida,* Rio de Janeiro, Francisco Alves, 1976.

Greisch, Jean, *Herméneutique et Grammatologie,* CNRS, 1977.

Hasumi, Shigehiko, *Foucault, Deleuze, Derrida* (in Japanese), Japan, Asahi Shuppansha, 1978.

Giovannangeli, Daniel, *Ecriture et Répétition: Approche de Derrida,* Paris, 10/18, 1979.

Lacoue-Labarthe, Ph., and Nancy, J.-L., eds., *Les Fins de l'homme: A partir du travail de Jacques Derrida,* Symposium at Cerisy-la-Salle of July 22 to August 2, 1980, Galilée, 1981, texts by Agacinski, Allen, Borch-Jacobsen, Brémondy, Burger, Carroll, Courtine, Escoubas, Feher, Ferry et Renault, Fischer, Fynsk, Gasché, Gearhart, Granoff, Hamacher, Hollier, Hovald, Imbert, Irigaray, Johnson, Kambouchner, Kofman, Lacoue-Labarthe, Laporte, Lewis, Lichtenstein, Loraux, Lyotard, Madaule, Marin, McDonald, Moscovici, Nancy, Payant, Petitot-Cocorda, Pinchard, Pujol, Rey, Rogozinski, Spivak, Toyosaki, Wipf.

Hartman, Geoffrey H., *Saving the Text: Literature/Derrida/ Philosophy,* The Johns Hopkins Univ. Press, 1981.

Kemp, Peter, *Doden og maskinen: Introduktion til Derrida,* Copenhagen, Bibliotek Rhodos, 1981.

Culler, Jonathan, *On Deconstruction, Theory and Criticism after Structuralism,* Routledge & Kegan Paul, London, 1982 (B).

Levesque, C., McDonald, Ch., eds., *L'Oreille de l'autre: Otobiographies, transferts, traductions,* texts and discussions, contributions by E. Donato, R. Gasché, C. Lévesque, P. Mahony, C. McDonald, F. Péraldi, E. Vance. Montréal, VLB, 1982.

Major, R., ed., *Affranchissement du transfert et de la lettre,* symposium about *La Carte postale* April 4–5, 1981. Texts by Bouazis, Huber, Lemaigre, Lembeye, Petitot, Rabant, Sempé, Torok, Trilling, Viderman, Ed. Confrontation, 1982.

Ryan, Michael, *Marxism and Deconstruction: A Critical Articulation,* Baltimore, The Johns Hopkins Univ. Press, 1982.

Krupnick, M., ed., *Displacement: Derrida and After,* texts by G. C. Spivak, T. Conley, P. de Man, S. Handelman, M. Krupnick, H. Rapaport, M. Ryan, G. Ulmer, Indiana Univ. Press, 1983.

Petrosino, Silvano, *Jacques Derrida e la legge del possibile,* Naples, Guida Editori, 1983.

Kofman, Sarah, *Lectures de Derrida,* Paris, Galilée, 1984.

Magliola, Robert, *Derrida on the Mend,* Indiana, Purdue Research Foundation, 1984.

Smith, J., Kerrigan, W., eds., *Taking Chances: Derrida, Psychoanalysis and Literature,* texts by A. Bass, D. Carroll, W. Kerrigan, J. H. Miller, A. Ronell, S. Weber, The Johns Hopkins Univ. Press, 1984.

Staten, Henry, *Wittgenstein and Derrida,* The Univ. of Nebraska Press, 1984.

Battaglia, Rosemarie Angela, *Presence and Absence in Joyce, Heidegger, Derrida, Freud,* S.U. of N.Y. at Birmingham, 1985.

Bernasconi, R., Wood, D., *Derrida and Différance,* texts by R. Bernasconi, W. Brogan, D. F. Krell, J. Llewelyn, G. Ormiston, D. Wood, Parousia Press, 1985.

Graham, J. F., ed., *Difference in Translation,* texts by A. Bass, C. Chase, J. F. Graham, B. Johnson, P. E. Lewis, R. J. Matthews, R. Rand, Cornell Univ. Press, 1985.

Ihde, D., Silverman, H., eds., *Hermeneutics and Deconstruction,* texts by J. D. Caputo, R. Gasché, N. J. Holland, A. Lingis, J. Margolis, D. Olkowski, G. L. Ormiston, T. Sheehan, S. H. Watson, State Univ. of New York Press, 1985.

Megill, Alan, *Prophets of Extremity: Nietzsche, Heidegger, Foucault, Derrida,* Univ. of California Press, 1985.

Slawek, Tadeusz, *The Outlined Shadow: Phenomenology, Grammatology, Blake,* Katowice, Uniwersytet Slaski, 1985.

Taylor, Mark C., *Errance. Lecture de Derrida. Un essai d'a-théologie postmoderne,* Le Cerf, 1985.

Ulmer, Gregory L., *Applied Grammatology: Post(e)-Pedagogy from Jacques Derrida to Joseph Beuys,* The Johns Hopkins Univ. Press, 1985.

Breton, S., Guibal, F., *Altérités: Jacques Derrida et Pierre-Jean Labarrière,* Osiris, 1986.

Gasché, Rodolphe, *The Tain of the Mirror: Derrida and the Philosophy of Reflection,* Harvard Univ. Press, 1986.

Harvey, Irene E., *Derrida and the Economy of Différance,* Indiana Univ. Press, 1986 (B).

Ijsseling, Samuel, *Jacques Derrida,* texts by S. Ijsseling, P. Moyaert, R. Bernet, J. Deryckere, E. Berns, A. Burms, Ambo, 1986 (B).

Laruelle, François, *Les Philosophies de la différence,* Paris, PUF, 1986 (partly on J.D.).

Leavey, John P., Jr., *Glassary* (with an essay by G. L. Ulmer), Univ. of Nebraska Press, 1986.

Lisse, Michel, *Auteurs contemporains: Patrick Modiano, Jacques Derrida, Maurice Blanchot,* Bruxelles, Hatier, 1986(B).

Llewelyn, John, *Derrida on the Threshold of Sense,* Macmillan, 1986 (B).

McDonald, Christie, *Dispositions: Quatre essais sur les écrits de Rousseau, Mallarmé, Proust et Derrida,* Hurtebise, Quebec, 1986.

Carroll, David, *Paraesthetics: Foucault, Lyotard, Derrida,* Methuen, 1987.

Egebak, Niels, *Skriftens Simulacrum: Traek of Jacques Derridas "metode,"* Viby (Denmark), Kimaere, 1987.

Englert, Klaus, *Frivolität und Sprache: Zur Zeichentheorie bei Jacques Derrida,* Essen, Verlag Die Blaue Eule, 1987.

Heimonet, Jean-Michel, *Politiques de l'écriture: Bataille/Derrida,* Univ. of North Carolina, 1987.

Norris, Christopher, *Derrida,* Harvard Univ. Press, 1987(B).

Sallis, J., ed., *Deconstruction and Philosophy: The Texts of Jacques Derrida,* texts by R. Berezdivin, R. Bernasconi, J. D. Caputo, R. Gasché, I. E. Harvey, D. F. Krell, J. R. Leavey, Jr., J. Llewelyn, H. J. Silverman, S. Watson, D. Wood, Univ. of Chicago Press, 1987.

Behler, Ernst, *Derrida—Nietzsche, Nietzsche—Derrida,* Schöning, 1988.

Iofrida, Manlio, *Forma e materia: Saggio sullo storicismo antimetafisico di Jacques Derrida,* Pisa, ETS Editrice, 1988.

Kimmerle, Heinz, *Derrida zur Einführung,* Hamburg, Soak im Junius Verlag, 1988 (B).

Menke-Eggers, Christoph, *Die Souveränität der Kunst. Ästhetische Erfahrung nach Adorno und Derrida,* Frankfurt., Athenäum, 1988.

Neel, Jasper, *Plato, Derrida and Writing,* Southern Illinois Univ. Press, 1988.

Percesepe, Gary John, *Future(s) of Philosophy: The Marginal Thinking of Jacques Derrida,* American Univ. Studies, 1988.

Brunette, Peter, Wills, David, *Screen/Play: Derrida and Film Theory,* Princeton Univ. Press, 1989.

Corlett, William, *Community without Unity: A Politics of Derridian Extravagance,* Duke Univ. Press, 1989.

Cartoon by David Levine for an article by John R. Searle entitled "The Word Turned Upside Down," *New York Review of Books,* 1983.

Hart, Kevin, *The Trespass of the Sign: Deconstruction, Theology and Philosophy,* Cambridge Univ. Press, 1989.

Michelfelder, D., Palmer, R. E., eds., *Dialogue and Deconstruction: The Gadamer-Derrida Encounter,* texts by H.-G. Gadamer, R. Bernasconi, J. D. Caputo, F. Dallmayr, G. Eisenstein, P. Forget, M. Frank, D. F. Krell, G. B. Madison, D. Michelfelder, N. Oxenhandler, R. Palmer, H. Rapaport, J. Risser, J. Sallis, C. Shepherdson, R. Shusterman, J. Simon, State Univ. of New York Press, 1989.

Morimoto, Kazuo, *From Derrida to Dogen: "Deconstruction" and "The Annulment of the Body and the Spirit,"* Fukutake Books, 1989 (in Japanese).

Peretti, Cristina de, *Jacques Derrida: Texto y deconstrucción: Prólogo de Jacques Derrida,* Barcelona, Editorial Anthropos, 1989(B).

Rapaport, Herman, *Heidegger and Derrida: Reflections on Time and Language,* Univ. of Nebraska Press, 1989.

Silverman, H., ed., *"Derrida and Deconstruction," Continental Philosophy II,* texts by R. Berezdivin, R. Bernet, W. Brogan, J. D. Caputo, D. Chaffin, B. Flynn, I. E. Harvey, C. Howells, D. Judovitz, S. Kofman, H. J. Silverman, H. Volat-Shapiro, E. Wyschogrod, Routledge, 1989.

Takahashi, Nobuaki, *Derrida's Thought,* Tokyo, 1989 (in Japanese).

Wood, David, *The Deconstruction of Time,* Humanities Press, 1989 (on Nietzsche, Husserl, Heidegger et Derrida).

Ferraris, Maurizio, *Postille a Derrida: Con due scritti di Jacques Derrida,* Turin, Rosenberg & Sellier, 1990 (B).

Forrester, John, *The Seductions of Psychoanalysis: Freud, Lacan and Derrida,* Cambridge Univ. Press, 1990.

Peñalver, Gomez Patricio, *La Deconstrucción: Escritura y filosofía,* Barcelona, Montesinos, 1990 (B).

Resta, Caterina, *Pensare al limite: Tracciati di Derrida,* Guerini, Milan, 1990.

Ruby, Christian, *Les Archipels de la différence: Foucault, Derrida, Deleuze, Lyotard,* Félin, 1990.

Sychrava, Juliet, *Schiller to Derrida, Idealism in Aesthetics,* Cambridge Univ. Press, 1990.

Thiel Detlef, *Über die Genese philosophischer Texte: Studien zu Jacques Derrida,* Fribourg/ Munich, Alber, 1990.

Special Issues of Journals

Tijdschrift voor Filosofie, no. 1, March 1968, H. Parret, K. Schumann.

Exil. Tidsskrift for litteratur og semiologie, no. 3, October 1972, texts by P. A. Brandt, E. Krause-Jensen, N. L. Knudsen, O. A. Olsen, E. Svejgaard. Braband/Copenhagen, Vinten.

Les Lettres françaises, no. 1429, March 29–April 4, 1972, *Hommages réunis par Jean Ristat,* texts by R. Barthes, C. Backès-Clément, H. Damisch, B. Dufour, J. Genet, J. Gillibert, J.-J. Goux, D. Hollier, R. Laporte, A. Masson, C. Ollier, J.-M. Rey, J. Ristat, P. Thévenin, J.-N. Vuarnet.

Le Monde, June 14, 1973, *Jacques Derrida le déconstructeur,* ed. by L. Finas, texts by Ch. Delacampagne, L. Finas, R. P. Droit, Ph. Sollers, Tim.

L'Arc, Jacques Derrida, ed. C. Clément, texts by C. Buci-Glucksmann, H. Cixous, D. Giovannangeli, E. Jabès, R. Laporte, E. Levinas, S. Lotringer, F. Laruelle, C. Ollier, no. 54, 1973.

Sub-stance, no. 7, fall 1973, *Literature . . . and Philosophy? The Dissemination of Derrida,* texts by C. Bandera, E. Donato, J. Ehrmann, J. Leroy, C. Lévesque, M. Pierssens.

Dometi 1–2, *Jacques Derrida,* texts by J. Acin, J. Barkovic, Miscevic, S. Zizek, Yugoslavia, 1977.

The Oxford Literary Review 3, no. 2, 1978, *Derrida,* texts by M. Cousins, V. Descombes, M. Ellmann, K. Mulligan, J.-L. Nancy, A. Wordsworth.

Research in Phenomenology, no. 8, *Reading(s) of Jacques Derrida,* texts by D. B. Allison, R. Berezdivin, K. Itzkowitz, D. Janicaud, J. Leavey, A. Lingis, H. J. Silverman. Humanities Press, 1978.

Kris. Kritik. Estetik. Politik, no. 16, September 1980, *Derrida/Blanchot,* texts by H. Engdahl, C. J. Malmberg, A. Olsson, Stockholm.

Nuova Corrente, no. 84, 1981, *Derrida o la lezione di calcolo,* ed. Stefano Agosti, texts by S. Agosti, A. Calzolari, D.

Carroll, H. Cixous, M. Ferraris, B. Graciet, D. Kambouchner, J. Risset, G. Sertoli, A. Zanzotto. Genova, Tilgher (B).

Teori Praksis, no. 9, 1981, *Filosofi, politik og psykoanalyse J. Derrida,* texts by P. A. Brandt, N. Egebak, P. Kemp, E. Krause-Jensen, S. E. Larsen, Kongerslev, Denmark, GMT.

Semeia: An Experimental Journal for Biblical Criticism, no. 23, 1982, *Derrida and Biblical Studies,* ed. R. Detweiler, texts by J. D. Crossan, J. P. Leavey Jr., H. N. Schneidau, The Society of Biblical Literature, Scholars Press, USA.

Contemporary Literary Criticism, Jacques Derrida 24, ed. Sharon R. Gunton, texts by D. Donoghue, M. Grene, G. H. Hartman, D. Hoy, D. G. Marshall, J. N. Riddel, R. Rorty, E. Said, M. Wood, Gale, Michigan, 1983.

Tijdschrift voor filosofie, Jacques Derrida, texts by S. Weber, R. Bernet, V. Vasterling, Leuven, 1983.

Nuova Corrente, nos. 93–94, 1984, *Decostruzione tra filosofia e letteratura,* symposium of Urbino, July 23–26, 1984, texts by G. Almansi, M. Ferraris, S. Fish, J. F. Graham, S. Hanson, D. Kujundzic, M. Lydon, P. de Man, P. Pucci, S. Rosso, L. R. Schehr, S. Weber, Genova, Tilgher (B).

Rivista da Estetica, year 25, no. 17, 1984, *Estetica e decostruzione,* texts by R. Burger, G. Carchia, M. Ferraris, C. Fynsk, R. Gasché, J. Margolis, L. Marin, M. Sbisa, J. Snyder, F. Vercellone, Turin, Rosenberg & Sellier.

Diacritics, winter 1985, *Marx after Derrida,* ed. S. P. Mohanty, texts by T. Eagleton, T. S. Lewis, A. Parker, G. C. Spivak, R. Terdiman, S. Weber.

Maldoror, no. 21, 1985, *Jacques Derrida—Primeras (p)referencias,* ed. C. Pellegrino, texts by L. Block de Behar, G. Grundman, G. Hartman, S. Kofman, R. E. Monegal, Montevideo.

Synteesi, no. 3, 1985, special edition on J.D. and deconstruction, texts by J. Culler, R. Gasché, O. Pasanen, Helsinki.

Dang-Dai, no. 4, January 1986, contributions by Chang Han-Liang, Li Yüeh, Li Yung-shih, Peking.

The Journal of the British Society for Phenomenology, no. 3, October 1986, *The Philosophy of Jacques Derrida,* texts by

J. D.'s initials in a drawing by André Masson for a special issue of *Les Lettres Françaises,* in 1972.

R. Berezdivin, J. D. Caputo, R. Gasché, I. E. Harvey, R. Platt, T. M. Seebohm.

De/Constructie. Kleine diergaerde voor kinderen van nu 1, Restant XV, 2, Antwerp, Records of Congress "De/Constructie", April 15, 1987, texts by R. Bernet, P. Buyck, G. Groot, S. Houppermans, G. Lernout.

De/Constructie. Kleine diergaerde voor kinderen van nu, 2, texts by E. Borms, S. Briosi, P. Buyck, C. Norris, E. Oger, C. Struyker Boudier, V. Vasterling, N. Wallace.

Confrontation, no. 19, spring 1988, *Derrida,* texts by A. Bass, D. Carroll, W. Kerrigan, J. H. Miller, A. Ronell, S. Weber.

Pratt Journal of Architecture 2, 1988, *Form, Being, Absence: Architecture and Philosophy,* texts by L. Breslin, E. Feingold, J. Knesl, S. Perella, M. C. Taylor, M. Wrigley, New York.

Religion and Intellectual Life, no. 2, winter 1988, *Deconstruction,* texts by W. Cutter, R. Detweiler, C. Raschke, G. Sheppard, M. Taylor. New Rochelle, New York.

Spirale 82, October 1988, *Jacques Derrida* (Dossier), texts by M. La Chance, G. Leroux, C. McDonald, G. Michaud, Montreal.

Anthropos, no. 93, February 1989, *Jacques Derrida: Una teoría de la escritura, la estrategia de la deconstrucción. Presencia del pensiamento de Jacques Derrida en España,* texts by M.-J. Abella Maeso, R. del Castillo Santos, A. N. Dobarro, F. Duque, M. Ferraris, J. Garcia, J. S. Guerrero, J. A. Mayorga Ruanœ, J. M. Peña, M. Peñalver Mariano, P. Peñalver Gomez, C. de Perretti Peñaranda, J. M. Ripalda, M. E. Vazquez, Barcelona.

Anthropos, Antologías temáticas, no. 13, March 1989, texts by J. J. Acero, L. F. Carracedo, E. P. Mecloy, P. Peñalver, C. de Peretti, Barcelona.

Deconstruction. Omnibus Volume, texts by A. Benjamin, G. Bennington, D. Lodge, J. Griffiths, P. Crowther, S. Tigerman, London, Academy Editions, 1989.

El Independiente, no. 12, December 24, 1989, *Jacques Derrida* (Dossier), texts by F. Duque, P. Peñalver Gomez, C. de Peretti, F. Perez, V. Bozal, J. M. Ripalda, J. P. Tudela, Madrid.

Critical Inquiry, no. 4, summer 1989, *On Jacques Derrida's "Paul de Man's War,"* texts by J.-M. Apostolidès, J.

Brenkman et J. Law, J. Culler, W. W. Holdheim, M. Perloff, J. Wiener, Univ. of Chicago Press.

Redrawing the Lines. Analytic Philosophy, Deconstruction, and Literary Theory, texts by J. Law, C. Norris, R. Rorty, H. Staten, S. Winspur, Univ. of Minnesota Press, 1989.

Revue philsophique de la France et de l'étranger, no. 2, April–June 1990, *Derrida,* ed. Catherine Malabou, texts by G. Agamben, R. Bernet, M. Banchot, R. Brague, G. Granel, M. Haar, D. F. Krell, R. Laporte, N. Loraux, J.-F. Lyotard, R. Major, C. Malabou, J.-L. Nancy, J. Sallis, B. Stiegler, J. Taminiaux, Paris, PUF.

Deconstruction and the Possibility of Justice, 28 participants, *Cardozo Law Review* 11, nos. 5–6, New York, 1990.

Les Lettres françaises, no. 4, December 1990, texts by C. Malabou, C. Margat, R. Michel.

6. Articles on Jacques Derrida

From a list of more than one thousand articles (classified by Elisabeth Weber in alphabetical order of author within each year), I have had to make brutal and unfair selections. To limit the arbitrariness of this procedure, I have varied the criteria (dates, places, subjects, situations). G.B.

Deguy, Michel, "Husserl en seconde lecture," *Critique,* no. 192, May 1963.

Carabelli, Giancarlo, "L'esperienza della scrittura," *Tempo presente* 606, June 1963.

Lacroix, Jean, "Ecriture et métaphysique selon Jacques Derrida," repr. in *Panorama de la philosophie française contemporaine,* Paris, PUF, 1966.

Perniola, Mario, "Grammatologia ed estetica," *Rivista di Estetica* 3, 1966.

Vuilleumier, J., "L'irruption du dehors dans le dedans," *La Tribune de Genève,* October 1–2, 1966.

Wahl, François, "L'écriture avant la parole?" *La Quinzaine littéraire,* May 2, 1966.

Bonnefoy, Claude, "Un nouveau philosophe, Jacques Derrida met en question toute la pensée contemporaine," *Arts-Loisirs,* June 1967.

Châtelet, François, "Mort du livre?" *La Quinzaine littéraire,* no. 15, October 31, 1967.

Ehrmann, Jacques, "Qui parle?" *Manteia,* no. 1, 1967.

Granel, Gérard, "Jacques Derrida et la rature de l'origine," *Critique,* no. 246, November 1967 (repr. in *Traditionis traditio,* Paris, Gallimard, 1972).

LaCroix, Jean, "La parole et l'écriture," *Le Monde,* November 18, 1967.

Penel, A., "Comment échapper à la philosophie? Jacques Derrida met en question la pensée occidentale," *La Tribune de Genève,* November 15, 1967.

Smith, F. Joseph, "Jacques Derrida's Husserl Interpretation," *Philosophy Today* 9, 1967.

Wahl, François, "Forcer les limites," *La Quinzaine littéraire,* no. 32, July 15–31, 1967.

Agosti, Stefano, "L'écriture et la différence," *Strumenti Critici* 2, no. 1, February 1968.

Châtelet, François, "Qui est Jacques Derrida? La métaphysique dans sa clôture," *Le Nouvel Observateur,* November 20–December 20 1968.

Robert, Jean-Dominique, "Voix et phénomène: à propos d'un ouvrage récent," *Revue philosophique de Louvain* 66, 1968.

Scherer, René, "Clôture et faille dans la phénoménologie de Husserl," *Revue de métaphysique et de morale,* no. 3, July–September, 1968.

Wahl, François, "La philosophie entre l'avant et l'après du structuralisme, II, La structure, le sujet, la trace," in *Qu'est-ce que le structuralisme?,* Paris, Seuil, 1968.

Benoist, Jean-Marie, "'Présence' de Husserl," *Les Etudes philosophiques* 4, 1968.

Boyer, Philippe, "Déconstruction: le désir à la lettre," *Change,* no. 2, 1969, *La Destruction* (repr. in *L'Ecarté(e),* Paris, Seghers-Laffont, 1973).

Catesson, Jean, "A propos d'une pensée de l'intervalle," *Revue de métaphysique et de morale,* no. 74, 1969.

Sollers, Philippe, "Un pas sur la lune," *Tel quel,* no. 39, autumn 1969 (and in *The Times Literary Supplement,* September 25, 1969).

Visscher, Luce F. de, "Des privilèges d'une grammatologie," *Revue philosophique de Louvain,* August 1969.

De Man, Paul, "Rhétorique de la cécité: Derrida lecteur de Rousseau," *Poétique,* no. 4, 1970.

Marchant, Patricio, "Presencia y escritura" (introduction to his translation of "Ousia et Grammè"), *Tiempo y Presencia,* Santiago de Chile, 1971.

Anonymous, "Scription, matérialisme dialectique Derrida-Marx," *Scription Rouge* (Organe de la science marxiste révolutionnaire textuelle), no. 1, May 1972.

Beigbeder, Marc, "*La Grammatologie* de Jacques Derrida," in *Contradiction et Nouvel Entendement,* Paris, Bordas, 1972.

Clemens, Eric, "Sur Derrida: Alternance et dédoublement," *TXT,* no. 5, Rennes, Bruxelles.

Egebak, Niels, "Et notat til en Derrida—Oversaettelse," *Exil. Tidsskrift for litterratur og semiologi,* no. 2, August 1972, Copenhagen, Vinten.

Favale, C., "La linguistica strutturale e Jacques Derrida," *Il Protagora* (1972), 80–81.

Finas, Lucette, "Derrida 'marque' Valéry," *La Quinzaine littéraire,* November 15–30, 1972.

Gelley, Alexander, "Form as Force," *Diacritics* 2, no. 1, spring 1972.

Goux, Jean Joseph, "*La Dissémination* de Jacques Derrida," *Les Lettres françaises,* no. 1455, October 11–17, 1972.

Guibal, Francis, "Philosophie, langage, écriture," *Etudes* 5, May 1972.

Jackson, John E., "Jacques Derrida: Un auteur ardu, mais le seul philosophe contemporain qu'admire Heidegger," *Journal de Genève,* December 2, 1972.

Kelemen, Janos, "Jacques Derrida A grammatologiarol," *Valosag* 25, no. 7, Budapest, 1972.

Klein, Richard, "Prolegomenon to Derrida," *Diacritics* 2, no. 4, winter 1972.

Parret, H., "Over de 'notie' van schriftuur," *Tijdschrift voor Filosofie* 34, 1972.

Singevin, Charles, "La pensée, le langage, l'écriture et l'être," *Revue philosophique de la France et de l'étranger* 162, no. 2, April–June 1972, and no. 3, July–September 1972.

Toubeau, Hélene, "Le *Pharmakon* et les aromates," *Critique,* nos. 303–304, August–September 1972.

Zaner, Richard M., "Discussion of Jacques Derrida's 'The

Ends of Man,'" *Philosophy and Phenomenological Research,* March 1972.

Anonymous, "La crise du signe et de l'impérialisme. Trotsky/articulation historique/Derrida," *Scription Rouge* (op. cit.), no. 5, September–November 1973.

Beyssade, Jean-Marie, "'Mais quoi, ce sont des fous': Sur un passage controversé de la Première Méditation," *Revue de métaphysique et de morale,* 1973.

Brague, Rémi, "En marge de *La Pharmacie de Platon* de Jacques Derrida," *Revue philosophique de Louvain* 71, May 1973.

Delacampagne, C., "Un coup porté à la métaphysique," *Le Monde,* June 14, 1973; "Condillac et le 'frivole,'" *Le Monde,* December 20, 1973.

Giovannangeli, Daniel, "Code et différence impure," *Littérature,* no. 12, December 1973.

Girard, René, "Lévi-Strauss, Frye, Derrida and Shakespeare Criticism," *Diacritics* 3, no. 3, fall 1973.

Anonymous, "Subersiv Gedacht," *Der Spiegel,* June 10, 1974.

Anquetil, Gilles, "*Glas,* le nouveau livre de Jacques Derrida," *Les Nouvelles littéraires,* no. 2457, October 28–November 3, 1974.

Autrand, Charles, "Mais qu'écrit donc Derrida?" *Cahiers L'Envers et l'Endroit,* May–June 1974.

Bass, Alan, "'Literature'/Literature," *Velocities of change: Critical Essays from MLN,* Johns Hopkins Univ. Press, 1974.

Blanchard, Gérard, "A propos de *Glas,*" *Communication et Langages,* no. 26, 1974.

Benoist, Jean-Marie, "L'inscription de Derrida," *La Quinzaine littéraire,* no. 182, March 1, 1974.

Delacampagne, C., "Derrida hors de soi," *Critique,* no. 325, June 1974.

Egebak, Niels, "Mimesisproblematikken hos Jacques Derrida," Knudsen, N. L., Olsen, O. A. eds. *Subjekt og Tekst,* Kongerslev, GMT, 1974, Denmark.

Jackson, John E., "Le dernier Derrida—un livre détestable d'une vulgarité immense. Un livre diabolique," *Le Journal de Genève,* December 15, 1974.

J. D.'s initials in a drawing by André Masson for a special issue of *Les Lettres Françaises,* in 1972.

Jannoud, Claude, "L'Evangile selon Derrida: sur Hegel et Genet," *Le Figaro littéraire,* November 30, 1974.

Kerr, Fergus, "Derrida's Wake," *New Blackfriars* 55, no. 653, October 1974.

Larmore, C., "Reading Russell, Readying Derrida," *Cambridge Review,* no. 2219, March 1974.

Lévy, Bernard-Henry, "Derrida n'est pas un gourou," *Magazine littéraire,* no. 88, May 1974.

Loriot, Patrick "*Glas*—de Jacques Derrida," *Le Nouvel Observateur,* no. 256, December 9–15, 1974.

Malmberg, Bertil, "Derrida et la sémiologie: Quelques notes marginales," *Semiotica II,* no. 2, 1974.

Margolin, Jean-Claude, "Les marginalia de Derrida," *Revue de synthèse,* nos. 73–74, January–June 1974.

Mehlman, Jeffrey, "Orphée scripteur: Blanchot, Rilke, Derrida," *Poétique,* no. 20, 1974.

Merlin, Frédéric, "Derrida ou la philosophie en éclats," *Les Nouvelles littéraires,* no. 2415, January 7, 1974; "Après Mallarmé, Pour qui sonne le glas," *Les Nouvelles littéraires,* no. 2461, November 25, 1974.

Pachet, Pierre, "Une entreprise troublante," *La Quinzaine littéraire,* no. 197, November 1, 1974.

Perlini, T., "Ontologia come violenza," *Nuova Corrente,* 63, 1974.

Van Hoovert, Michel T., "La stratégie corruptrice de Jacques Derrida," *Gazette de Lausanne,* January 19, 1974.

Agosti, Stefano, "*Glas,* libro scandoloso: Per chi suona questa campana," *Il Giorno,* January 15, 1975.

Ames, Van Meter, "Art for Art's Sake Again?" *The Journal of Aesthetics and Art Criticism* 33, no. 3, 1975.

Bandera, Cesareo, "Literature and Desire: Poetic Frenzy and the Love Potion," *Mosaic* 8, 1975.

Benoist, Jean Marie, "Le Colosse de Rhodes," *L'Art vivant,* no. 54, December 1974–January 1975.

Boyer, Philippe, "Le point de la question," *Change* 22, "L'imprononçable, l'écriture nomade," March 1975.

Delacampagne, C., "Hegel et Gabrielle, le premier 'livre' de Jacques Derrida," *Le Monde,* January 3, 1975.

Hartman, Geoffrey H., "*Monsieur Texte:* On Jacques Derrida, his *Glas,*" *The Georgia Review* 29, no. 4, winter 1975, p. 759–97.

Jabès, Edmond, "Lettre à Jacques Derrida sur la question du livre," in *Ça suit son cours,* Fata Morgana, 1975.

Lamizet, Bernard, et Nef, Frédéric, "Entrave double: le glas et la chute," *Gramma,* no. 2, April 1, 1975.

Laruelle, François, "Le style di-phallique de Jacques Derrida," *Critique,* no. 334, March 1975.

Lascault, Gilbert, "La peinture d'Adami telle qu'on l'écrit," *La Quinzaine littéraire,* June 16, 1975.

Meschonnic, Henri, "L'écriture de Derrida," *Les Cahiers du chemin,* no. 24, April 15, 1975.

Miguez, José Antonio, "Derrida, Jacques *La Diseminación,*" *Arbor* 92, no. 360, 1975.

Miller, J. Hillis, "Deconstructing the Deconstructers," *Diacritics,* no. 2, summer 1975.

Parret, Herman, "Grammatology and Linguistics: On Derrida's Interpretation of Linguistic Theories," *Poetics* 4, no. 1, March 1975.

Toyosaki, Koitchi, "Mobile Supplements" (in Japanese), Epaves ed., Tokyo, 1975.

Altieri, Charles, "Wittgenstein on Consciousness and Language: A Challenge to Derridean Literary Theory," *MLN,* no. 6, December 1976.

Castellana, M., "Il post-strutturalismo di Jacques Derrida," *Il Protagora* (1976).

Delacampagne, C., "Derrida et Deleuze," *Le Monde,* April 30, 1976.

Ferguson, Frances C., "Reading Heidegger: Jacques Derrida and Paul de Man," *Boundary* 2, no. 2, winter 1976, repr. by Indiana Univ. Press, 1979.

Giovannangeli, Daniel, "Jacques Derrida: une pensée de la répétition," *Annales de l'Institut de philosophie,* Brussels, 1976.

Grene, Marjorie, "Life, Death, and Language: Some Thoughts on Wittgenstein and Derrida," *Partisan Review* 43, 1976.

Laruelle, François, "La scène du vomi, ou comment ça se détraque dans la théorie," *Critique* 347, April 1976.

Leavey, John, "Derrida and Dante: Differance and the Eagle in the Sphere of Jupiter," *MLN,* no. 1, January 1976.

McLaughlen, Kathleen, "Reading anew: A study of critical

methods through the texts of Jacques Derrida," *DAI* 36, 1976.

Mecchia, Renata, "L'interpretazione della linguistica saussuriana e la duplice nozione de 'scrittura': Jacques Derrida," *Lingua e stile* 2, 1976.

Mehlman, Jeffrey, "Ruse de Rivoli: Politics and Deconstruction," *MLN* 91, no. 5, October 1976.

Nemo, Philippe, "L'aventure collective d'un chercheur solitaire: Derrida et le *Greph,*" *Les Nouvelles littéraires,* February 12, 1976.

Riddel, Joseph, "From Heidegger to Derrida to Chance . . . ," *Boundary* 2, 4, no. 2, winter 1976, and in Spanos, W. V. ed., *Heidegger and the Question of Literature: Toward Postmodern Literary Hermeneutics,* Indiana Univ. Press, 1979.

Stefan, Jude, "Sur L'Archéologie du frivole," *Les Cahiers du chemin,* no. 28, October 15, 1976.

Abrams, M. H., "The Limits of Pluralism II: The Deconstructive Angel," *Critical Inquiry* 3, no. 3, spring 1977, Univ. of Chicago Press.

Agosti, Stefano, "Il fantasma segreto dell'inconscio," *Il Giorno,* March 2, 1977.

Garver, Newton, "Derrida on Rousseau on Writing," *The Journal of Philosophy* 74, no. 11, November 1977.

Heath, Stephen, "Of Derrida," *Canto,* winter 1977.

Johnson, Barbara, "The Frame of Reference: Poe, Lacan, Derrida," *Yale French Studies,* nos. 55–56, 1977, *Literature and Psychoanalysis.*

Leavey, John, "Undecidables and Old Names," preface to *Ed. Husserl's Origin of Geometry: An Introduction,* New York, Nicolas Hays Ltd., 1977; repr. Nebraska Univ. Press, 1989.

Lemaitre, M., "Borges . . . Derrida . . . Sollers . . . Borges," *Revista Iberoamericana* 43, 1977.

McDonald, D., "Derrida and Pirandello," *Modern Drama* 20, 1977, 4.

Miers, Paul, "Avertissement: Fourfold Vortex Formulations of *Différance* in Derridean Cryptograms," *MLN* 92, 1977, 5.

Pachet, Pierre, "Une réélaboration de la théorie freudienne

de l'inconscient," *La Quinzaine littéraire,* no. 253, April 1, 1977.

Peretti, Cristina de, "'Ereignis' y 'Différance.' Derrida, intérprete de Heidegger," *Anales del seminario de metafísica* 12, 1977, Madrid.

Rorty, Richard, "Derrida on Language, Being, and Abnormal Philosophy," *The Journal of Philosophy,* no. 11, November 1977.

Spivak, Gayatri C., "Glas-Piece," *Diacritics,* no. 3, fall 1977.

Berns, Egide E., "*De Grammatologie* van J. Derrida," *Wijsgerig perspectief op maatschappij en wetenschp* 19, no. 1, 1978–79.

Bogel, Fredric V., "Deconstructive criticism: the logic of Derrida's différance," *Minnesota Center For Advanced Studies: Language, Style and Literary Theory* 6, 1978.

Carroll, D., "History as Writing," *Clio* 7, 1978.

Ciampa, Maurizio, "Il fattore di Derrida," *Rinascita,* no. 21, May 26, 1978.

Fynsk, Christopher I., "A Decelebration of Philosophy," *Diacritics,* summer 1978.

Janicaud, Dominique, "Presence and Appropriation: Derrida and the Question of an Overcoming of Metaphysical Language," *Research in Phenomenology* 8, 1978.

Rorty, Richard, "Philosophy as a Kind of Writing," *New Literary History* 10.

Cahen, Didier, "Faux-tableau de Derrida: investiture/peinture," *Critique,* no. 390, November 1979.

Giovannangeli, Daniel, "Pour ne pas mourir de la vérité (Derrida écrit sur la peinture)," *Cahiers internationaux de symbolisme,* nos. 37–38–39, 1979.

Hoy, David C., "Forgetting the Text: Derrida's Critique of Heidegger," *Boundary* 2, 8, no. 1, 1979.

Kambouchner, Denis, "Derrida et le 'bottle-neck,'" *Le Nouvel Observateur,* August 27, 1979.

Kemp, Peter, "L'éthique au lendemain des victoires des athéismes: Réflexions sur la philosophie de Jacques Derrida," *Revue de théologie et de philosophie* 111, 1979.

McDonald, Christie, "Jacques Derrida's Reading of Rousseau," *The Eighteenth Century,* no. 1, winter 1979.

Monroe, Bill, "Derrière Derrida: The Narrative as a Socio-Intellectio Drama (in three acts)," *Chicago Literary Review,* December 7, 1979.

Olivier, Jean-Michel, "Hors cadre: La Vérité en peinture de Jacques Derrida," *Actuels* nos. 9–10, 1979.

Orr, Leonard, "A Derrida Checklist," *Sub-stance,* no. 22, 1979 (B).

Owens, Craig, "Detachment from the parergon," *October,* no. 9, summer 1979.

Reggiori, Danielle, "La Des-Textualización segun Derrida," *Cuadernos de Filosofía y Letras,* August 1979, Bogota.

Rodriguez, Mario, "Borges y Derrida," *Revista chilena di Literatura,* no. 13, April 1979.

Taguiev, Pierre, "Philosophie et peinture," *Opus international,* no. 72, 1979.

Whitford, Margaret, "Derrida's Grammatology—A Philosophy with a Difference," *The Literary Review,* November 30–December 13, 1979.

Wood, D. C., "Introduction to Derrida," *Radical Philosophy,* no. 21, spring 1979.

Wordsworth, Ann, "Considerable Texts," *The Oxford Literary Review* 4, no. 1, autumn 1979.

Boyer, Philippe, "Lettre d'amour d'un philosphe," *Libération,* June 6, 1980.

Clément, Catherine, "*La Carte postale* de Jacques Derrida: Le livre d'amour d'un philosophe," *Le Matin,* April 29, 1980.

Delacampagne, Christian, "Une singulière carte postale," *Le Monde,* April 4, 1980.

Goldberg, S. L., "The Deconstruction Gang," *London Review of Books,* vol. 2, no. 10, May 22–June 4 1980.

Major, René, "Spéculer sur Derrida avec Freud," *La Quinzaine littéraire,* no. 325, May 15–31, 1980.

Norris, Christopher, "The Polymetaphorical Mailman: Jacques Derrida," *Times Literary Supplement,* July 4, 1980.

Olivier, Jean-Michel, "*La Carte postale—De Socrate à Freud et au delà,* de Jacques Derrida," *Actuels,* 12–13, 1980.

Pachet, Pierre, "Amour et philosophie," *La Quinzaine littéraire,* no. 325, May 15–31, 1980.

Petitdemange, Guy, "Les traversées de la fin: Spinoza. Kant. Derrida," *Recherches de science religieuse,* 1980.

Spivak, Gayatri C., "Revolutions That as yet Have No Model: Derrida's *Limited Inc.,*" *Diacritics,* no. 4, winter 1980.

Wood, David, "Style and Strategy at the Limits of Philosophy: Heidegger and Derrida," *The Monist* 63, no. 4, October 1980.

Wood, David, "Derrida and the Paradoxes of Reflection," *Journal of the British Society for Phenomenology* 2, no. 3, October 1980.

Boyer, Philippe, "Il était une fois un philosophe (à propos de Derrida)," *Politique Hebdo,* April 27–May 3, 1981.

Boyne, Roy, "Alcibiades as Hero: Derrida/Nietzsche?" *Sub-stance* 28, 1981.

Cacciari, Massimo, and Ciampa, Maurizio, "Sul Fondamento: Nietzsche letto da Derrida," *Il Centauro,* no. 1, January–April 1981.

Clément, Catherine, "Jacques Derrida met l'API en accusation", *Le Matin,* February 14–15, 1981.

Cumming, Robert D., "The Odd Couple: Heidegger and Derrida," *Review of Metaphysics* 34, March 1981.

Davies, John L., "Derrida and a Theory of Meaning," in *Theories of Meaning—Education, Television,* Institute of Education, London Univ., 1981.

Engdahl, Horace, and Malmberg, Carl Johan, "Kommentar til Glas," *Kris* 20/21, 1981, Stockholm.

Ferraris, Maurizio, "Derrida e l'ontologia della scrittura, Differenze: La filosofia francese dopo lo strutturalismo, Multhipla, Milan, 1981.

Hobson, Marian, "Jacques Derrida's Scroll-Work," *The Oxford Literary Review* 4, no. 3, 1981.

James, Carol P., "Reading Art through Duchamp's *Glass* and Derrida's *Glas,*" *Sub-stance* 31, 1981.

Parker, Andrew, "Taking Sides (on History): Derrida Re-Marx," *Diacritics* 11, September 1981.

Schor, Naomi, "Duane Hanson Truth Sculpture" (chap. "Derrida/Kant"), *Fragments: Incompletion and Discontinuity,* L. D. Kritzman and J. Parisier Plottel, eds., nos. 8–9, New York, 1981.

Bernet, Rudolf, "Is the Present Ever Present? Phenomenology and the Metaphysics of Presence," *Research in Phenomenology* 12, 1982.

Boehm, Rudolf, "A Tale of Estrangement: Husserl and Contemporary Philosophy," *Research in Phenomenology* 12, 1982.

Culler, Jonathan, "Convention and Meaning: Derrida and Austin," *New Literary History* 13, 1981–82.

Gane, Mike, "Textual Theory: Derrida," *Economy and Society* 2, no. 2, May 1982.

Handelman, Susan, "Reb Derrida's Scripture," in *The Slayers of Moses: The Emergence of Rabbinic Interpretation in Modern Literary Theory,* State Univ. of New York Press, 1982.

Hejdanek, Ladislas, Dr., "L'affaire du philosophe Jacques Derrida," *Les Temps modernes,* no. 429, April 1982.

Henning, E. M. "Foucault and Derrida: Archaelogy and Deconstruction," *Stanford French Review,* fall 1981.

Hobson, Marian, "Deconstruction, Empiricism, and the Postal Services," *French Studies* 34, no. 3, July 1982.

Howells, Christina, "Sartre and Derrida: qui perd gagne," *Journal of the British Society for Phenomenology,* January 1982.

Ihde, Don, "Phenomenology and Deconstructive Strategy," *Semiotica* 41, 1982.

Lawlor, Leonard, "Temporality and Spatiality, a Note to a Footnote in Jacques Derrida's Writing and Difference," *Research in Phenomenology* 12, 1982.

Liberman, Kenneth, "The Economy of Central Australian Aboriginal Expression: An Inspection from the Vantage of Merleau-Ponty and Derrida," *Semiotica* 40, 1982.

Meyerowitz, Rael, "The Uncanny Sun," *The Hebrew University Studies in Literature,* autumn 1982, Jerusalem.

Nevo, Ruth, "The Waste-Land: Ur-Text of Deconstruction," *New Literary History* 13, no. 3, spring 1982.

Van Luijk, Henk, "Jacques Derrida Filosoferen tegen het zere been," *Elseviers Magazine,* no. 20, May 22, 1982.

Wolosky, Shira, "Derrida, Jabès, Levinas: Sign-Theory as Ethical Discourse," *Prooftexts: A Journal of Jewish Literary History* 2, 1982, Johns Hopkins Univ. Press.

Wood, David, "Time and Interpretation" (on J.D. and Heidegger), in Wood, D. and Bernasconi, R., eds., *Time and Metaphysics: A Collection of Original Papers,* Parousia Press, Warwick.

Wright, Edmond, "Derrida, Searle, Contexts, Games, Riddles," *New Literary History* 13, no. 3, spring 1982.

Bennington, Geoff, "Theory: They or We?" *Paragraph: The Journal of the Critical Theory Group* 1 (on J.D. and Lyotard), Cambridge, 1983.

Cohen, R. A., "The Privilege of Reason and Play: Derrida and Levinas," *Tijdschrift voor Filosofie,* year 45, no. 2, June 1983.

Ferraris, Maurizio, "Derrida: La grammatologia e la 'verita in pittura'" and "Da Loos a Derrida," in *Tracce: Nihilismo, moderno, postmoderno,* Multhipla, Milan, 1983.

Ferrero Carracedo, Luis, and De Peretti, Cristina, "La Recepción en España del pensamiento de Jacques Derrida," *Revista de Filosofía,* 2d series, 6, 1983, Madrid.

Forrester, John, "Who is in Analysis with Whom? Freud, Lacan, Derrida," *Economy and Society* 13, no. 2, 1983.

Frankel, Margherita, "Vico and Rousseau through Derrida," *New Vico Studies* 1, 1983.

Gasché, Rodolphe, "Joining the Text from Heidegger to Derrida," in J. Arac, W. Godzich, and W. Martin, eds., *The Yale Critics: Deconstruction in America,* Univ. of Minnesota Press, 1983.

Godzich, Wlad, "The Domestication of Derrida," in J. Arac, W. Godzich, and W. Martin, eds., *The Yale Critics: Deconstruction in America,* Univ. of Minnesota Press, 1983.

Grisoni, Dominique A., "Le phénomène Derrida," *Le Magazine littéraire,* no. 196, June 1983.

Harvey, Irene E., "Derrida and the Concept of Metaphysics," *Research in Phenomenology* 13, 1983.

Nancy, Jean-Luc, "La voix libre de l'homme," in *L'Impératif catégorique,* Paris, Flammarion, 1983.

Waldenfels, B., "Auf den Spuren der Schrift (Jacques Derrida)," in *Phänomenologie in Frankreich,* Suhrkamp, 1983.

Wyschogrod, Edith, "Time and Non-Being: Derrida and

Quine," *Journal of the British Society for Phenomenology* 14, no. 2, May 1983.

Yaeger, Patricia, "Coleridge, Derrida and the Anguish of Writing," *Sub-stance* 39, 1983.

Yeh, Michelle, "The Deconstructive Way: A Comparative Study of Derrida and Chuang Tzu," *Journal of Chinese Philosophy* 10, 1983, Honolulu.

Casey, Edward S., "Origin(s) (of) Heidegger/Derrida," *The Journal of Philosophy* 31, no. 10, October 1984.

D'Amico, Robert, "Text and Context: Derrida and Foucault on Descartes," *The Structural Allegory,* in John Fekete, ed., Univ. of Minnesota Press, 1984.

Dean, Williams, "Deconstruction and Process Theology," *The Journal of Religion* 64, 1984.

Delacampagne, Christian, "Derrida: Le droit à la philosophie," *Le Nouvel Observateur,* May 11–17, 1984.

Donato, Eugene, "Ending/closure: On Derrida's Ending of Heidegger," *Yale French Studies,* no. 67, 1984.

Gadamer, Hans-Georg, "Et pourtant: puissance de la bonne volonté (une réplique à J.D.)," *Revue internationale de philosophie,* no. 151, 1984, fasc. 4, *Herméneutique et Neostructuralisme: Derrida-Gadamer-Searle,* Univ. of Brussels/PUF.

Keenan, Tom, "Jacques Derrida: *Signéponge/Signsponge,*" *Critical Texts,* Yale Univ.

Marion, Jean-Luc, "La percée et l'élargissement: Contribution à l'interprétation des *Recherches logiques,*" *Philosophie,* nos. 2 and 3, 1984, repr. *Réduction et Donation,* PUF, 1989.

Ormiston, Gayle L., "Traces of Derrida: Nietzsche's Image of Woman," *Philosophy Today,* summer 1984.

Rorty, Richard, "Deconstruction and Circumvention," *Critical Inquiry* 11, no. 1, September 1984.

———, "Signposts along the Way That Reason Went," *London Review of Books,* February 16–29, 1984.

Sallis, John, "Heidegger/Derrida—Presence" (Symposium Heidegger/Derrida), *The Journal of Philosophy* 81, no. 10, October 1984.

Schrift, Alan D., "Reading Derrida Reading Heidegger Reading Nietzsche," *Research in Phenomenology* 14, 1984.

Shapiro, Gary, "Peirce and Derrida on First and Last Things," *University of Dayton Review* 17, no. 1, 1984.

Spivak, Gayatri C., "Love me, Love My Ombre, Elle," *Diacritics,* winter 1984.

Wheeler, Samuel C., "Indeterminacy of French Interpretation: Derrida and Davidson," *Truth and Interpretation,* Blackwell, 1984.

Wills, David, "Post/Card/Match/Book/Envois/Derrida," *Sub-stance 43,* vol. 13, no. 2, 1984.

Wright, Elizabeth, "Post-structural Psychoanalysis: Text as Psyche—Derrida and the Scene of Writing," in *Psychoanalytic Criticism, Theory and Practice,* Methuen, 1984.

Anonymous, "The Derrida Room," *In-S-Omnia: Invisible Seattle's Omnia,* no. 1, 1985, Seattle.

Adams, Michael Vannoy, "Deconstructive Philosophy and Imaginal Psychology: Comparative Perspectives on Jacques Derrida and James Hillman," *Journal of Literary Criticism* 2, no. 1 (June 1985), Allahabad, India.

Benstock, Shari, "From Letters to Literature: *La Carte postale* and the Epistolary Genre," *Genre* 18, fall 1985.

Bernet, Rudolf, "Die ungegenwärtige Gegenwart: Anwesenheit und Abwesenheit. Husserls Analyse des Zeitbewußtseins," *Phänomenologische Forschungen* 14, 1985, Fribourg and Munich, Alber.

Block de Behar, Lisa, "Jacques Derrida, un filósofo inaudito," *Jaque,* Montevideo, October 10, 1985.

Caputo, John D., "Three Transgressions: Nietzsche, Heidegger, Derrida," *Research in Phenomenology* 15, 1985.

Chang, Briankle G., "The Eclipse of Being: Heidegger and Derrida," *International Philosophical Quarterly,* June 1985.

Cobb-Stevens, Richard, "Derrida and Husserl on the Status of Retention," *Analecta Husserliana* 19, 1985.

Dearin, Ray D., "On Signéponge/Signsponge by Jacques Derrida," *Quarterly Journal of Speech,* May 1985.

Ferraris, Maurizio, "Note. Habermas, Foucault, Derrida. A proposito di 'neoilluminismo' e 'neoconservatismo,'" *Aut aut* 208, July–August 1985.

Fynsk, Christopher, "The Choice of Deconstruction," *Rivista di estetica,* no. 17, Turin, 1985.

Gadamer, Hans-Georg, "Decostruzione e interpretatzione," *Aut aut* 208, July–August 1985.

Habermas, Jürgen, ". . . Derridas Kritik am Phonozentrismus," *Der Philosophische Diskurs der Moderne,* Suhrkamp, 1985.

Jardine, Alice A., "The Hysterical Text's Organs: Angles on Jacques Derrida," in *Gynesis: Configurations of Woman and Modernity,* Cornell Univ. Press, 1985.

Krell, David Farrell, "A Hermeneutics of Discretion," *Research in Phenomenology* 15, 1985.

Lawson, Hilary, "Derrida," *Reflexivity: The Post-modern Predicament,* London, 1985.

Leitch, Vincent B, "Derrida's Assault on the Institution of Style," in J. M. Heath and M. Payne, eds., *Text, Interpretation, Theory,* Bucknell Univ. Press, 1985.

Llewelyn, John, "Levinas, Derrida, and Others 'Vis-à-Vis,'" in *Beyond Metaphysics? The Hermeneutic Circle in Contemporary Continental Philosophy,* Humanities Press, 1985.

Longxi, Zhang, "The Tao and the Logos: Notes on Derrida's Critique of Logocentrism," *Critical Inquiry* 11, no. 3, 1985.

McCannell, Juliet Flower, "The Temporality of Textuality: Bakhtin and Derrida," *MLN,* 1985.

Mauriès, Patrick, "Jacques Derrida, la déconstruction du monde," *Libération,* August 8, 1985.

Morot-Sir, Edouard, "On *Signéponge/Signsponge,*" *World Literature Today,* winter 1985.

Parker, Andrew, "Between Dialectics and Deconstruction: Derrida and the Reading of Marx", in G. S. Jay and D. L. Miller, eds., *After Strange Texts: The role of theory in the study of literature,* Univ. of Alabama Press, 1985.

———, "Response to Jacques Derrida's 'Mnemosyne, a lecture for Paul de Man,'" *Critical Exchange,* no. 17, winter 1985.

Peñalver, Patricio, "Jacques Derrida: La clausura del Saber," in *La Voz y el Fenómeno* (preface to the Spanish translation), Valencia, Pre-textos, 1985.

Rodriguez Monegal, Emir, "Borges y Derrida: boticarios," *Diario* 16, "Culturas," Madrid, December 22, 1985.

Vazquez García, Manuel, "Platon o Mallarmé: filosofía y literatura en Derrida," *Aurora: Revista de filosofía, no. 3, June 1985, Valencia.*

Avtonomova, N. S., "Language and Epistemology in Derrida's Thought," *Critical Analysis of Research Methods in Contemporary Bourgeois Philosophy* (in Russian), Moscow, 1986.

Campbell, Colin "Deconstruction and All That, from Yale's Critical Jungle," *International Herald Tribune,* February 14, 1986.

———, "The Tyranny of the Yale Critics," *The New York Times Magazine,* February 9, 1986.

Campolo, Lisa D., "Derrida and Heidegger: The Critique of Technology and the Call to Care," *Journal of the American Academy of Religion* 53, no. 3, 1986.

Caputo, John D., "Hermeneutics as the Recovery of Man," in B. R. Waechterhauser, ed., *Hermeneutics and Modern Philosophy,* State Univ. of New York Press, 1986.

Cohn, Robert G., "Notebook: Derrida at Yale," *The New Criterion,* May 1986.

———, "Introduction: A Derridean Pre-text," *Journal of the British Society for Phenomenology* 17, no. 3, October 1986.

———, "Metaphorics and Metaphysics: Derrida's Analysis of Aristotle," *Journal of the British Society for Phenomenology* 17, no. 3, october 86.

Hobson, Marian, "Les négations de Derrida," in D. Kelley and I. Llasera, eds., *Cross-References: Modern French Theory and the Practice of Criticism,* 1986.

Irwin, John T., "Mysteries We Reread, Mysteries of Rereading: Poe, Borges, and the Analytic Detective Story; also Lacan, Derrida and Johnson," *MLN* 101, no. 5, December 1986.

Jackson, John E., "Une 'parole de la circoncision,'" *Journal de Genève,* July 5, 1986.

Lévy, Bernard-Henri, "Le marteau de Jacques Derrida (1975)," *Questions de principe* 2, Paris, Grasset, 1986.

Mazzoldi, Bruno, "La f(r)icción del chisme entre Foucault y Derrida," *Texto y Contexto,* May–August 1986, Bogota.

———, "Reseña (la postal de Socrates a Freud. Nota sobre Derrida)," *Falsas Riendas: Revista de arte y pensamiento* 1, no. 1, October–December 1986, Bogota.

Melville, Stephen W., "A Context for Derrida," in *Philoso-*

phy Beside Itself: On Deconstruction and Modernism, Univ. of Minnesota Press, 1986.

Münster, Arno, "Die 'Differänz' und die 'Spur': Jacques Derridas Dekonstruktion der abendländischen Metaphysik," *Spuren in Kunst und Gesellschaft,* no. 16, July–August 1986, Hamburg.

Norris, Christopher, "Deconstruction Against Itself: Derrida and Nietzsche," *Diacritics,* no. 4, winter 1986.

———, "Names. Signéponge/Signsponge," *London Review of Books,* February 20, 1986.

———, "On Derrida's 'Apocalyptic tone': Textual Politics and the Principle of Reason," *Southern Review* 19, no. 1, March 1986, Univ. of Adelaide, South Australia.

Peñalver, Mariano, "Gadamer—Derrida: de la recolección a la diseminación de la verdad," *ER: Revista di filosofía,* no. 3, May 1986, Seville.

Pradhan, S., "Minimalist Semantics: Davidson and Derrida on Meaning, Use and Convention," *Diacritics,* spring 1986.

Rapaport, Herman, "Applied Grammatology," *Sub-stance* 50, 1986.

Sprinker, Michael, "Deconstruction in America," *MLN,* December 1986.

Staten, Henry, "Rorty's Circumvention of Derrida," *Critical Inquiry,* winter 1986.

Toyosaki, Koitchi, "Speech Act Without Presence: The Performative in Derrida" (in Japanese), in *Hoko no shukusai,* ed. Asahi, November 1986.

Behler, Ernst, "Deconstruction versus Hermeneutics: Derrida and Gadamer on Text and Interpretation," *Southern Humanities Review,* summer 1987.

Bennington, Geoff, "Demanding History," in *Poststructuralism and the Question of History,* Cambridge Univ. Press, 1987.

Bernet, Rudolf, "Jacques Derrida, *Husserls Weg in die Geschichte am Leitfaden der Geometrie*" (preface to the German translation of *Edmund Husserl, L'Origine de la géométrie*), Fink, 1987.

Berns, Egide, "Jacques Derrida" (biography and partial bibliography), *Kritisch denkerslexicon* 3, 1987.

Bernstein, Richard, "Serious Play: The Ethical-Political

Horizon of Jacques Derrida," *The Journal of Speculative Philosophy,* Penn. State Univ. Press, 1987.

Cahen, Didier, "Introduction à l'entretien avec Jacques Derrida," (heading "Vers la déconstruction"), *Digraphe,* no. 42, December 1987.

Caputo, John D., "Derrida, a Kind of Philosopher: A Discussion of Recent Literature," *Research in Phenomenology,* 1987.

Cornell, Drucilla, "The Poststructuralist Challenge to the Ideal of Community," *Cardozo Law Review,* April 1987.

Dallmayr, Fred R., "Critical Encounters Between Philosophy and Politics," in *Hermeneutics and Deconstruction: Gadamer and Derrida Dialogue,* Univ. of Notre Dame Press, 1987.

Di Martino, Carmine, "Derrida all'origine," *Introduzione a Husserl, L'origine della geometria,* Italian translation, Jaca Book, 1987.

Droit, Roger-Pol, "Jacques Derrida et les troubles du labyrinthe," *Le Monde,* December 4, 1987.

Groys, Boris, "Yes, Apocalypse, Yes, Now," (in Russian), *Beseda: Review of Philosophy and Religion,* no. 5, Leningrad, 1987.

Harvey, Irene E., "Dekonstruktion lähteillä: Kant, Nietzsche, Heidegger ja Derrida," *Tiede & Edistys,* Finland.

Haverkamp, Anselm, "*Paradigma* Metapher, *Metapher* Paradigma—Zur Metakritik hermeneutischer Horizonte (Blumenberg/Derrida, Kuhn/Foucault, Black/White," *Poetik und Hermeneutik* 12, Fink, 1987.

Hobson, Marian, "History Traces," in *Post-structuralism and the Question of History,* Cambridge Univ. Press, 1987.

Ijsseling, Samuel, "Mijn 'favorit' Jacques Derrida," *Streven: Cultureel maatschappelijk,* Louvain, 1987.

Jacquet, Claude, "'Nes. Yo' in Joyce, Oui-Rire Derrida," in B. Benstock, ed., *James Joyce Literary Supplement,* Univ. of Miami, November 1987.

Kujundzic, Dragan, "Nacrz za jednu Derideologiju," *Knjizevnarec,* no. 295, February 25, 1987, Belgrade.

Laruelle, François, "L'Autre non-thétique: La critique de Levinas et de Derrida," *Philosophie et Nonphilosophie,* Mardaga, 1987.

Loy, David, "The Clôture of Deconstruction: A Mahayana Critique of Derrida," *International Philosophical Quarterly* 105, March 1987.

Maggiori, Robert, "Derrida tient Heidegger en respect," *Libération,* November 17, 1987.

Magliola, Robert, "Chinese Buddhism and Derridean Deconstruction," *Chung Wai: Literary Monthly,* Taïwan, 1987.

Monegal, Emir, "Borges/deMan/Derrida/Bloom, La deconstrucción 'Avant et après la lettre,'" *Diseminario: La desconstrucción, otro descubrimiento de America,* Montevideo, 1987.

Norris, Christopher, "Against a New Pragmatism: Law, Deconstruction, and the Interests of Theory," *Southern Humanities Review,* fall 1987.

———, "Against Post-modernism: Derrida, Kant and Nuclear Politics," *Paragraph* 9, Oxford Univ. Press, 1987.

Rapaport, Herman, "Forecastings of Apocalypse: Ashberry, Derrida, Blanchot," in D. G. Marshall, ed., *Literature as Philosophy, Philosophy as Literature,* Univ. of Iowa Press, 1987.

Scibilia, Giovanni, "Oltre Derrida: Rousseau e la coscienza retorica del paradosso," *Strumenti critici,* September 1987.

Silverman, Hugh J., "The Limits of Logocentrism" and "Self-decentering Derrida incorporated," in *Inscriptions: Between Phenomenology and Structuralism,* Routledge, 1987.

Spivak, Gayatri, "Speculations: On Reading Marx after Derrida," in *Post-structuralism and the Question of History,* Cambridge Univ. Press, 1987.

Todd, Jane Marie, "The Philosopher as Transvestite: Textual Perversion in Glas," in D. G. Marshall, ed., *Literature as Philosophy, Philosophy as Literature,* Univ. of Iowa Press, 1987.

Weber, Samuel, "Reading and Writing chez Derrida," and "The Debts of Deconstruction and Other Related Assumptions," in *Institution and Interpretation,* Univ. of Minnesota Press, 1987.

Wood, David, "Heidegger after Derrida," *Research in Phenomenology* 17, 1987.

Wordsworth, Ann, "Derrida and Foucault Writing the History of Historicity," in *Post-structuralism and the Question of History,* Cambridge Univ. Press, 1987.

Benjamin, Andrew, "Derrida, Architecture and Philosophy," *Deconstruction in Architecture: Architectural Design* 58, nos. 3–4, London, 1987, repr. in *Deconstruction: Omnibus Volume,* London, 1988.

Bennington, Geoffrey, "Deconstruction and the Philosophers (The Very Idea)," *Oxford Literary Review* 10, nos. 1 and 2, 1988.

Berman, Art, "Post-Structuralism II: Derrida" and "Deconstruction in America," in *From New Criticism to Deconstruction,* Univ. of Illinois Press, 1988.

Bernasconi, Robert, "Deconstruction and Scholarship," *Man and World* 21, no. 2, 1988.

Carroll, David, "L'invasion française dans la critique américaine des lettres," *Critique,* April 1988.

Cornell, Drucilla, "Post-structuralism, the Ethical Relation, and the Law," *Cardozo Law Review,* no. 6, August 1988.

Critchley, Simon, ". . . Derrida's Reading of Hegel in *Glas,*" *Bulletin of the Hegel Society of Great Britain,* no. 18, autumn/winter 1988.

Ferraris, Maurizio, "Dallo spirito al fuoco," *Aut aut,* no. 225, May–June 1988.

———, "Heidegger e il male dello spirito," *Alfabeta,* no. 106, February 1988.

Givone, Sergio, "Derrida," *Storia dell'Estetica,* Bari, 1988.

Harvey, Irene, "Structures of Exemplarity: Poe, Freud, Lacan, and Derrida," in *The Purloined Poe: Lacan, Derrida, and Psychoanalytic Reading,* The Johns Hopkins Univ. Press, 1988.

Llewelyn, John, "Derrida: The Origin and End of Philosophy," in H. J. Silverman, ed., *Philosophy and Non-Philosophy since Merleau-Ponty, Continental Philosophy I,* Routledge, 1988.

———, "Glasnostalgia," *Bulletin of the Hegel Society of Great Britain,* no. 18, autumn/winter 1988.

Pelissier, Alain, "Jacques Derrida: La déconstruction—un projet?" *Revue internationale d'architecture et de design* 380, October–November 1988.

Peretti, Cristina de, "Precisiones en favor de Derrida," *La Balsa de la Medusa,* no. 7, 1988, Madrid.

Russo, Adelaide M., "An Exchange of Tokens: Michel Leiris, Marcel Duchamp and Jacques Derrida," *Bucknell Review* 31, no. 1, 1988, *Criticism, History, and Intertextuality,* R. Fleming and M. Paybe, eds.

Sartiliot, Claudette, "Herbarium, Verbarium: The Discourse of Flowers," *Diacritics,* winter 1988.

Scibilia, Giovanni, "Derrida e i dialoghi dell'altro," *Alfabeta,* no. 110–111, 1988.

Ulmer, Gregory, "The Puncept of Grammatology," in *On Puns: The Foundation of Letters,* Blackwell, 1988.

Wills, David, "Supreme Court," *Diacritics,* no. 3, 1988.

Zuccarino, Giuseppe, "Modalità di lettura-scrittura in Derrida," *Nuova Corrente* 35, 1988.

Baptist, Gabriella, "Die andere Seele des Geistes," *Philosophische Rundschau* 36, no. 4, Tübingen, 1989.

———, "La scrittura sfalsata: *Glas* e *La Carte postale* di Jacques Derrida," *Intersezioni,* year 9, no. 2, August 1989.

Behler, Ernst, "Flamme, Glut und weiße Asche: Jacques Derrida wandelt auf Martin Heideggers Pfaden, Vom Geist," *Frankfurter Allgemeine Zeitung,* December 18, 1989.

Belo, Fernando, "Nietzsche, Heidegger, Deleuze, Derrida: os filosofas da diferança ou O bando dos quatro . . . ," *Journal de Letras* 21, no. 3, Lisbon, 1989.

Chnaiderman, Miriam, "Algumas entreconsideraçoes a J. Lacan e J. Derrida," in *O Hiato Convexo: Literatura e psicanalise,* São Paulo, 1989.

Critchley, Simon, "The Chiasmus: Levinas, Derrida and the Ethical Demand for Deconstruction," *Textual Practice,* no. 1, April 1989.

De Man, Paul, "Jacques Derrida, *Of Grammatology,*" in Lindsey Waters, eds., *Critical Writings 1953–1978,* intr. by L. Waters, Univ. of Minnesota Press, 1989.

Elias, Hanna, ". . . or the text beyond Mourning," *Al Yom Essabeh* (in Arabic), Paris, April 17, 1989.

Ferraris, Maurizio, "Jacques Derrida e il dibatto sulla decostruzione," *Cultura e scuola,* no. 110, April–June 1989.

Fish, Stanley, "With the Compliments of the Author: Reflections on Austin and Derrida," in *Doing What Comes Naturally: Change, Rhetoric, and the Practice of Theory in Literary and Legal Studies,* Duke Univ. Press, 1989.

Flynn, Bernard Charles, "Chair et textualité: Merleau-Ponty et Derrida," *Les Cahiers de philosophie,* no. 7, spring 1989, Lille.

Gaudin, Claude, "L'inscription: Remarques sur la déconstruction du platonisme par Jacques Derrida," *Revue de philosophie ancienne* 7, no. 1, 1989, Brussels.

Jihad, Kadhim, "Impossible Mourning and the Grateful Memory," *Al Yom Essabeh* (in Arabic), Paris, February 20, 1989.

———, "Translation in Search of Its Poetics," *ibid.,* May 19, 1989.

Lukacher, Ned, "Writing on Ashes: Heidegger *Fort* Derri*da," Diacritics,* nos. 3–4, winter 1989.

Norris, Christopher, "Deconstruction, Postmodernism and Philosophy: Habermas on Derrida," *Praxis International* 8, January 1989.

———, "Derrida's 'Vérité,'" *Comparative Criticism* 2, 1989.

Peretti, Cristina de, "Jacques Derrida-Paul de Man: la responsabilidad de la amistad," *ABC literario,* March 4, 1989.

———, "El texto escrito de la filosofía," ibid., November 11, 1989.

Petitdemange, Guy, "Jacques Derrida: Le rappel à la mémoire," *Etudes,* no. 4, October 1989.

Rorty, Richard, "From Ironist Theory to Private Allusions: Derrida," in *Contingency, Irony and Solidarity,* Cambridge Univ. Press, 1989.

———, "Is Derrida a Transcendental Philosopher?" *The Yale Journal of Criticism,* no. 2, spring 1989.

Sallis, John, "Flight of Spirit," *Diacritics,* nos. 3–4, winter 1989.

Sartiliot, Claudette, "Telepathy and Writing: Jacques Derrida's *Glas,*" in *Paragraph,* vol. 12, Oxford Univ. Press, 1989.

Scibilia, Giovanni, "Dire il tempo: Derrida lettore di Heidegger. Un percorso," *Paradigmi: Rivista di critica filosofica,* no. 20, May–August 1989, Schena.

Ulmer, Gregory, "Otobiography" and "'Derrida at the

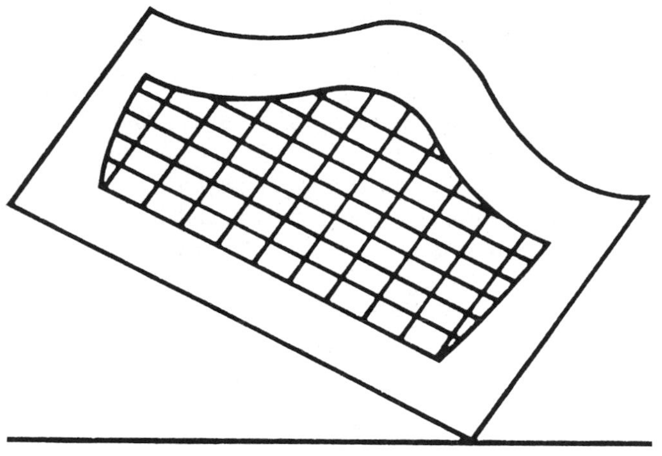

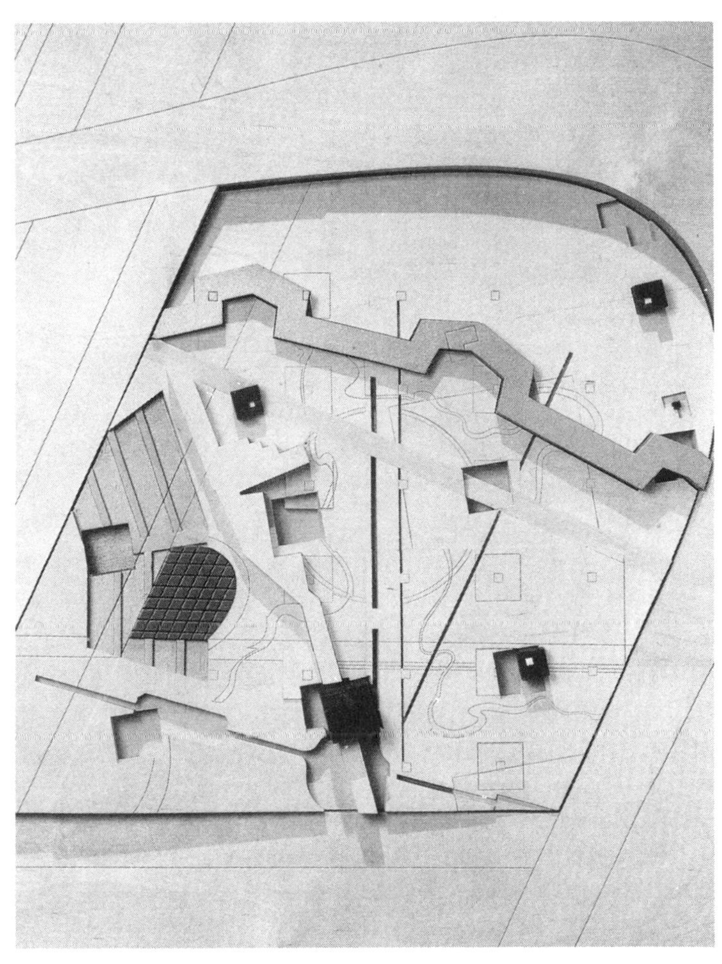

Choral Work, a book in progress and a construction project for the Parc de la Villette. The American architect Peter Eisenman and Derrida are working together on this at the request of Bernard Tschumi (see "Why Peter Eisenman Writes Such Good Books," tr. Sarah Whiting, in *Architecture and Urbanism* (Tokyo, 1988), 113–24). To the left, a drawing by Derrida; to the right, the final model by Eisenman.

Little Bighorn': A Fragment," in *Teletheory: Grammatology in the Age of Video,* Routledge 1989.

Wills, David, "Deposition: Introduction to Right of Inspection (Droit de regards)," *Art & Text,* no. 38, autumn 1989, Melbourne.

Wood, Philip R., "Derrida Engagé and Post-structuralist Sartre: A Redefinition of Shifts in Recent French Philosophy," *MLN* no. 4, September 1989.

Bennington, Geoffrey, "Towards a Criticism of the Future," in D. Wood, ed., *Writing the Future,* Warwick Studies, Routledge, 1990.

Berns, Egidius, "Derrida's huishouding," in *Algemeen nederlands tijdschrift voor wijsbegeerte* 82, no. 4, October 1990, Amsterdam.

Calzolari, Andrea, "Jacques Derrida o il lavoro du Penelope. Esergo," in G. Zuccarino, ed., *Palinsesto, I modi del discorso letterario e filosofico,* Marietti, Genova, 1990.

Eribon, Didier, "Le militant de la philo: Le nouveau combat de Jacques Derrida," *Le Nouvel Observateur,* October 25–31, 1990.

Ferraris, Maurizio, "Classico Derrida," *L'Indice,* no. 9, 1990.

Jay, Gregory S., "De-nominations: From Marx to Derrida," in *America the Scrivener, Deconstruction and the Subject of Literary History,* Cornell Univ. Press, 1990.

LaCoste, Jean, "'L'improbable débat' de Derrida avec la philosophie anglo-saxonne," *La Quinzaine littéraire* 550, March 1, 1990.

Lascault, Gilbert, "Des espaces peuplés d'aveugles," *La Quinzaine littéraire* 566, November 16, 1990.

Lisse, Michel, "Le motif de la déconstruction et ses portées politiques," *Tijdschrift voor filosofie,* no. 2, June 1990.

Maggiori, Robert, "Derrida et Searle en viennent aux mots," *Libération,* April 26, 1990.

———, "Plaidoyer pour une reine," *Libération,* November 15, 1990.

Moroncini, Bruno, "La lettera disseminata e l'inventione della verità: Poe, Lacan, Derrida," in *Palinsesto* (cf. Calzolari, *supra*).

Norris, Christopher, "Habermas on Derrida"; "How Not to Read Derrida"; "Derrida and Kant," in *What's Wrong with Postmodernism, Critical Theory and the Ends of Philosophy,* Harvester, 1990.

Radloff, Bernhard, "*Das Gestell* and *L'écriture* : The Discourse of Expropriation in Heidegger and Derrida," in *Heidegger Studies* 5, Berlin, 1990.

Sallis, John, "Heidegger/Derrida—Présence," in *Délimitations: La phénoménologie et la fin de la métaphysique,* Aubier, 1990 (original text, 1986).

Seguin, Louis, "Une certaine idée de la philosophie," *La Quinzaine littéraire* 564, October 16, 1990.

Vattimo, Gianni, "Derrida e l'oltrepassamento della metafisica," preface to reissue of *La Scritura e la Differenza,* Einaudi, 1971–90.

SUPPLEMENTAL BIBLIOGRAPHY

1. Book by Jacques Derrida

Points de suspension . . . (Paris: Galilée, 1992)

2. Articles by Jacques Derrida

"Afterw.rds. Or, at Least, Less Than a Letter about a Letter Less," tr. by G. Bennington. In *Afterwords,* ed. N. Royle. Tampere, Finland.

"Autour de Paul de Man," *Les papiers du Collège International de Philosophie,* no. 11 (Paris): with M. Deguy, E. de Fontenay, A. Garcia Düttmann, and M.-L. Mallet (session of March 10, 1990, regarding *Mémoires—pour Paul de Man*).

"La philosophie demandée," *Bulletin de la société française de philosophie,* session of November 24, 1990, January–March 1991. Paris: Armand Colin.

"Lettre," *Césure: Revue de la convention psychanalytique,* no. 1: "Destins du savoir," September 1991, Paris.

"Lettre à Francine Loreau," in *Max Loreau 1928–1990.* Brussels: Editions Lebeer Hossmann, 1991.

"Prière d'insérer" (apropos of *Dits et récits du mortel* by M. Bénézet, 1977). In: *Ubacs,* no. 10, Rennes, 1991.

Summary of Impromptu Remarks, 58 minutes, 41 seconds. In *Anyone,* ed. Cynthia C. Davidson. New York, 1991.

"Du 'sans prix' ou le 'juste prix' de la transaction," in *Les philosophes et l'argent.* Editions Le Monde, 1992, Paris.

"Donner la mort," in *L'éthique du don: Jacques Derrida et la pensée du don,* eds. J-M. Rabaté and M. Wetzel. Editions Métayer–De Léobardy (distribution, Seuil), 1992.

"Etre juste avec Freud: L'histoire de la folie à l'age de la psychanalyse," in *Penser la folie: Essais sur Michel Foucault,* Galilée, 1992.

"Générations d'une ville," *Lettre internationale,* no. 33, 1992, Paris.

"Heidegger's Ear: Philopolemology (Geschlect IV)", tr. by J. P. Leavey, Jr., in *Commemorations: Reading Heidegger,* ed. John Sallis. Bloomington, Indiana University Press, 1992.

"Lignées," *Le genre humain,* nos. 24, 25, 1992, Paris, Seuil.

"Nous autres Grecs," in *Nos Grecs et leurs modernes,* ed. B. Cassin. Paris, Editions du Seuil, 1992.

"Passions: 'An Oblique Offering,'" tr. by D. Wood, in *Derrida: A Critical Reader,* ed. David Wood. Cambridge, Blackwell, 1992.

"Post-Scriptum," tr. by John Leavey, Jr., in *Derrida and Negative Theology.* Albany, SUNY, 1992.

"Syllabe," in *La poésie comme avenir: Essai sur l'oeuvre de Michel Deguy* by J.-P. Moussaron. Presses Universitaires de Grenoble, 1992.

"L'atelier de Valerio Adami: Le tableau est avant tout un système de mémoire." Participation at a round table, in *Rue Descartes,* no. 4. Paris, Editions Albin Michel, 1992.

"Résistances," in *L'analyse,* Editions TER, 1992.

3. Interviews

"Contra los consensos," with Y. Roucaute, in *Diario,* no. 16, June 30, 1990. Spain.

"Im Grenzland der Schrift," with E. Weber, in *Spuren in Kunst und Gesellschaft,* no. 34135, October–December 1990. Hamburg.

"Après coup," with M. Ferraris, in *Stéphane Mallarmé: Poesie*. Milan, Arnoldo Mondadori Editore, 1991.

"Contresignatures," with J. Daive, in *Fig. 5,* Paris, Fourbis, 1991.

"Canons and Metonymies," with R. Rand, in *Logomachia: The Conflict of Faculties,* ed. R. Rand. Lincoln, University of Nebraska Press, 1992.

"This Strange Institution Called Literature," with D. Attridge, in Jacques Derrida, *Acts of Literature,* ed. D. Attridge. New York, Routledge, 1992.

4. Works on Jacques Derrida

Books

Boyne, Roy, *Foucault and Derrida: The Other Side of Reason,* London and Boston, Unwin Hyman, 1990.

Coward, Harold, *Derrida and Indian Philosophy,* Albany, SUNY, 1990.

Kultermann, Udo, *Kunst und Wirklichkeit: von Fiedler bis Derrida; Zehn Annäherungen,* Munich, Scaneg, 1991.

Major, René, *Lacan avec Derrida. Analyse désistentielle,* Paris, Mentha, 1991.

Schällibaum, Urs., *Geschlechterdifferenz und Ambivalenz: Ein Vergleich zwischen Luce Irigaray und Jacques Derrida,* Vienna, Passagen, 1991.

Bernstein, J. M., *The Fate of Art: Aesthetic Alienation from Kant to Derrida and Adorno,* Pennsylvania State University Press, 1991.

Critchley, Simon, *The Ethics of Deconstruction: Derrida and Levinas,* London, Blackwell, 1992.

Kaufmann, Linda, *Special Delivery: Epistolary Modes in Modern Fiction,* Chicago, University of Chicago Press, 1992, chap. 3 on Derrida's *The Post Card.*

McKenna, Andrew J., *Violence and Difference: Girard, Derrida, and Deconstruction,* Urbana and Chicago, University of Illinois Press, 1992.

Special Issues of Journals and Readers on Jacques Derrida

A Derrida Reader: Between the Blinds, ed. Peggy Kamuf. New York, Columbia University Press, 1991.

Magazine littéraire, no. 286, *Jacques Derrida: La déconstruction de la philosophie.* Texts by P. Bougon, D. Cahen, R. Klein, G. Lascault, M. Lisse, P. de Man, R. Major, J. H. Miller, G. Petitdemange, R. Rorty. Interview with Derrida. "Une 'folie' doit veiller sur la pensée." Paris, March 1991.

Delo, xxxviii, nos. 1 and 2, January–February; nos. 3 and 4, March–April, 1992. Belgrade (in Serbian). (Two volumes.) Texts by O. Savic, W. Welsch, S. Zizek, N. Miscevic, M. Frank, H. Staten, P. Bojanic, G. Bennington, A. Erjavec, etc.

Derrida: A Critical Reader, ed. David Wood. Texts by G. Bennington, R. Bernasconi, J. Derrida, M. Frank, M. Haar, I. Harvey, J. Llewelyn, J-L. Nancy, C. Norris, R. Rorty, J. Sallis, D. Wood. Bibliography, A. Leventure with T. Keenan. Blackwell, 1992.

Acts of Literature, ed. Derek Attridge. New York and London, Routledge, 1992.

L'ethique du don: Jacques Derrida et la pensée du don, eds. J-M. Rabaté and M. Wetzel. J. Derrida, C. Malabou, R. Major, M. Lisse, D. Wills, M. Calle-Gruber, G. Bennington, P. Marratti, H. de Vries, J-P. Moussaron, E. Weber, A. David. Métayer–De Léobardy, 1992.

5. Some Articles on Jacques Derrida

Menke, Christoph, "'Absolute Interrogation': Metaphysikkritik und Sinnsubversion bei Jacques Derrida," *Philosophisches Jahrbuch der Gorre-Gesellschaft* 97, no. 2, 1990: 351–66.

Schleifer, Ronald, "The Rhetoric of Mourning: Jacques Derrida and the Scene of Rhetoric," in *Rhetoric and Death: The Language of Modernism and Postmodern Theory.* Urbana and Chicago, University of Illinois Press, 1990.

Shimizu, Mariko, "On *The Post Card:* What's the Name of the Game? (II)," *Lumières,* no. 4, 1990. In English, published in Japan.

Taylor, Mark C., "Non-negative Negative Theology," *Diacritics* 20, no. 4, 1990. Johns Hopkins University Press.

Ulmer, Gregory L., "Theory Hobby," *Art and Text,* no. 37, September 1990. Melbourne, Australia.

Benstock, Shari, "The Post Card in the Epistolary Genre," in *Textualizing the Feminine: On the Limits of Genre.* Norman and London: University of Oklahoma Press, 1991.

Gadamer, Hans Georg, "Et pourtant: puissance de la bonne volonté (une réplique à Jacques Derrida)," in *L'art de comprendre.* Ecrits II. Paris, Aubier, 1991.

Gächter, Sven, "Jean-François Lyotard und Jacques Derrida: Totalität in Fetzen," *Du,* no. 11, November 1991, Zurich.

Glusberg, Jorge, "De la Modernidad a la Deconstrucción," *Revista de estetica,* no. 8, 1991. Centro de Arte y Comunicación, Buenos Aires.

Morimoto, Kazuo, "La réflexion de Derrida sur l'université'—L''abîme' et les 'barrières,'" *Surugadai University Studies,* no. 5, 1991.

Ripalda, José, "Philosophie als Dichtung und Verdichtung," *Deutsche Zeitschrift für Philosophie* 39, no. 4, 1991: 415–430.

Takahashi, Nodnahi, "Présence et déconstruction: Sur la pensée de Jacques Derrida," *Jitsuzonshiso-Ronshu Annals of Existential Thought,* no. 6, 1991. Edited by the Japanese Society of Existential Thought, Japan.

Vlaisavljevic, Jugoslav, "Husserl's Legacy in Derrida's Grammatological Opening," *Analecta Husserliana* 36: 101–17. Netherlands, 1991.

Abdel-Jaouad, Hédi, "Derrida: L'Algérie ou l'enfance troglodyte," *Cahiers d'études maghrébines,* no. 4, "Villes dans l'imaginaire: Marrakech, Tunis, Alger," January 1992.

Bernardo, Fernanda, "O Dom do Texto: a Leitura como Escrita-o Programa gramatologico de Derrida," *Revista Filosofica de Coimbra* 1, no. 1, 1992. Portugal.

Critchley, Simon, "The Problem of Closure in Derrida (Part One)," *Journal of the British Society for Phenomenology* 23, no. 1, 1992.

de Vries, Hent, "Anti-Babel: The 'Mystical Postulate' in Benjamin, de Certeau and Derrida," *MLN* 107, no. 3, April 1992, Baltimore, Johns Hopkins University Press.

Dosse, François, "Derrida ou l'ultra-structuralisme," in *Histoire du structuralisme II: Le chant du cygne, 1967 à nos jours.* Paris, Editions La Découverte, 1992.

Hobson, Marian, "Dans la caverne de Platon: Heidegger, Derrida," *Littérature,* no. 85, February 1992. Paris, Larousse.

Pappalardo, Stefano, "Rythmos e differenza ontologica: L'evento ritmico da Platone a Derrida," *Itenerari filosofici,* year 2, January–April 1992.

ILLUSTRATION SOURCES

Archives Derrida (clichés Seuil), 5, 21, 57, 89, 189, 249, 269, 324, 337, 338, 339, 340ab, 341, 342, 343, 347, 351, 369, 377, 381, 387, 406, 407.—Archives Pontigny-Cerisy, 344, 345.—Bibliothèque nationale, Paris, 67, 251.—Bodleian Library, Oxford, 365.—Bulloz, 81.—M. Chassat/Louvre, 353.—Suzanne Doppelt, 11, 35.—Film Forum 1, New York, 349.—Daniel Franck, 223.—Gamma/Andersen, vii.; Fontanel, 346.—Giraudon, 17, 29, 109.—Jean-Pierre Guillerot, 352.—Ian Hlavaty, 183, 307.—Roger-Viollet, 149, 195, 357.—Salvaro, 350.—Sygma, 348.